The Legend of
BABY DOE

The Legend of

The Life and Times of

Books by John Burke

WINGED LEGEND

DUET IN DIAMONDS

BUFFALO BILL

THE LEGEND OF BABY DOE

Contents

Illustrations follow page 144.

The Legend of
BABY DOE

Prologue

OBVIOUSLY there was something both cinematic and operatic about the career of Elizabeth McCourt Doe Tabor, the legendary Baby Doe, sometimes referred to as the Silver Queen of Colorado and more often as "that shameless hussy." It arched over a large segment of Western history like one of those effulgent rainbows in an Albert Bierstadt painting of the Rockies, all the more brilliantly because she was a prototype of the modern American woman. Forty years ago a film titled *Silver Dollar* somewhat inadequately celebrated the life of our heroine in colors even gaudier than a Bierstadt painting. Some years later an opera based on the same theme was written by John La Touche and Douglas Moore and produced for the first time, most fittingly, among the Yankee Baroque splendors of the Central City Opera House, and later it was staged to considerable acclaim at the Metropolitan Opera and the Brussels International Festival.

Her whole life unreeled in the fashion of a scenario, easily adaptable to film, opera stage, or even to a daytime television serial—if that art form dared to venture into the past—beginning with the lurid backdrop of the timberland flames which several times destroyed her native city and ending with the mountain blizzard which attended her last moments on a slag-crusted slope outside the mining camp that provided her fabulous life-style. It was the story of a beautiful and venturesome young woman who knew what she wanted and went for it straight as a plumb line. At a time when most people clung to the conventions and certainties of the Victorian Age, she behaved as though the rules had been rewritten for her benefit. She liberated herself without help from—indeed, against opposition from—her own sex. And found herself paying a Faustian penalty for the bargain she had struck with fate. There was the decade she spent as consort of the lordliest of the silver magnates, and almost four decades in which she clung with stoic courage, alone and neglected, to the magic mountain which produced so much of her husband's wealth. Her story had the classical symmetry of events closing to a full circle.

She was one of those rare creatures of the fabled West in which some men and women still appear in triple-power magnification, which accounts for their durability in the American view of their past. If much of the glamour was laminated onto a few bare facts, nonetheless Baby Doe's story is more real, though often less believable, than what history and biography have randomly made of her contemporaries like Calamity Jane, Belle Starr, Buffalo Bill, Billy the Kid, Wild Bill Hickok, and others who have suffered from an elephantiasis of the journalistic or literary imagination. Baby Doe's legend was lived in full view of her goggle-eyed contemporaries and can be documented step by step, unlike, for instance, some of the adventures credited to Calamity Jane or the casualty list which issued from the barrel of Hickok's six-shooter. Headlines were her footnotes.

Legends concerning Baby Doe appear in a flood of prismatic light, warped by a sense of what America was a hundred years ago and what, less picturesquely, it has become. Anything seemed possible to the adventurous spirit of the last century. Ambitions were fulfilled through mere luck, the quickness of a trigger finger, being in the right place at the right time—or the eternal allure of sapphire-blue eyes and an impressive thorax.

A man could go West with nothing more than a wide pair of shoulders or a promising streak of larceny, and make his fortune overnight. A young woman from an Eastern slum could journey to a mining camp, attach herself to a dance hall or to one of the naughtier establishments, and marry the richest man in the territory. It happened. Not often enough to make the gamble a wise one in the actuarial sense, but enough to contribute some of the gaudier dyes which color the legendary West.

What makes the story of Baby Doe worth the telling and retelling is the quirky, unconquerable spirit which carried her through a lifetime almost majestic in its defiance of conventional wisdom.

BOOK I

Shameless Hussy

1. *The Pocket Venus from Oshkosh*

FROM early childhood on, the girl born and christened as Elizabeth Bonduel McCourt promised to be a disturbing element in whatever bit of the world she chose to inhabit.

She was a beautiful child, a Dresden figurine, with golden hair and striking blue eyes. Botticelli himself would have been fascinated by her hair and eyes and the porcelain tone of her skin. She was a pocket Venus even while she still wore hair ribbons and sucked on licorice sticks. And even as a child she exercised her budding charm on the opposite sex, preferring that occupation, akin to a kitten sharpening its claws, to playing with other little girls. Real live men, smelling of tobacco and whiskey, were more interesting than cooing over dolls.

The earliest vital statistics are scanty because her hometown was destroyed by fire several times and the usual records are missing. It seems fairly certain, however, that she was born in 1854 in Oshkosh, Wisconsin, and christened at St. Peter's Roman Catholic Church. Her middle name was bestowed by a celebrated French missionary to the Indians, Father Florimond Bonduel, who had spent twelve years among the Menominees who roved the Northern forests before the white man destroyed them with ax, whipsaw, and fire. Father Bonduel was a frequent visitor at the McCourt home, which was one of the more substantial in Oshkosh.

Her parents were devout Irish immigrants who had brought fourteen children, including Elizabeth, into the world. Several of the children died in infancy, but Elizabeth was the fourth daughter, and came along at a time when her ambitious and energetic father had established himself in the New World. Peter McCourt was born in 1818 in County Armagh, a part of the Ulster province in which the Catholics were greatly outnumbered by the Protestants and therefore had every reason to seek friendlier shores. First he migrated to Canada, then across the border to Utica, New York, and finally settled in the lumbering center of Oshkosh. His trade was tailoring, and he prospered in a town enlivened with sudden new wealth. With a partner he was soon able to open a clothing and custom-tailoring establishment.

Oshkosh may seem a curious starting point for a career as adventurous and unconventional as Baby Doe's. It is one of those small cities which seem to epitomize the stodginess of Middle America. For many years vaudeville comedians got themselves an easy laugh merely by mentioning Oshkosh, Keokuk, or Kalamazoo. Its other claim to universal attention was the nationally advertised slogan of a manufacturer of overalls: "Oshkosh, B'Gosh!"

During Elizabeth McCourt's childhood, however, Oshkosh was neither a tank town nor a vaudeville joke, but a roaring frontier boomtown. It served as headquarters for a brawling and rapacious pack of lumber barons. And no doubt that boomtown atmosphere, with its fireside tales of overnight fortunes, of Brobdingnagian types wresting wealth from the Northern forests, of people who knew what they wanted and grabbed it for themselves (characters accurately limned by the late Edna Ferber's *Come and Get It*), was as great an influence on the imagination of a bright, impressionable girl as the catechism drilled into her at St. Peter's. At least a seedling of ambition was planted by the expansive talk of her father's friends and customers, men with diamond stickpins and voices booming with confidence that Oshkosh would grow bigger than Milwaukee, maybe even Chicago.

The source of all that newly discovered prosperity, real and imagined, was the great white-pine forests which covered most of northern Wisconsin. During the years following the Civil War, there was a building boom and a clamoring market for lumber. Thus Oshkosh, on the shores of Lake Winnebago, was the center of a bonanza measured in millions of board feet. In the nearby Chippewa River valley stood one-sixth of all the nation's white pine, and the forests of northern Wisconsin accounted for an estimated 130 billion board feet of high-grade lumber.

Never mind that within two generations those endless (but not quite) stands of pristine timber would be leveled as millions of board feet were pirated from government land by the lumber barons. The size of that forest-leveling operation was almost incomprehensible except in statistics: the famous Chippewa River logjam of 1869, for instance, saw 130 million feet of logs piled like straws in a mountain twenty to thirty feet high and two miles long.

Oshkosh literally roared with the effort of processing and shipping out that ceaseless flood of timber. Long trains of lumber barges coursed through the middle of the town on their way to the seventeen sawmills, six shingle mills, and three planing mills on the shore of Lake Winnebago. Oshkosh not only processed that timber, but provided an advanced base for the swaggering magnates of the industry, the middlemen, the millers, and shippers. They also provided the ambience of high living, of gambling on one's own prowess, of unconscionable grabbing and getting, of devil-take-the-hindmost competition, in which Elizabeth McCourt was raised. A Republican lumber magnate named Philetus Sawyer, a five-term Congressman and two-term Senator, was a ringleader of the wrecking crew which, according to the great Wisconsin reformer Senator Robert M. LaFollette, Sr., "undermined every semblance of representative government in Wisconsin."

Elizabeth's childhood was filled with the clashing echoes of

baronial struggles for dominance in the Northern forests. One of
the more violent conflicts was the Beef Slough War which broke
out when she was twelve. Frederick Weyerhaeuser, soon to glory
in the title of "lumber king of the world," acquired the monopoly
known as the Beef Slough Booming Company in 1872. Consequently, there was a struggle between those mill operators on the
Wisconsin rivers who were determined to saw the logs and ship
out the milled lumber themselves, and those on the Mississippi,
who wanted the logs processed in their mills in Illinois. The Beef
Slough Booming Company favored the Mississippi mill owners
until the sawmill operators in the Chippewa valley organized an
army of 200 hobnailed bravos who cut loose the rival companies'
booms, opened up their storage ponds, and sent their timber
tumbling down the spring flood of the Mississippi.

And there was plenty of violence close at hand to give an
impressionable child the idea that a malletlike fist was more
admirable than a kindly heart. On Saturday nights Oshkosh was
the Barbary Coast of the hinterlands. Hundreds of German,
Irish, and Scandinavian lumberjacks descended on the town with
their pay to spend their weekends drinking and brawling. There
was a malady locally known as Loggers' Smallpox, which was
caused by one lumberjack jumping on a fallen adversary's face
with his calked boots.

Oshkosh was afloat in the greenbacks earned by that ava-
lanche of boards, beams, shingles, and toothpicks which stripped
the Northern pine forests, but there was a price to be paid for its
prosperity. It was boastfully, then ruefully, known as the Sawdust
City. It was, in fact, a huge tinderbox; a rude and jerrybuilt
Pompeii living under the lip of its own Vesuvius. Resinous pine
would burst into explosive flame and burn like an oilfield. The
Peshtigo fire of October, 1871, burned over 1,280,000 acres,
destroyed two billion trees, and left more than a thousand
persons dead.

And Oshkosh itself, with pine slabs and sawdust drifted around
the foundations of the frame buildings, was a fireman's nightmare. Disastrous fires had swept the town in 1859, 1866, and

1874. Each time it was rebuilt with wood rather than stone or brick.

Then came the afternoon of April 28, 1875. In midafternoon, as usual, Elizabeth stopped in at Cameron & McCourt, her father's store, to spend the hours until closing. Then as later she avoided the company of her own sex as much as possible. She loved to linger behind the counters with their scent of tweed, worsted, and broadcloth intermingling with that of cigar smoke —hearty masculine smells. She had long ago decided that her ambitions would not take her in the direction of ladies' sewing circles, quilting bees, or parish teas. And more than anything, being a daddy's darling, spoiled as none of her sisters were by Peter McCourt and her brothers, always conscious of her effect on men, she was delighted when one of the customers, passing to or from the sitting room, would stop and tell her father, "Beautiful daughter you have there, McCourt. Aren't you afraid someone will steal her away?"

That windy April afternoon she was given more to think about than the lickerish glances of her father's customers. A man on horseback came galloping down Main Street shouting, "Fire at Morgan's mill!"

Within a few minutes, the fire had spread from the sawmill section beyond Main Street, through lumberyards, and up to Main Street. Everything was built of wood, and the fire raced from the Chicago, Milwaukee & St. Paul depot and freight yard to the false-fronted, fretworked structures which housed Oshkosh's commerce and trade. The Harding Opera House went up like a torch and collapsed into a pile of burning debris within twenty minutes. The fire roared on up Main Street. Papa's store was right in its path, and there was nothing to do but clean out the cashboxes and flee.

Much of the residential section, including the McCourt house on oak-lined Algoma Street, was spared as the fire burned itself out shortly after midnight. An area a mile long and a quarter-mile wide, including the business district, had been turned into charcoal. At breakfast that morning Peter McCourt announced to the dozen faces grouped around the table, "We're just about cleaned out. I'll have to borrow money to build a new store—brick or stone this time, begod—but I don't know where I'll get the money to stock it."

McCourt had prospered with the times, with the lumber boom, but he had invested heavily in real estate. As an eager subscriber to the theory that Oshkosh would soon rival Chicago, he had bought lots all over town, but the boom was evaporating and no one was building cottages on his empty sites. He and his partner Cameron did manage to borrow $4,000 from the banks to build a two-story brick and stone structure at 62 Main Street to house the Cameron & McCourt clothing store, but by the time they opened their doors they found few customers waiting outside.

Almost 500 other supposedly fireproof buildings were built that year in the town of 17,000 population. Oshkosh, however, had passed its peak as a lumber outlet. And like many of his fellow optimists who believed the boom would last for decades, Peter McCourt was caught short. Before the fire his holdings were estimated at $75,000, a fair-sized fortune in 1875, but now he was in debt to the banks, the town was checkerboarded with his vacant and unwanted building lots, and men weren't able to afford much custom tailoring.

Elizabeth, however, wasn't greatly depressed by her father's business worries. Certainly her own capital assets were not depreciating as she entered adolescence. In her mid-teens she was already being nominated, as she knew only too well, as the "belle of Oshkosh." The competition was anything but formidable. Most of her rivals for that distinction were sturdy, flaxen-haired German girls; hausfraus in the making; dumplings for the homelier tastes.

Elizabeth, with her Celtic beauty, might have stepped out of the illuminated pages of the Book of Kells. The stuff of warrior-queens, Druid priestesses, ladies of the Fianna Fail.

At fifteen she attained her full height of 5 feet 2 inches; she had curly golden hair and eyes bluer than Lake Winnebago on a six inches of her calves to the Protestant mob! But Mr. McCourt was overruled by his wife and daughter.

The whole McCourt family turned out to watch Elizabeth the Saturday afternoon of the figure-skating contest, proud of her daring but secretly apprehensive about the reaction of their fellow spectators.

When Elizabeth skated out to take her turn at demonstrating her grace and inventiveness on the ice, a gasp went up from the crowd. The female leg, once its owner passed into puberty, was supposed to be a veiled mystery, terra incognita, except for fallen women and their patrons. Elizabeth McCourt was undeniably, exuberantly nubile, yet there she was flaunting her calves in full view of an audience of both sexes.

With her golden hair catching the sunlight under her little fur tippet, with her hands tucked demurely into her mink muff and her skirt swirling well above the ankles and displaying trim calves, she twirled and swooped through her figures. She was well aware of the fetching picture she made, the green costume highlighting her golden hair and blue eyes, having studied herself for hours in the pier-glass mirror at home. The ladies present watched in outrage, their menfolk with relish. When she skimmed over the ice in front of the judges' platform, she noted the appreciative smiles on their faces.

After the other contestants had made their anticlimactic appearances, the judges conferred briefly, then announced their decision. "First prize goes to Miss McCourt!" She skated out to receive her blue ribbon and a box of candy.

Among the young men of Oshkosh who treasured their glimpses of the daring Miss McCourt's "extremities," as decent people referred to them, was a handsome fellow named Harvey Doe, who was slightly older than Elizabeth.

Harvey began paying court to Elizabeth over the objections of his mother. His father was less concerned. Men would always be more tolerant of Elizabeth than their womenfolk.

Elizabeth fell in love in headlong fashion; she never did things

by halves and would always be ruled by impulses and intuitive
flashes. She was attracted by Harvey's stalwart frame, his
conventionally handsome looks, and perhaps most of all by the
fact that her peers considered him a "good catch." Furthermore,
when he came calling at the McCourt parlor, he enthralled the
whole family with his piano-playing and singing.

Not the least of Harvey Doe's attractions, perhaps, was the fact
that he came of one of the first families of Oshkosh. His father,
William Harvey Doe, Sr., had accumulated a sizable stake from
Colorado mining properties, then returned to Oshkosh to invest
heavily in the lumber industry. A Republican, naturally, he had
just served as mayor of Oshkosh for several terms. His brother,
the Reverend F. B. Doe, was the pastor of the Congregational
Church, which had provided Elizabeth with the opportunity to
catch the eye of the Reverend Doe's nephew.

"I met my love on the street," reads an inscription in the first
of the many scrapbooks Elizabeth would keep. She was referring
to Harvey Doe.

There were several reasons why young Harvey's courtship was
regarded with dismay by his family. The McCourts were Irish
Catholics, "Papists," and that was about as far down the social
scale as you could get and still hang onto a few shreds of
respectability. In that time a marriage between a Catholic and a
Protestant was almost a tragic affair, deplored by both religious
factions and a cause for recrimination in both the families
involved.

Furthermore, the senior Doe was a certified tycoon while Peter
McCourt was a "mere tailor." And there were political as well as
social, economic, and religious grounds for abhorring the idea of
a connection between the Does and McCourts. In the election of
1877, Doe Senior had been defeated for the mayor's office by a
dastardly Democrat, who was none other than Elizabeth's
brother-in-law, the up-and-coming Andrew Haben.

If that wasn't enough to discourage the young lovers, there was
to be considered the vengeful, self-dramatizing figure of Harvey's
mother, who howled for smelling salts the first time she heard

that Harvey was taking an interest in that "little snip of a Bessie McCourt." Harvey was a mama's boy, which was his burden but perhaps not his fault. He was the only male offspring in a family which included five adoring sisters. Young Harvey was so surrounded by female solicitude, not to mention possessiveness, that it was a wonder that he ever made such an independent decision as to court Elizabeth.

Mother Doe collapsed the day Harvey came home and announced that he intended to marry Elizabeth McCourt. In Mrs. Doe's opinion, Elizabeth was a Jezebel, a heartless flirt, a social climber, who would abandon Harvey the moment she got what she wanted; and in the coming years Mother would not hesitate to recall her warnings.

Thereafter she suffered what she claimed were heart attacks every time the subject of marriage came up.

The McCourts, rejoicing in what would later be termed "upward mobility" by the sociologists, were pleased by the prospect of Elizabeth marrying into such a distinguished family. They were willing to overlook Harvey's only defect in their eyes—Protestantism—provided the marriage ceremony were conducted under proper auspices, which was to say the priest of St. Peter's Church.

Peter McCourt's financial affairs were in such a depressed state that marrying off his youngest daughter was the only fair prospect on his horizon. Oshkosh was no longer a boomtown. The decline in the lumber market had caused a local depression. Even Harvey's father was so hard hit that he was talking about going back to Colorado and finding a new stake. Other businesses were failing almost daily, former magnificoes were hiring out as day laborers when they got the chance, and few of Peter McCourt's old customers could afford his quality merchandise. The day came, early in 1877, when the sheriff tacked a notice on the closed doors of Cameron & McCourt announcing that all its stock and fixtures were being sold to satisfy the firm's creditors.

Almost sixty years old, Peter McCourt had to start all over

again in a little tailor's shop provided, it was assumed, by his prosperous son-in-law Andrew Haben. Not his sons, but his sons-in-law, would always be McCourt's salvation. Now it was up to his children to make good in the world—the daughters by marrying wisely—and with all the iron bonds of Irish clanship see to it that their parents would have a decently comfortable old age.

Certainly young Elizabeth was doing her best to restore the family's fortunes. There was talk that Harvey would accompany his father out to the goldfields of Colorado. And if Mrs. Doe didn't succeed in stopping the marriage, Elizabeth would journey to El Dorado with her bridegroom and father-in-law.

The Celtic imagination being what it was and is, McCourt and his brood easily conjured visions of Elizabeth strolling around the nugget-strewn goldfields, picking up bits of the metal, and rapidly restoring her family to its former affluence.

Mrs. Doe stormed and pleaded and suffered one collapse after another but she failed to dissuade her only son from marrying into what were generically known, among the non-Irish, as "the shanty Irish." It took the display of a firm hand from Doe Senior to get Mrs. Doe's agreement to attend the ceremony, with all its heathen trappings, and not to play the mad scene from *Lucia* when her only son knelt, properly raised Congregationalist though he was, before a minion of the Pope.

Despite all the stormy portents, however, the wedding ceremony was performed smoothly enough. To avoid further abrasion of the Doe family's sensibilities, the twenty-three-year-old Elizabeth and the twenty-four-year-old Harvey were married not in St. Peter's Church but in the McCourt home. The ceremony was conducted by the Reverend James O'Malley. The bride was ravishing, never more innocently glowing than that day, June 27, 1877. Mrs. Doe was coldly self-contained but her husband managed to convey a paternal satisfaction.

There was a reception at which the two factions, Catholic and Protestant, the McCourts and their friends and the Does and their supporters, did not tend to amalgamate until the punch bowl was brought in and alcohol accomplished what simple humanity could not. Naturally there were many pessimists among the guests who predicted that Elizabeth would be a "handful" for Harvey, that the young bride was a willful creature who needed someone with more authority than the amiable Harvey could muster. And they were right, as pessimists usually are. Her high-spiritedness was as evident as her blond beauty.

Immediately after the wedding the bride and groom, accompanied by the latter's father, left by train for Colorado. It was a curious honeymoon with her father-in-law along as chaperon, but the urgency of recouping family fortunes would not yield to romantic sentiment. Her first glimpse of the Rockies from the train window, she later said, convinced her that marrying Harvey Doe was worthwhile no matter what kind of husband he would make. She felt that destiny had somehow pointed her toward those mountains, and for better or worse, like her marriage, her life would be contained beyond the timberline and among the towering snow peaks.

2. *The Birth of Baby Doe*

IN 1877 gold still colored the vision of those who trekked to the mountain mining camps of Colorado. The silver bonanza was just in the offing. For almost twenty years, since the Pike's Peak rush of 1858–1859, the goldfields of Colorado, accessible only over rugged mountain trails, had attracted hundreds of thousands of people from all over the country who joined in crying the slogan: Pike's Peak or bust! Most of them reached the Pike's Peak region and were busted shortly thereafter. In 1859 alone more than 100,000 persons were estimated to have succumbed to the lure of mountain gold. For all but a lucky few it had been a costly illusion. Now the mining was largely in the hands of industrialists, and gold was no longer where you found it, but in the deep tunnels and shafts where you worked for a day's pay.

Occasionally a rugged individualist made a strike. That happened just often enough to keep optimists like the Does coming out to try their luck. In the fabulously productive California Gulch the gold yield recently had dropped to less than $20,000 a year. Only a few diehards still hoped the shining mountains would produce another bonanza.

When the Does arrived early in July, Denver was living more on its prosperous past than on future expectations. The senior

Doe went ahead to Central City to inspect his mining property while Elizabeth and Harvey had their honeymoon. After a two-week stay at the American House, they would join Harvey's father in the mountains and help to work his claim.

Elizabeth may have been something of a spoiled darling, a little too conscious of her beauty and overly expectant of its rewards, but there was a bedrock durability of character beneath the frivolity of a young bride. She had come out West with her husband and father-in-law determined to be a helpmate rather than an encumbrance. High on her personal agenda was the determination to help restore her family to its previous dignity; the McCourts were just then moving out of their large comfortable home on Algoma Street and into a small backstreet cottage.

Certainly she did not suffer from "pedestalism," as the late James Thurber once described a malady which afflicted many of those who pioneered the West. This syndrome, which has never been sufficiently investigated, resulted in a "decent" woman being placed on a pedestal so high it would have commanded the awe of St. Simeon of the Stylites.

Women of unimpeachable virtue were in such short supply that they were all but worshiped as divinities in dimity—a tight-lipped brigade, defensive about their prerogatives and quick to expel any sister suspected of doubting their worthiness, which young Mrs. Harvey Doe, Jr., had no intention of joining. Understandably, their hauteur was considerable, their influence out of all proportion to their intellect, and their demands on their menfolk outrageous (as testified by the numbers of grand pianos which were transported out West by riverboat and on muleback to overstuffed parlors in which reigned wives who felt culturally deprived without a Bechstein as part of the decor). Those women, unique and powerful only because of their scarcity, became both the terrorizing and civilizing forces of the frontier communities. Terrorizing because their advent meant the end of free-and-easy masculine rule, the closing of whorehouses and gambling saloons, the coming of lyceums, opera houses, Epworth Leagues, clean starched collars, china cuspidors, and other attributes of civilization the men had fled in the first place. Their astringent virtue and their willfulness were so notorious that when word circulated in an isolated camp that a "wife from the East" was joining her husband, there was a serious outbreak of depopulation, worse than if the whole Sioux nation was heading their way. As one Colorado historian has analyzed the attitude of frontier males:

"In their minds they could not associate 'sex' with a decent woman and stood in frightened, speechless awe of such remote and chilling goddesses. They were always unhappily ill at ease in their presence and at the first sign that a camp was about to become respectable and succumb to domesticity, the 'bad men' and many a law-abiding sourdough took to their heels and fled to the far frontier."

Elizabeth McCourt Doe was too warm and lively a spirit to become that sort of purse-lipped or simpering deity. There was too much of the adventuress in her makeup to aspire to admiration for any negative virtues she might possess, and she wasn't about to fit herself into a mold shaped by other hands. If she ever mounted a pedestal, it would most likely be to display a bit of shapely leg. She had early formed an independent opinion of the joys of respectability.

Her stay at the American House in Denver opened her eyes to what life could be like for those who were bold and quick enough to grasp the wherewithal. She was enthralled by the red-carpeted elegance of the hostelry, the moneyed self-assurance of its patrons, their easy assumption that they had been born to enjoy such privileges. Five years before, as she was told, the Grand Duke Alexis of Russia and his entourage had stopped off there on the way to buffalo-hunting with General Philip H. Sheridan and Buffalo Bill Cody. In the hotel's ballroom, Denver society had entertained the Grand Duke until the party broke up with word received that a buffalo herd had been sighted. It was easy for Elizabeth to imagine the bonanza kings in evening dress and their wives in satins, furs, and jewels.

In mid-July young Mr. and Mrs. Doe checked out of the

American House to join his father in Central City. They rode the train westward toward James Peak, a spectacular journey which took them along the lip of a steep canyon at the bottom of which ran Clear Creek, gray-colored from the tailings produced by the stamping mills upstream. Shortly before noon they reached the terminus in Gregory Gulch, in which were located Blackhawk, Mountain City, Central City, Nevadaville, and Dogtown. They got off the train at Blackhawk and took the stage for Central City, a mile up the gulch, whose once-flowering hillsides were now disfigured by the series of shantytowns, piles of rubble and slag, mine shafts, and ore-reduction mills.

Central City itself seemed to be the newest of the towns in Gregory Gulch because it had been destroyed by fire in 1874 (supposedly started by the lighting of joss sticks in Chinese Alley) and many of its buildings were red brick. The Teller House, where Mr. Doe had reserved a room for his son and daughter-in-law, stood as a symbol of all the wealth which had been wrested from the gold-bearing gulch. "The parlors are perfect marvels of elegance," as the local newspaper ululated. "They are furnished with the latest approved style in walnut and damask, and carpets of the finest Brussels. The piano—a Knabe square grand—has great volume and richness of tone, its strings clear and resonant as the finest Steinway. All the sleeping rooms, to the number of ninety, are tastefully fitted up with all the essential conveniences."

Yes, it looked as though the handsome young Mr. and Mrs. Doe would begin married life in style. They were greeted by Doe Senior, a bigger, bluffer, and heartier specimen than his son, and evidently a respected member of local society. Elizabeth may have been somewhat surprised to learn that her father-in-law was locally known as Colonel Doe, possibly because he looked and acted like a colonel. It was merely a courtesy title; Doe Senior had been eminently eligible for service in the Union Army but had bought himself a substitute to take his place in the ranks.

Elizabeth fell in love with the place at first sight. Just as she arrived, the mines were changing shifts at noon, and the miners,

tramping along in their heavy boots and swinging their lunch-
pails, were singing in melodious harmony. They were Cornishmen, "Cousin Jacks," Elizabeth was told, and undoubtedly
she warmed to them and their spirited manner; certainly she
could not remember sawmill workers singing on their way home
in Oshkosh. They touched the theatrical chord in her being and
seemed a portent of a more richly colored life than she had
known in settled and inhibited Wisconsin.

After a noonday dinner at the Teller House, she and Harvey
were taken out on a tour of inspection by Doe Senior. They
picked up Mr. Doe's two-seater buggy at John R. Morgan's
blacksmith shop, where the brake had just been repaired, and
then set out for his property, the Fourth of July mine, out near
Dogtown on Quartz Hill. It was not a particularly prepossessing
property at first glance, just a big hole in the ground.

Doe and his partner, Benoni C. Waterman, the owner of a
twenty-stamp quartz mill at Nevadaville, had acquired the claim
in 1871 but had never exploited it properly, as Doe Senior
explained. He had recently reached a new agreement with
Waterman. Doe would lease Waterman's half-interest for two
years, during which period the shaft would be sunk 200 feet
deeper and would be timbered. If a profitable vein of quartz were
located by those operations, Doe had the option of buying out
Waterman for $10,000 the first year or $15,000 the second. After
two years, if gold-bearing ore wasn't found, Waterman would be
free to sell his interest to anyone he chose.

Now for the beauty part. Doe Senior, as he explained to his
son and daughter-in-law on that barren hillside, had decided to
let Harvey work the mine in return for a large share of the
profits. If Harvey made good, he would be deeded the mine.

Elizabeth was thrilled by what, superficially, appeared to be a
munificent wedding present. Neither she nor her young husband
paused to reflect that, vague promises aside, Harvey would be
doing all the donkey work while his father took his ease. And if
the Fourth of July was so promising, why hadn't it been fully
exploited before?

Such niggling questions didn't occur to Elizabeth, any more than they did to Harvey, because they couldn't conceive of William Harvey Doe, Sr., ex-mayor and self-styled colonel with his grand manner, doing a con job on them. They also knew how Doe Senior had made his own fortune in these mountains, though not with his own hands. During the Civil War years, he had owned a number of claims in Gregory Gulch as well as a stamping mill and a miners' boardinghouse. Two mines in Prosser Gulch had been profitable, and in 1865 Doe Senior had sold out his interests to the Sierra Madre Investment Company of New York for a sizable fortune, most of which had vanished in his Wisconsin timber speculations. There was no reason, as Doe Senior emphasized, why Harvey couldn't work the Fourth of July and make his own fortune in a similar fashion.

Elizabeth listened to her father-in-law's expansive talk and stared down the opening of the mine which, she was certain, would make them wealthy. She had all the ancient Celtic faith in magic forces underground waiting to be released, or so her lengthy career of peering into tunneled earth would indicate. She may not have believed in leprechauns and fairy gold like her ancestors, but something in her blood stirred, some intuition or wisp of race memory responded to the idea of treasure underfoot.

She listened only half-attentively as Doe Senior told of his plans to have lawyers draw up the agreement with Waterman, then leave for Denver to look up the possibility of starting a business of some kind. They would have enough money to get the work started, but Harvey would have to pitch in with pick and shovel himself—his days as the centerpiece adored by his mother and five sisters were over. Time for Harvey to prove his manhood, now that he had taken on the responsibilities of marriage. Elizabeth was too busy speculating over how quickly they would strike a vein of gold to wonder whether she had just been given a magnificent wedding present or a pig in a poke.

That summer in the mountain mining camp Elizabeth began to suspect there were flaws or weaknesses in her husband's character which had been concealed from the general view by an amiable and winsome personality.

It was obvious that developing a mining property took something more than the exercise of vocal chords soulfully rendering "Home Sweet Home" at the grand piano in the lobby of the Teller House while Elizabeth dutifully turned the pages.

She began to assume an executive function, in fact, before the marriage was two months old. She got them moved out of the expensive quarters at the Teller House and into a cottage on Spring Street. It was dismaying how lackadaisical Harvey could be about getting the Fourth of July project under way; he preferred to loll among the knickknacks in their parlor complaining of the heat while the agreement with Benoni Waterman waited at the Gilpin County courthouse to be signed. The deed was ready on August 18, but it wasn't until September 6 that she coaxed Harvey into a buggy and drove him to the courthouse to have the document recorded.

As they left the courthouse, she remarked, "You ought to get work started on digging the shaft before the snow flies."

"Oh, don't worry," Harvey yawned in reply. "Everything will be all right."

Elizabeth was not inclined to share that attitude. She may have been considered a flibbertigibbet back in Oshkosh, but out here you grew up fast or you got left behind. The men who amounted to something, from her observation of the mini-magnates who patronized her father's store, didn't keep putting things off or stay home all day mooning at their wives.

Her father-in-law had introduced her to two men of substance in Central City, Joseph Thatcher, the president of the First National Bank, and Billy Bush, the proprietor of the Teller House, both vigorous men in their late thirties. Both gave her almost identical advice: "Get working on the mine before the snow comes."

A crew of Cornishmen was employed to start driving a shaft for the Fourth of July mine, and Elizabeth often rode out to watch the "Cousin Jacks" burrowing into the hillside she was still certain would make her a grand lady. All around was evidence that other people were making money out of their claims, at least enough to keep them working and meet their payrolls. On the road below, the heavy ore wagons trundled. On surrounding hillsides there was the steady beat of pumps and the shriek of steam hoists. Down below in Blackhawk you could see the narrow-gage railway hauling in machinery for mine shafts and for the stamping mills. The countryside was fairly humming with energy. A sort of renaissance had come to the Clear Creek region. After all the easily found gold was located, there had been a long hiatus during which thousands deserted the country. Then a new smelting process was developed by Professor Nathaniel P. Hill of Brown University, who made a fortune out of showing how lower-grade ores could be refined. Those with sufficient capital and extensive ore-bearing property became wealthier as hired labor and the stamping mills did their work for them. Others became members of an underclass to "toil day and night," as a contemporary observed, "weekdays and Sundays, in darkness, begrimed with dirt, amidst the clatter of machinery, under the drippings of shaft and tunnel."

Impressionable as she was, Elizabeth Doe realized that Harvey would either have to make the Fourth of July mine profitable or she would be consigned to the drab life of a day laborer's wife. Out here in the mountain towns there was no middle ground, no place for even the most personable losers. So she was determined to supply the driving force that Harvey so evidently lacked. That situation developed so quickly that one wonders whether her shrewd father-in-law hadn't foreseen what would happen and hoped that his very young daughter-in-law would succeed where Harvey was bound to fail. Certainly Doe Senior had not lingered long in Denver, after all, but had returned to Oshkosh.

One afternoon late in September Harvey came home to shatter whatever hopes she had that luck was riding with them. He had taken some samples of ore from the Fourth of July to an assayer in Nevadaville, who told him the samples weren't even worth testing. The assayer's report, as quoted by Harvey, was that "You might keep on sinking your shaft and strike a better vein. But those quartz lodes you've struck so far are too low-grade to bother working." Soon they wouldn't have enough money to keep the "Cousin Jacks" working.

"Why don't we sink another shaft?" Elizabeth suggested. "I'll go out every day and help you. We can't give up until we're certain the whole claim has been explored. All five hundred feet of it. You've got to keep trying, that's the difference between success and failure, according to Mr. Thatcher."

"Mr. Thatcher," Harvey grumbled, having heard that name mentioned far too often. "He doesn't grub around with a pick and shovel."

"I'll help," Elizabeth insisted. "I'll put on old clothes and grub right alongside you."

"What will people say?" Harvey groaned.

"Whatever they please," Elizabeth snapped. "I've never given a hoot."

At first light every morning, dressed like a "Cousin Jack," with her golden curls tucked under a grimy cap, Elizabeth drove out to the Fourth of July with her husband. The work force was split between them, with Elizabeth working beside the men driving the new shaft into Quartz Hill. Small as she was, though sturdier than she appeared, she hauled timbers for shoring up the tunnel, drove a team, flailed away with a pick. The mining editor of a short-lived Central City weekly came across the Fourth of July enterprise while making a tour of the mines in the gulch, and reported what many of his readers already knew—that a married woman was letting her caste down by doing a man's work: "I next reached the Fourth of July Lode, a mine which has not been worked for several years, but started up some months ago under the personal supervision of the owner, Mr. W. H. Doe and his wife. The young lady manages one half of the property while her liege lord manages the other. I found both at their separate shafts managing a number of workmen, Mr. Doe at his which is 70 feet, and his wife, who is full of ambition, in her new enterprise, at hers which is sunk 60 feet. This is the first instance where a lady, and such she is, has managed a mining property. The mine is doing very well and produces some rich ore."

The claim that the Fourth of July was yielding "rich ore" must have come from the unbashful Elizabeth, certainly not from her increasingly gloomy husband, who was regretting having left a sheltered life for this cold windswept hillside in a godforsaken gulch.

His distress was increased by the way Elizabeth was scandalizing the community, dressing like a man, strutting around, joining the singsongs of their Cornishmen, and acting like she didn't know a woman's place. Except for the sympathetic bank manager Joseph Thatcher, the Central City establishment was horrified by her conduct. Even Billy Bush, much as he might admire her spirit, avoided her. For Elizabeth Doe's declaration of independence came at an unhappy time for the majority of people who abhorred the possibility of social change. She seemed a harbinger of dangerous movements then agitating the people back East. With the last of the Indian wars just concluded, a female uprising was under way. American women were boldly suggesting that they had certain human and inalienable rights. One saucy creature had even presumed to offer herself for the Presidency. Nor were these mere journalistic alarms. Lucy Stone, the women's suffrage propagandist, who asserted that women should have the right to retain their maiden names after marriage, and did so herself, had lectured before audiences in Denver and Central City.

It may have seemed that Elizabeth Doe, in her "Cousin Jack" outfit, was marching under those banners, but she was no suffragette. She wore men's work clothes because you couldn't work a mine in a gingham frock; she was much happier parading down Main Street in her best sapphire-blue dress and attracting stares from every male past puberty and this side of senescence.

Everyone, except possibly a few female rivals, agreed that Elizabeth Doe was the most beautiful young woman in the several towns which clung to the slopes of Gregory Gulch. The rough work on Quartz Hill had not harmed her peaches-and-cream complexion and her figure was more supple than ever. There were secret lechers who would waste half a morning hoping to catch a glimpse of her on the street.

There is no record of exactly how Elizabeth Doe became Baby Doe, but according to legend a miner watching her tripping down Main Street one day loudly remarked to his companion, "There goes a beautiful baby." Whoever applied the sobriquet, it stuck forever. Only her family and those who knew her well would ever call her Elizabeth, Bessie, or Lizzie.

"Baby" only added to her notoriety locally, and it wasn't long before presumably well-meaning friends of the Doe family were sending letters to Mother Doe in Oshkosh informing that easily shocked lady that her daughter-in-law was the scandal of Central City.

Actually, by that time she had stopped working on the Fourth of July and become a somewhat restless housewife again. Operations on Quartz Hill had been shut down since Harvey ran out of the money his father had left as a subsidy, had borrowed all he could from the banks, and owed several restive creditors.

Harvey, sensibly enough, decided he would have to work in someone else's mine and arranged for a job in the Bobtail Tunnel near Blackhawk. Baby—a name Harvey detested—stormed in protest. Mucking in somebody else's mine meant he was giving up on their shared dream of finding a bonanza under Quartz Hill; and a dream, as her later life amply demonstrated, was more important to Baby than food on the table. Perhaps, too, she comprehended what a struggle it had been for the McCourts to raise themselves to the middle-class level and could not abide the thought of slipping back into the lower, wage-earning class. Whatever her motive, she strongly opposed the idea of Harvey joining the ranks of day labor.

She wouldn't listen to his argument that "I've been brought up by self-respecting people who spend only what they've got. We haven't got the money to fulfill the agreement of timbering the mine, and besides it's too long a gamble. I don't know enough about carpentry and mining. It's better for me to learn what I'm about first by taking a steady job. Then, when I know more, and maybe have saved up some money of our own, we can try developing the mine."

She could not stop him from clumping off to the Bobtail, but she would not give up her ambition to strike it rich. She hadn't come West to make sandwiches for Harvey's lunchpail. That taste of the sweet life under the crystal chandeliers of the American House in Denver had shown her what people could do with money, and she would not be satisfied with less. She believed in taking a gamble, not in plodding toward a distant goal.

Carried along by the thrust of that determination to be rich or to be nothing, she prevailed over Harvey's conservative instincts. The Does sent them $250 for Christmas, 1877. Harvey wanted to use it in paying off their debts, but she badgered him into investing it in other claims, $50 for one on the Stonewall Ledge in Prosser Gulch, $165 for three claims near the English-Kansas mine on Quartz Hill.

The Does, not yet married a year, moved into cheaper quarters over a store in a red-brick building on the main street of Blackhawk. Harvey had lost his job at the Bobtail Tunnel and got another. The few hours Harvey had to spare from a long shift in the mine and sleeping like a dead man were largely occupied by trying to pacify Baby. She resented living in one room over a store. She emphasized that she didn't expect to spend the rest of her life as a day laborer's wife. It didn't help matters when she learned that in addition to the thousand dollars they owed the First National—a loan arranged chiefly, perhaps, through Baby's persuasiveness—Harvey had secretly engaged a carpenter named Peter Richardson to shore up the botched timbering job Harvey had done in his shaft of the Fourth of July mine. Now Richardson was suing him for $485.

Nor did it help in the least when her in-laws suddenly appeared. Only a severe attack of the shingles had kept Mother Doe from hastening to Central City after receiving detailed accounts of her daughter-in-law's scandalous behavior. Baby was no longer exhibiting herself in men's clothes, but to Mrs. Doe's censorious eye she was not only a bad housekeeper but brazenly independent, saucy, and flippant. Mrs. Doe expected nothing better from the low-class Irish.

Poor Harvey found himself caught in the crossfire between his mother, who was again trying to lasso him with her apron strings, and his resentful wife. He began drinking a little too much, and soon would be drinking a lot too much even by local reckoning. The only thing he had to be grateful for was that the two warring females were separated by the distance between Central City and Blackhawk, though half the circumference of the world would have been better.

The senior Does settled down for a time in Central City, where Doe Senior opened a mining office and tried to straighten out the tangled affairs of the Fourth of July mine. (During the next decade that property, having been sold to more energetic developers, was provided with deeper shafts and produced about $200,000 in high-grade ore. Baby Doe's hunch had been right, after all.) Later, they moved to Idaho Springs, where Father Doe prospered and perhaps was relieved when Mother Doe decided to go back to Oshkosh and supervise their daughters' lives.

Even without her mother-in-law's help, Baby and Harvey became virtually estranged in the summer of 1878. Aside from Harvey's ineffectuality, the reason appeared to be Baby's restless craving for more attention and admiration than Harvey could spare from his duties underground.

With her distaste for housework and for the society of other females, she found time dragging as she passed into her eighteenth year. Down the street in Blackhawk was a clothing store operated by Jacob Sandelowsky and Sam Pelton. She had always liked hanging around her father's clothing store, and the Sandelowsky & Pelton store became her comforting substitute. It didn't bother her in the least that she often caught Jake Sandelowsky staring at her in a possibly speculative manner.

The handsome, black-haired Jake, then about thirty years old, was a Polish Jew brought to this country by his parents when he was a boy. He was raised in Utica, New York, but came out West when he was eighteen. For several years he had been a partner of Sam Pelton in the clothing store. He was a somewhat reckless gambler and had the reputation of being a ladies' man, more vulgarly known as a skirt-chaser, but that did not dismay Baby Doe. She frankly welcomed Jake's friendship. He had a lively sense of humor and a dashing style. Poor Harvey, who had neither, also liked Jake—at first. Jake often came to their place for dinner or took them out to a restaurant. With a man on each arm, making her entrance with a touch of the regal manner, Baby Doe naturally caused envy in other women. Understandably there was a streak of narcissism in Baby's character, fostered by years of admiration and envy. Soon the Gregory Gulch gossip factories were almost as busy as its stamping mills.

The scrapbooks she treasured recorded an indiscreet amount of information on the development of her relationship with Jake Sandelowsky. On that evidence, it was innocent enough, at least to begin with. One page conveys her delight at having two men in attendance on her, when the trio appeared at the New Year's Hop given by the Blackhawk Club on January 12, 1878, at Marsh and Buffington's Hall. Harvey had never learned to dance, so Jake twirled her off for every number . . . and how the wallflowers muttered to each other and the older women shook their heads!

The possibility of a more or less romantic triangle did not escape those watchful eyes. Yet gossip was restrained by the fact that Harvey and Jake were, from all outward appearances, such good friends.

Baby caught a wild bird and tried to keep it in a cage—the symbolism may have escaped her—but the creature pined away for its freedom and died. She was sentimental enough to insist that the bird be given a proper burial, which she was too saddened to attend. In her scrapbook may be found notations, "Feathers out of my dead bird's wing that Jake and Harvey buried on the mountain back of Jake's store," and underneath some dried yellow flowers pasted to the page, "Picked these flowers near my bird's grave, the day Jake showed me its grave."

She and Harvey and Jake attended the gala opening of the Central City Opera House, an institution still thriving part time, on March 4 and 5, 1878. A little later they watched the Central City grand parade. They were an increasingly ill-assorted trio. Harvey was frequently out of work, and it was common knowledge—true in this case—that Jake was often buying the groceries for the Doe table.

That would have been hard enough for Harvey to take, even if it hadn't been for the gossip which reached even his ears. Baby Doe, it was whispered, thought a lot more of Jake Sandelowsky than she did of her husband. Always the indiscreet chronicler of her own life, Baby verified the rumors with a page of her scrapbook on which pressed blue gentians were pasted over the caption, "Jake gave me these September 25, 1878, the night of the festival in his store when we sat on the schoolhouse steps together. He kissed me three times and oh! how he loved me and he does now."

Undoubtedly Jake's attentions were the reason for a quarrel which sent Harvey storming out of their home and caused him to disappear from Gregory Gulch for a time. During that interval, she was dependent upon Jake for food and rent, evidently, since Harvey had abandoned the role of provider and protector; she was too proud to ask the Does for money, and her own family back in Oshkosh was barely getting by. On the evidence of her scrapbook, there was no doubt now who was Number 1 in her life. Under a photograph of Jake, which proudly displayed his outsized gold watchchain, she pasted clippings of poems with such titles as "Dreamers," "The First Meeting," and "Possession." There was also room for a picture of Harvey in a silk topper, pudgy-faced and rather hangdog, as well he should have been, with the quotation beneath: "A wound from the tongue is worse than a wound from the sword; for the latter affects only the body, the former the spirit, the soul. . . ."

To regularize the situation, she went to work temporarily as manager of the ladies' wear department of Sandelowsky &

Pelton. At least that covered her living expenses until Harvey returned and assumed his responsibilities.

At night she and Jake often dressed up and sallied over to the Shoo-Fly, a noisy and free-swinging variety hall with a reputation which caused respectable women to hurry past its batwing doors, eyes averted, even in the daytime. It was housed in a brick building on Nevada Street and included a barroom, a dance hall, a small theater, private rooms for gambling, and bedrooms available for hourly rental upstairs. If Jake wanted to hang out there and take a whirl at the tables while she sipped champagne, it was all right with Baby Doe, whose reputation was the last and least of her worries. Chary as she was of the society of respectable women, she made friends with the dance-hall girls and did not bridle when they frankly told her, "Why don't you get rid of that mama's boy husband of yours? With your looks, you can get any man around." Baby was inclined to agree with them. She liked Jake better than anyone she knew, but she had set her matrimonial sights higher than the proprietor of a clothing store. Her husband—whether it were Harvey or his imagined successor—would have to provide her with the silks, furs, and jewels she fervently believed were her due.

Sometime late in November, 1878, with Harvey still among the missing, but not greatly lamented, Baby learned that she was pregnant. The news came at a bad time for reasons other than that her husband, and her child's presumed father-to-be, had vanished: all the towns in the goldfield gulches of central Colorado were electrified by news of the silver strikes around Leadville. Another bonanza had been struck. Everyone, including Baby, with her own mining interests, wondered whether their claims, like the played-out gold mines of Leadville, might not also produce the carbonates from which molten silver was smelted. What a botheration for the abandoned wife, widely regarded as the *femme fatale* of the mine towns, to be burdened with a prospective baby! She had already started digging a shaft into the Troy claim she and Harvey had acquired on Quartz Hill with the Christmas money from the Does, working all by herself with a pick and shovel. If that didn't pan out, she was thinking of joining the rush to the Leadville area.

Father Doe learned that she was with child and, while Mother Doe was sternly uninterested in her daughter-in-law's condition, declared that she and Harvey must reconcile for the sake of his coming grandchild. He provided Baby with funds while a search was instituted for his vanished son. Harvey was found in some mysterious fashion and a tentative sort of reconciliation was arranged, with the result that they took rooms in the Mueller Block in Central City. The elder Mr. and Mrs. Doe shortly thereafter moved to Idaho Springs, where Doe Senior became a local bigwig, president of the bank, a member of the Colorado legislature in 1880, and speaker of the house in 1881.

Harvey got a job on the night shift in a mine, while Baby Doe waited out her pregnancy. Evidently she regarded the reconciliation a mere formality, a cursory bow to the conventions, because she kept meeting Jake Sandelowsky nights after Harvey went to work. There was further evidence in her own scrapbook that the relationship with Jake was more than a friendship. Indiscreet as always, she pasted in her scrapbook the receipted bill from a New York jeweler dated March 11, 1879, for "three diamonds, $1,185 . . . three solid gold puff bracelets, $250 . . . one solid gold cross, $50."

Harvey fortunately did not come across that item in Baby Doe's record of her life, but that spring he did overhear some drunken miners gossiping about the paternity of Baby Doe's baby, which they assigned to Jake Sandelowsky. About the same time he had asked his father for enough money to develop the Troy mine and was refused. The combination of those two events caused Harvey to drink heavily; there was a violent row with Baby which she terminated by flinging a chunk of ore at his head, and Harvey took off again.

Once again Father Doe arranged a reconciliation, apparently convinced that most of the trouble was his son's weakness and instability. Baby Doe and their coming child might make a man out of him.

The child, however, was stillborn on July 13, 1879. Both Harvey and Jake were in attendance, which caused much shaking of heads and rattling of tongues in Central City. Harvey was so flustered by the emergency that Jake had to run for the midwife. Baby did not linger over the loss of her first child, but only noted laconically in her scrapbook that "My baby boy had dark, dark hair, very curly, and large blue eyes."

Harvey's behavior became more erratic after the baby's death and he was largely an absentee husband, though it would be months before she made up her mind to divorce him. No doubt she hesitated over taking that step largely because of the Catholic proscription against divorce. They had been married by a priest in a Catholic ceremony, and in that situation there was no loophole. In the eyes of the Church she would always be Mrs. Harvey Doe. She bided her time even after she caught him lurching out of a parlor house in Central City.

The idea of joining the rush to Leadville assumed a greater importance than shucking off poor old Harvey. Jake and his partner were going to open a store in the new boomtown. He urged her to look the place over, so in December she took the Colorado Central narrow-gauge line over to Georgetown, then the stage over the high Argentine Pass to Leadville, where she checked into the Clarendon Hotel next to the Tabor Opera House. The "Cloud City" was humming, all right. Her old friend Billy Bush had taken over management of the Clarendon. In the past year Leadville had grown from 1,200 population to 16,000. Freight wagons, prairie schooners, buggies, and all sorts of conveyances created a perpetual traffic jam on the main thoroughfare. Teamsters just in from the mountain runs jostled Chicago bankers, New York speculators, and Denver mining engineers on the boardwalks. Madame Gallat, the French dressmaker, had opened her salon for the wives of the newly rich. For the solace of the menfolk there were the parlor houses operated by Madams Frankie Paige, Minnie Purdy, Carrie Linnel, Molly Price, Molly Day, and Sallie Purple. Champagne flowed nightly at the Tontine Club, where George Fryer (who made the prime discovery on Fryer's Hill) squandered half a million dollars and then committed suicide. The whole town was febrile with excitement; the air was scented with money, and banks were springing up on every corner. Only a fool could go broke in a place like this.

Baby Doe was dazzled by what she saw and the tales of sudden wealth she heard, but she stayed only a few days. There were other matters to be resolved in Central City. What about Harvey, for whom she felt a vestigial loyalty and affection? What about Jake, who hinted at succeeding Harvey as her husband?

With all the possibilities to which her visit to Leadville opened her eyes, it seemed ridiculous to Baby Doe to stay married to Harvey. Even without the diagnosis to be later supplied by Sigmund Freud for cases such as Harvey's, she understood that he was permanently handicapped by Mother Doe's devouring love. It was too bad, but she had tried for almost two years to snap the silver cord and had failed. She already had the pretext for legally shedding him as her husband, having caught him leaving Lizzie Preston's parlor house.

The end of her first marriage came about prosaically enough, though her well-wishers in Central City had hoped for more fireworks.

Harvey's side of the story was conveyed in a pathetically misspelled and occasionally incoherent letter he sent his parents on March 29, 1880. It was more self-revelatory than any charges Baby could have made against him, and read:

"You have of corse herd before this of my sad sad loss in loosing my darling Babe I am heart broken about it I shal go crazey about it. I know I shal for my dear Father & Mother it was not my fault that I went into that parlor house.

"Let me tell you about it and then I hope you will not blame me. There is a man in this town who was trying to sell my mine for me. We had been looking all over town for a man who said he could sell it so we hunted all over for him. So this man said let us look in Lizzie Preston's for him. I told him I did not go into such places as that. Well he says if you want to sell your mine to this man we have got to find him tonight for he is going away in the morning so I told him if he would not stay in there I would go right in and right out again.

"So I went in and who should be a cross the street and she saw me going in there. Just as I was going to go out Babe came there and caught me and she did act like a perfect lady and conducted herself so nicely in such a place as that.

"Now my dear Father & Mother do not blame me. I went in there on business of great importance to me I can assure you. I was so hard up I did not have any money nor nothing to eat in the house and I thought if I could find this man I might get some money for him to help me out. I did not go in that place with any bad intentions no no I love my darling wife to much to ever disgrace her in that manner. I have been as true to her as any man could be to his wife so I went into that parlor house thinking I might get some money I might get some money to help us along in the world.

"God only knows I have had a hard time of it for the past two years trying to get along in the world and get ahead so I could get a home for us that we might live happy and enjoy ourselves.

"Even my own father has worked against me and wherever he could hinder me from making money he has done so. I hope and sincerely pray my dear parents you will not blame me and do try and get Babe to come back to me and for she is all I have got in this world. Do try to persuade her to come back to me and do not blame her for I did not do any harm at all. Babe has got a piece of property which I gave her a year ago which she can sell and I sincerely hope and pray she will come back to me. Hoping now that my dear parents you will look into this sad sad affair is the earnest wish of your Loving Son, Harvey."

The man was such a consistently luckless type one can almost believe his story of innocently wandering into the parlor house.

Perhaps Baby Doe also believed it, but she was determined to obtain a divorce despite the pleas from her family back in Oshkosh not to risk excommunication from the Church. They weighed heavier with her than anything Harvey could say or her father-in-law's appeal to give the marriage another try.

Her plan to divorce Harvey on charges of adultery and non-support was, however, circumvented by Doe Senior. To avoid any further scandal, she was persuaded to sue for divorce in Denver and to charge only non-support. She testified that Harvey had been such a poor provider that she had been forced to sell their furniture, her jewelry, and some of her clothing. The judge, being male, was sympathetic and immediately granted her a decree. In return for obtaining the divorce with a minimum of scandal, and not seeking alimony, Baby was given an unstated sum for the Troy claims which Harvey had signed over to her.

She never saw Harvey or any of the Does again. Harvey drifted around the Colorado mining camps for several years until the death of his father in 1884. When Doe Senior's estate was settled, he accompanied his mother back to Oshkosh and worked occasionally as a janitor or night watchman. Mother Doe, at least, was content.

Now Baby Doe was footloose again. Jake was urging her to join him in Leadville. He was a fine fellow and had lightened her burdens, but she had larger ambitions.

During her stay in Leadville the previous December, she had listened intently to all the talk about the town's Number 1 citizen and chief beneficiary of the silver bonanza, Horace A. W. Tabor. He was a full-blooded fellow with a restless eye, by all accounts; his only handicap a vinegary New England wife. She was determined to meet this Mr. Tabor. Early that spring of 1880 she packed up and left Central City for Leadville and her fated meeting with the Silver King.

3. *King of the Mountain*

THE man now framed in Baby Doe's sights was as fortunate in other men's eyes as her first husband was unfortunate. Horace Austin Warner Tabor's run of luck during a dozen years of his life was the wonder of the West at a time when sheer chance touched so many lives. A Midas of the baser metal, for a time, everything he touched seemingly turned to silver.

The mountains seemed to have been waiting for his appearance to upend their cornucopia. Only seemed, however, because for twenty years before his first big strike he had scrabbled around the Rockies not much more successfully than hundreds of other gold-hunters.

Eugene Field, the poet who was presently writing a column for the Denver *Tribune*, described him in a pungent paragraph just as he attained the status of a leading magnate: "Stoop-shouldered; ambling gait; awkward with hands; black hair, inclined to baldness; large head; rugged features; big black mustache which spreads at ends; dresses in black; magnificent cuff buttons of diamonds and onyx; no public speaker; generous and charitable; carried his hands in his pockets; worth 8 million dollars."

Plainly there was little aside from the qualities of luck and persistence to distinguish him from hundreds of thousands of fellow stampeders to the Colorado mining camps. He was, however, remarkable for the rapid expansion of his ego even among the lordly array of nineteenth-century magnates, who were convinced that acquisition of wealth showed that God specially favored them, and for the scale of his ambitions, which made even John D. Rockefeller, Sr.'s seem like the dreams of an underpaid bookkeeper. He was neither smarter nor stronger than those who failed to find their fortunes in the gold and silver camps. In some ways he was the greatest fool of the lot, therefore on a more human scale than a Rockefeller or a Mellon or a Carnegie. It was just his foibles, his unabashed delight in being rich, rich, rich, his determination to convert wealth into sensual enjoyments of all kinds that made him a legendary figure among the bonanza kings, while those who hung onto their money and their wizened wives and their respectability are memorialized only by an occasional bronze plaque or a pigeon-dappled statue which no one can identify.

Horace Tabor was born in Holland, Vermont, on November 26, 1830, to Sarah and Cornelius Tabor, the latter a failed farmer and country schoolmaster. His attendance at the village school was marked by much fistfighting and practical joking, and was terminated when he went to work at the local general store. After the death of his mother, his father remarried and his new stepmother did not take to him, so Horace left home to join a brother who practiced the stonecutter's trade in Massachusetts. Once he had acquired a journeyman's skills, Horace went out on his own and spent his youth and young manhood working for quarries in various New England states. In 1857 he was employed by an Augusta, Maine, quarry owner named Pierce. His employer had a prim, angular daughter named Augusta, who was then twenty years old but considerably more mature than Horace. She persuaded him there were better things in life than fighting and drinking. The fact she took the trouble to reform him suggested to Horace that she must be in love with him, that being the only sure sign of love from a decent American woman of her time.

Aside from being a "good influence," she offered herself as a substitute for the maternal love of which death had deprived him. He was too earthy a fellow for a marriage based on such a narrow foundation, but seemingly he needed someone like Augusta if he didn't want to wind up like his brother Thomas in his drunkard's early grave. They were married shortly after the Panic of 1857 struck; times were hard for men who worked with their hands, but there was always the opportunity offered by the free lands and supposedly limitless rewards of the Golden West.

The brawny and swarthy Horace, with his frail and pallid, but inwardly tough and determined wife, went out to Kansas with the three-hundred-dollar wedding present from her father as their working capital. They traveled by train to St. Louis, by riverboat from there to Westport, Kansas, where they bought a yoke of oxen, a wagon, farming tools and seed, then proceeded to an abandoned homestead on the prairie near Manhattan. The times were ominous, the territory was a battleground on which anti-slavery and pro-slavery factions (Border Ruffians, the Abolitionists called them) fought it out. The isolated homestead and deserted cabin claimed by the Tabors probably had belonged to a Southern family rudely dispossessed by the anti-slavery faction.

Augusta wrote in the diary which, along with her other writings, forms the record of Horace Tabor's first marriage, and which presents a not entirely unbiased viewpoint, that she would never forget the cold spring morning they moved into the cabin. Her eyes were accustomed to the forested slopes of Maine; here there was nothing but flat treeless prairie for a hundred miles all around. "To add to the desolation of the place, one of the Kansas winds was blowing furiously. Sitting upon an open prairie, one half mile from any cabin, was my future home—a log cabin, 12 by 16 feet; not an outhouse, or a stone or stick in sight. I was ushered in, and the only piece of furniture in the room was a No. 7 cook stove that was confiscated from the Border Ruffians' brotherhood. I sat down upon the old trunk, the only thing to sit on, and the tears began to flow copiously. Why I felt so badly I could not tell, for I had not been deceived. I knew the house stood upon an open prairie. I could not realize how lonely it could be. Then we had seen so many Indians on the way, and I feared them. . . ."

She had come from a modestly comfortable home in which there were servants to do the domestic chores, but "after a few hours I dried my tears, cleaned up the cabin, and prepared the first meal that I had ever tried to cook. . . ."

Horace tried farming for a couple of years, broke the sod on his land, put in seed, and watched the first crop shrivel for lack of rain. The 1858 crop was better, but there was no market for his produce. Augusta lived in constant fear of the rattlesnakes which coiled up in corners of the cabin. She was even more worried by Horace's involvement in the politics and paramilitary actions of the Free Soil movement and feared that he might lose his life in the skirmishes with the Border Ruffians.

Kansas seemed to offer little opportunity for a better life, at least not until the contest over the slavery issue was decided. News of the Pike's Peak gold rush seemed to offer an escape from the bleak and hazardous life on the Kansas prairie. In February of 1859, Augusta wrote in her diary that Horace heard reports of the Colorado bonanza and was eager to join the stampede, although their first and only child, Nathaniel Maxcy, had just been born. "He told me I might go home to Maine, but I refused to leave him, and upon reflection he agreed . . . Mr. Tabor worked at the Fort through March and April, earning money for the outfit. The fifth day of May we gathered together our scanty means, bought supplies for a few months, yoked our oxen and cows, mounted to our seats in the wagon, and left with the determination of returning in the fall, or as soon as we made enough money to pay for the one hundred and sixty acres of Government land and buy a little stock."

They joined the human wave which in the summer of 1859 rolled up over the plains and into the Colorado mountains. The perils and hardships of that journey under the canvas of a covered wagon were naturally harder on Augusta, with an infant son to care for, than on the brawny Horace. "Indians followed us all the time," she recorded in her diary, "and though friendly, were constantly begging and stealing. Every Sunday we rested, if rest it could be called. The men went hunting while I stayed to guard the camp, wash the soiled linen, and cook for the following week . . . My babe was teething and suffering from fever and ague, and required constant attention day and night. I was weak and feeble, having suffered all the time I lived in Kansas with the ague. My weight was only ninety pounds." Yet she did not regret her decision to stay with Horace, because loyalty to her husband was the first rule of her life. Though not a romantic like her husband, she was touched by the pristine beauty of the Colorado frontier, "the antelope, the great herds of buffalo, the wild flowers I gathered, the bright mornings, the fragrant atmosphere . . . I was a girl then, filled with enthusiasm. . . ."

In mid-June they reached the tent and log-cabin city of Denver, and then pushed on toward the mountain goldfields. Horace was confident that his experience as a stonecutter gave him an edge over the thousands of other greenhorns venturing into the mountains; he was no stranger to hard rock, he was just under thirty and he was determined to hack his fortune out of those gulches and mountainsides reputedly streaked with gold-bearing ore. For all his qualifications, however, Horace Tabor wasn't much luckier than most of the others who stampeded to Colorado during the next two decades.

The Tabors' first venture in prospecting took them to Clear Creek, where Horace pitched a tent for Augusta and her baby and set off with a group of other men to look for gold. "Leaving me and my sick child in a seven-by-nine tent that my own hands had made," she noted in her diary, "the men took a supply of provisions on their backs, a few blankets, and left on the morning of the glorious Fourth. How sadly I felt, none but God in whom I then firmly trusted, knew. Twelve miles from a human soul save my babe! The only sound I heard was the lowing of the cattle . . . Three long weary weeks I held the fort."

Horace and his companions returned emptyhanded. Once more they were on the move, toward Gregory Gulch this time, then and always tugged along by the latest rumor of gold strikes

farther into the mountain wilderness. "The road was a mere
trail; every few rods we were obliged to stop and widen it,"
Augusta wrote. "Many times we unloaded the wagon and by
pushing it, helped the cattle up the hills. Often night overtook us
where it was impossible to find a level place to spread a blanket.
Under such circumstances we drove stakes into the ground,
rolled a log against them, and lay with our feet against the log.
Sometimes the hill was so steep that we slept almost up-
right. . . ."

They arrived at a place later called Idaho Springs, where as
Augusta proudly recalled, "I was the first white woman there, if
white I could be called after camping out three months." As
always, Augusta, despite her frailty and the necessity of caring
for an ailing child, pitched in and provided the logistic support
for Horace's prospecting; the difference between Tabor's even-
tual success and the failure of most of his fellow gold-hunters was,
in one word, Augusta; his mainstay was her strength of character
and her determination to do her share. "The men cut logs," she
related, "and laid them up four feet high, then put the
seven-by-nine tent on for a roof. Mr. Tabor went prospecting. I
opened a 'bakery,' made bread and pies to sell, and sold milk
from the cows we had brought." She also nursed a prospector
felled by what she diagnosed as "mountain fever," and another
who had suffered a gunshot wound.

Horace Greeley, with two other New York journalists, visited
the Gregory Gulch diggings that summer, and was enthralled by
panning out his own gold from the creek. He tried to discourage
others from joining the Gregory Gulch stampede, however,
because "there are said to be five thousand people already in this
ravine, and hundreds more are pouring in daily . . . Nearly
every pound of provisions and supplies of every kind must be
hauled by teams from the Missouri River . . . Part of this
distance is desert. To attempt to cross it on foot is madness—suicide—murder . . . A few months hence—probably by the
middle of October—this whole Alpine region will be snowed
under and frozen up . . . We beg the press generally to unite

with us in warning the whole people against another rush to these gold-mines. . . ."

That first summer Tabor found no gold, but Augusta did rather well as a baker. They were warned of mountain snowslides and went back to Denver to spend the winter. "I had been very successful with my bakery in that camp, making enough money to pay for the farm in Kansas and keep us through the winter. Arriving in Denver, we rented a room over a store. It was the first roof I had slept under for six months."

Early the next spring, hitching up their oxen to their battered wagon, they trekked into the mountains again. Their destination was California Gulch, where about fifty miners, mostly Southerners, were profitably placer-mining a few hundred feet below the timberline. Augusta and her baby were almost lost during a treacherous river crossing. At California Gulch Horace staked out claims, built a cabin of green logs, sawed up the wagon to provide furniture. While he worked his sluice boxes that summer, Augusta presided over a boardinghouse, then opened a general store and post office which contained the only pair of gold-weighing scales in the camp. The settlement began growing and was renamed Oro City, with the celebrated Father Machebeuf building a log church and the Methodists establishing a chapel. Within a few months, in fact, there were 10,000 persons in California Gulch, attracted by reports of rich finds. Horace panned out $5,000 in gold that summer but the man on the claim below his made $80,000.

Augusta was the only woman in the camp that summer, and revered accordingly—not for feminine charm or beauty but for her strength of character. She settled disputes, bound up wounds, dispensed advice which was largely unheeded. Another woman drifted into the settlement. She was named "Red Stocking," a whore who had made her fortune before the snow fell, but Augusta never got to know her. She disapproved of mining-camp mores on practical as well as on religious grounds. "The miners," she observed, "would clean up their boxes, get their gold weighed, go to town (where Leadville now stands), spree all

night, and return dead broke in the morning to commence
again."

California Gulch was soon panned out, and many of its
temporary residents went elsewhere. They were particularly
vexed by the heavy red sand which made placer-mining for gold
difficult in that gulch. Since there were no geologists on the
scene, no one suspected the presence of a combination of lead
and silver—not until almost twenty years later.

The Tabors returned to Denver that winter, and Horace was
considerably irked when Augusta, the custodian of the family
funds, took the train back to Kansas and used $1,000 of their
summer earnings to buy more land in Kansas. "Show me the
farmer who can get gold out of potatoes," he snorted.

He would never go back to hardscrabble farming, no matter
how dim the prospects of striking it rich in the mining camps. For
the next eight years they summered in Buckskin Joe, where they
kept a small general store for the miners of the region, and
wintered in Denver, where Augusta presided over a boardinghouse. They got by. In 1868 they moved back to Oro City in
California Gulch when new finds were made and a small
stamping mill was opened. During the next ten years Horace
played poker and occasionally worked a sluice box while
Augusta managed the store and acted as postmistress. Later,
recording the impressions of those years in a sketch, "Cabin Life
in the Rockies," which was eventually published as a magazine
article, that time seemed quite pleasant and eventful to Augusta,
though they did little to satisfy the restless ambitions of her
husband.

"Tabor," she recalled, "wanted our boy to go into the store,
but I wanted him to go to school. I told him I would go into the
store and do all the boy could. I went into the store and he found
I was a better hand at keeping the books than he was. I made all
the returns for the post office for seven years, and during that
time only one paper was sent back for correction." The Tabor
store also served as the gold exchange, and Augusta risked the
dangers of being hijacked by high-graders when the dust and

nuggets were transported to Denver. "I have been taken along a great many times when Mr. Tabor was going to Denver with treasure, because he thought he would not be so liable to be attacked. I have carried gold on my person many a time. He would buy all the gold that he could and we would carry it down ourselves rather than trust the express, because our express was often robbed . . . If anyone came along he would rather search him [Tabor] than me. Then there were some miles that we could not ride our horses on account of the wind, it blew so fiercely. In some places it was so steep we had to hang onto our horses' tails."

Obviously Augusta was one helpmate in a million. She might nag him about his poker playing and whiskey drinking, but without her hand on the reins Horace might have gone the way of so many other gold-rushers and died of starvation, of a bullet over a card table, or of alcoholism. She saved him for the luck that awaited him. All that had a bearing on what happened when luck did come their way, and Horace discovered that the straitlaced, God-fearing, hardworking woman—her face becoming more severe every year, especially after she started wearing pince-nez glasses which made her look like a retired missionary —was not quite what he needed to enhance the life of the luckiest man in the West.

Oro City and the other settlements in California Gulch were slowly sliding into the status of ghost towns late in the seventies, but the Tabors stayed on at their store. Tabor was close to fifty and had all but abandoned his hopes of striking it rich. He no longer went out prospecting because it was agreed that the gulch was played out. When the Santa Fe and the Denver & Rio Grande railroads began competing for the right of way through the Royal Gorge of the Arkansas, a bitter and murderous rivalry, Horace did right well for himself cutting the timber for the Santa Fe builders' ties.

Then came intimations that all those grubby citizens of the gulch who had hung on through the years had been sitting on an unsuspected treasure trove, not of gold, but silver. Nobody had even considered the possibility of silver until a metallurgist named A. B. Wood went into partnership with Uncle Billy Stevens, a veteran prospector, who had been working over some of the old placer claims. Wood discovered large lead deposits, and knew silver was often found in combination with lead.

Stevens had come to California Gulch with the intention of starting large-scale placer-mining for gold. He was convinced that with an adequate water supply for hydraulic operations, he and Wood could wring a fortune out of the old tailings and the bluffs on both sides of the gulch. For that purpose he organized the Oro Ditch and Fluming Company, with the backing of Eastern capitalists, and built a twelve-mile ditch from the headwaters of the Arkansas River.

Stevens and Wood cleared a profit of 20 to 30 percent annually on their placer operations, but soon became interested in the "heavy porphyry" formations to be found throughout the gulch. That was stuff which other gold-obsessed miners scorned as less than worthless. "The 'liquid mud' and the masses of unwieldy 'dirty black rock,' " as one Leadville historian wrote, "still clogged Georgia Rockers, sluice boxes and Long Toms, still hindered digging. Outside of grumbling and cursing only a few of the miners did anything to solve these galling problems. During all the years of placer mining in the gulch few thought of carbonate ores bearing silver—the majority thought of gold and gold alone. Although these prospectors covered the hills thoroughly, they were looking for blossom rock which indicated gold. They ignored the lead carbonates with their hidden silver treasure."

Stevens, the real discoverer of Leadville silver, not Tabor, who merely was one of those who capitalized on it, collected specimens of various strata in California Gulch and submitted them to an assayer. Some of the rocks assayed at forty ounces of silver per ton.

That was in 1875, when those remaining in California Gulch could think of nothing but making another gold strike. Wood and Stevens kept quiet about their discovery and began buying up claims along the presumed vein of silver-bearing carbonates.

They began working several mines in a modest fashion, without attracting much interest, and continued plugging away even after reading newspaper reports from Washington stating that Congress was considering a bill that would close down silver-mining operations as a danger to the gold standard. The question of the gold content of the dollar was beginning to agitate the electorate in a manner which seems curious to a later generation which accepts without a murmur a coinage containing neither silver nor gold and based on little more than blind faith.

A Chicago merchant prince named Levi Leiter, who was Marshall Field's partner and the future father-in-law of the British proconsul Lord Curzon, passed through the region, visited the Wood and Stevens properties, and bought out Wood's interest for $40,000. The new partnership of Leiter and Stevens extended the operation.

That news animated a number of sourdoughs who had been ignoring the possibilities of anything but gold in California Gulch. Silver strikes flashed over the horizon. A new rush was in the making. George Fryer, who had operated a lunch counter in Fairplay, bought a piece of what became known as Fryer's Hill and worked the claim himself. Using only a pick and hand drills, he burrowed fifty feet down until striking white-green porphyry, and below that a mucky layer of carbonates.

The whole hill was layer on layer of silver-bearing ore. Four Irish roustabouts located the Little Chief nearby, worked it for a year, and sold out for $400,000. Smelting companies were moving in furnaces at the lower end of the gulch. Oro City was moved to the site of the old Slabtown and renamed New Oro City, and the Tabors also set up their home and general store in the new location, adding a four-room cabin which Tabor grandly advertised as a hotel.

Horace, so often disillusioned by gold rushes that quickly petered out, watched the booming of California Gulch with a cynical eye. Thousands of more hopeful people came flooding in, and the Tabor general store–post office–hotel prospered accordingly. Largely because of his long residence, he was referred to as the First Citizen of Leadville, as New Oro City and several surrounding shantytowns were now christened. Early in 1878 he was elected mayor of Leadville and began construction on a brick building on Harrison Avenue and Chestnut Street. His chest began to expand; at last Horace Tabor, familiarly known as Hod, was a Big Man; people were so taken with his backslapping exuberance, his expansive personality, that there was talk he would be proposed for higher elective office.

Augusta, fearing that Horace would come a cropper, frowned on all this. She knew that he possessed no more than average mental capacity, which she considered insufficient for holding public office. If there was anything her Yankee soul abhorred, it was the spectacle of a man getting too big for his britches. The idea of Hod running a fair-sized city, as Leadville was becoming, seemed ridiculous. He hadn't even been able to keep the accounts straight when the Oro City post office had no more than a hundred patrons. Perhaps her trepidations, which she was too straightforward to conceal, opened the first sizable crack in their marriage. A man who was getting as important as Hod Tabor didn't want a Cassandra type casting doubts on his new eminence. Why couldn't the woman rejoice in his growing stature among his fellow citizens?

Some new honor seemed to come Horace's way almost every month. There was talk of naming the newly organized fire department the Tabor Hose Company. Everyone deferred to him when questions of municipal management arose—whether to form a vigilante group, for instance, to control the growing lawlessness, the incoming tide of thugs, high-graders, sharpers, pimps and prostitutes, and tinhorn gamblers. And all Augusta could do was cringe at the thought of her husband, whom she respected but did not overestimate, making big decisions, and hope that greater honors and responsibilities did not come his way. It was plain to Horace that Augusta could cope splendidly with hard times, but feared affluence as a good Christian fears hellfire. It almost seemed—and this thought has struck American men for continuing generations—that a man needed one wife to help him through the early struggles and another to help him enjoy his success.

A tremendous stroke of luck came to Horace in the most prosaic way. It was borne by the unlikeliest messengers: two ragged and hungry-looking prospectors who looked as though they hadn't eaten for a week, shaved for a month, bathed for a year, or changed their clothes since the Battle of the Little Bighorn.

Those two men, the tailings of so many gold rushes, were August Rische and Theodore Hook. Rische was a cobbler from Missouri, Hook a former iron puddler from Pennsylvania. They had joined earlier rushes to Colorado and wound up in the mining camp of Fairplay, where they struck up a friendship, and later a partnership, because both were Germans. Their entire wealth at the moment consisted, as someone later remembered, of a pick, a shovel, and a dog almost as woebegone as his masters.

They sidled into Tabor's general store on a Sunday morning, April 21, 1878, and mumbled through a plea for a grubstake. They had a hunch about a hill outside of town, they explained. They had staked a claim but needed provisions to work it. They were willing to cut Tabor in for a third interest in return for supplies.

Tabor had never seen a worse pair of credit risks, and he had heard the same tale a thousand times. Probably they didn't even have a claim. But Rische, as he would recall, was "the worst played-out man I ever met," and more out of pity than hope of a return on his investment he agreed to the proposition.

They filled gunnysacks with the groceries they needed and as an afterthought hooked onto a jug of Tabor's whiskey. The bill came to $64.75. Loaded down with provender, they staggered away, with their benefactor certain he would never see them again.

Horace didn't even tell Augusta about grubstaking Rische and

Hook because she would either disapprove of his foolishness or, if she approved of a charitable gesture, would quote the Bible at him ("Bread cast upon the waters . . .").

Rische and Hook headed out of town, pausing occasionally to swig from the jug of whiskey, and dumped their supplies on a hillside not far from George Fryer's New Discovery mine.

For a week they burrowed into the loose rock formation, with Rische swinging the pick at the bottom of their hole and Hook operating the windlass. Nothing promising showed up until they had dug twenty-five feet down. Rische's pick then chipped into a layer of rich carbonate. Sheer luck had guided them. A few feet either way and they would have missed the vein. They had bored into the hillside, as a report of the United States Geological Survey later determined, "at the only point on the whole area of the hill where rock in place comes to near the surface."

They immediately christened the mine the Little Pittsburgh, because Hook had once labored in the Pittsburgh steel mills. Further exploring their find, they discovered that they had struck a thirty-foot "drift" of high-grade silver ore. Before informing their silent partner, they loaded a ton of ore into a wagon and hauled it to the nearest smelter, where they were paid $800 for the load.

Now they told Tabor about the Little Pittsburgh's brilliant prospects. He knew what to do immediately; he had been in training for this moment for the past twenty years. Laborers were hired to start gouging out the ore, and a whole convoy of wagons to haul the stuff to the smelter. Then Tabor uncorked a quart of whiskey and he and his two partners celebrated their stroke of luck.

Within two months Horace Tabor was on his way to becoming a wealthy as well as an influential citizen of Leadville. The Little Pittsburgh was producing $20,000 a month. At that point Theodore Hook was overcome by forebodings about the deleterious effects of sudden, unexpected, and possibly undeserved wealth. He had begun to suspect that Rische, eyeing him strangely, was planning to do away with him. Undoubtedly Mr.

Hook, despite his temporary pathological symptoms, was the most sensible man of the trio. He sold his interest in the Little Pittsburgh to the other two partners for $100,000, treated himself to a trip to Germany, returned to Colorado, prospered on a fertile farm in the lowlands, and left a considerable estate to the Odd Fellows orphanage at Canon City. Rische held out a little longer against the same kind of qualms and intimations which Hook had experienced. Finally he sold his interest in the Little Pittsburgh to David H. Moffat, a Denver man who had built the Denver & South Park Railroad, for $265,000. Rische then dabbled in other mining ventures, bought an ornately furnished saloon in Denver, and with the help of a notable swarming of barflies drank up the profits. He ended up as night watchman in the state capitol building.

Tabor, the third partner, aimed a great deal higher.

He promptly sold his general store, established the Bank of Leadville in his new brick building on Harrison Street, installed himself as president (though still unable to tot up a column of figures), and prepared to join the ranks of the new silver tycoons.

Thus began the trajectory of a spectacular career. "The Little Pittsburgh," as a contemporary historian of the state noted, "started Tabor on the road to become a millionaire. It exalted him to the headship of men of affairs in his own state, caused him to be chosen Lieutenant Governor, sent him to the Senate of the United States, all within two or three years, and almost before he had recovered from the dazzling bewilderment of the marvelously rapid transition from obscurity and poverty to princely wealth and importance among his fellows." The speed of that transition, in fact, would induce a vertigo of the psyche from which he never quite recovered.

Rarely has there been a longer or more lucrative winning streak than Tabor's. On an investment of $64.75 he had already realized a profit of $500,000.

Now, David Moffat and his attorney, a suave and slippery fellow named Jerome Napoleon Chaffee, whose sinuous maneuvers would prove too much for a man of Tabor's uncomplicated

personality, wanted to buy out Tabor's interest in the Little
Pittsburgh for one million in cash. It was an attractive offer.
Tabor would be provided with the capital to try out his luck on
other properties. Furthermore, he would be given a large chunk
of stock in the Little Pittsburgh Consolidated, a corporation
capitalized at $20,000,000. Tabor agreed to the proposition, and
before the autumn leaves drifted down found himself a millionaire. Another million came his way when New York speculators
boomed the stock of Little Pittsburgh Consolidated from $5 to
$30 a share on the New York Stock Exchange.

His luck was really phenomenal. Again its bearer was an
unlikely mining-camp type. Just as Rische and Hook represented
the figure of the luckless prospector, his new unwitting benefactor
was the equally familiar con man of the goldfields. Chicken Bill
Lovell was a specialist in salting mines; that is, taking a worthless
shaft and planting high-grade ore, obtained elsewhere, at the
bottom and then selling the mine to someone who didn't know
better.

Lovell had appeared in Leadville shortly after George Fryer
made the first important find. He located a claim near the New
Discovery on Fryer's Hill, dug down twenty feet, and being as
lazy as most crooks, gave up the task. As he watched the water
seeping into his hole, he decided to salt the mine. He borrowed a
wagon, sneaked over to the Little Pittsburgh one night, loaded on
the rich ore from Tabor's property, and dumped it down his own
shaft.

It was purest con man's humor to peddle his salted mine to the
man who had unknowingly provided the salt. He went over to
Tabor's office and told the new millionaire he had struck a rich
vein, but that water had flooded his shaft and he didn't have the
money or patience to undertake pumping operations. Would
Tabor be willing to buy his claim for $40,000? Tabor hardly
paused to consider the matter before writing out the check.

Lovell fled town before Tabor could investigate the possibilities of his acquisition. Tabor hired a crew of ten workmen to

drain Chicken Bill's shallow pit. He then discovered that Lovell had salted the mine with ore from the Little Pittsburgh.

Leadville roared at Tabor's discomfiture, and Augusta muttered about "a fool and his money." The blow to his self-esteem was unbearable, so Horace ordered his miners to keep digging, a decision based partly on wounded pride and the consideration that Lovell's claim was close enough to the New Discovery's lode to make it a possibility. After all, Lovell had only dug twenty feet down.

Tabor's crew dug just eight feet deeper after pumping out the mine, and struck what was later described as the "richest body of ore ever found on Fryer's Hill." Tabor christened it the Chrysolite and proceeded to make himself another fortune in a matter of a few months. The ore taken from the Chrysolite was bringing in $100,000 monthly when it caught the eye of Eastern capitalists, who now regarded Leadville Silver as the Number 1 speculative issue. Tabor agreed to incorporation of the Chrysolite Mining Company with a capitalization of $10,000,000; he sold his stock when its price rose from $5 a share to $45. And that company stayed in existence until 1927, the longest-lived of all the enterprises founded by Horace Tabor.

His third visitation from Lady Luck followed quickly, even as other ventures were proving to be bad guesses. He was throwing his chips all over the board. Like everyone else he was infected by the speculative fever raging in the region, to the point that one mining company was organized by a group of Leadville housewives. He was shoving his money around like a drunken roulette player, placing his chips on the Maid of Erin, the Scooper, the Union Emma, the Tam O'Shanter, the Hibernia, the Wheel of Fortune, and other properties. Many turned out to be oreless holes in the landscape.

Then came the proposition that he buy the Matchless mine on Fryer's Hill, that tree-shorn mound of carbonate. He bought the Matchless for $117,000 and sank $40,000 more settling conflicting claims. Much more was needed to develop the mine, but

Tabor hung in there. Finally his workmen struck a thick vein of carbonate. And the Matchless turned out to be the crowning triumph of his career. Through the years it brought in an estimated $11,000,000.

Leadville now was imprinted on the national consciousness, like Sutter's Creek and the Comstock Lode, and a river of bullion flowed down from the mountains. Tabor's name was a byword for phenomenal luck. Since it was generally believed that Providence smiled broadest on those who deserved it the most, Horace Tabor, having leaped in one year from obscurity to the greatest prominence and wealth, became a towering figure. The Republican Party insisted that he run for lieutenant governor on its ticket, and he was elected to that post in November of 1878, a mere seven months after he had grubstaked Rische and Hook. The Republicans, of course, planned to divert some of his millions into their state treasury.

Leadville itself he regarded as his personal creation. Where would it be without the acumen which developed three rich mines, without the political wisdom and the generally acclaimed builder's talent of its first mayor?

Augusta, of course, might point out that Leadville was rapidly becoming the wickedest place on earth; that Tabor's good luck had resulted in the importation of unholy amounts of greed, vice, and dissipation. Some people might call it the Magic City, but a decent person would be more likely reminded of Sodom, Port Said, or Dodge City. Even the town-booming local newspaper took note of the violence that coexisted with prosperity early in 1879. "Leadville never sleeps," the journal observed. "The theaters close at three in the morning. The dance houses and liquoring shops are never shut. The highwayman patrols the street in quest of drunken prey. The policeman treads his beat to and fro. The music at the beer halls is grinding low. A mail coach has just arrived. There is a merry party opposite the public school. A sick man is groaning in the agonies of death. Carbonate Hill with her scores of briefly blazing fires is Argus-eyed. Three shots are heard down below the old courthouse. There is a fight in a State Street casino. A woman screams. The sky is cloudless. A man stands dreaming in front of the Windsor looking at the stars—he is away from home.

"A barouche holding two men and two women comes rushing up Chestnut Street. Another shot is heard down near the city jail. A big forest fire lights up the mountains at the head of Iowa Gulch. 'Give you the price of a bed, did you say?' 'Yes, I've not seen a bed for a week. Believe me, kind sir, I'm sick and in need of a friend. Help me, stranger, and as true as I live I'll repay your kindness.' The clock on the Grand Hotel points to one. Shots are heard from Carbonate Hill. The roar of revelry is on the increase. The streets are full of drunken carousers taking in the town."

That vignette, of course, could only skim the surface of what it was like to live in Leadville as its boom was cresting. Any vice imaginable was tolerated and catered to, any sort of crooked dealing (provided it was successful) was laughed off, but poverty was unforgivable and the color of your skin was crucial. An unofficial but harshly worded decree was circulated throughout the territory warning that Leadville was for white men only. The hardworking Chinese, who had appeared in most mining camps from Colorado to California, and did the washing and cooking and other chores at bargain prices, were most particularly forbidden to settle in or even enter Leadville. Three Chinese laundrymen from Fairplay slipped in through the blockade one night, were seized, taken to an arroyo outside of town, shot to death, and thrown down an abandoned mine shaft.

Banditry of all kinds had become endemic in Leadville. "Footpads were to be found lurking in every corner, lying in wait for belated businessmen or wealthy debauchers on their way home," as a regional historian recounted. "The ominous command, 'Hold up your hands,' accompanied by the click of a pistol, was heard almost nightly, and the newspaper reporter who failed to secure one or more holdups during his daily rounds felt that he had failed in one of the duties of his profession. Men were robbed within the shadows of their own doors, stripped of their

valuables in their own bedchambers . . . Men whose duties
compelled them to be out late at night walked with naked pistols
in their hands, and not infrequently with a second in reserve,
taking the middle of the street to avoid being ambushed from
dark corners. . . .

"One young man, a confidential employee of a prominent
company, in a fit of drunken bravado, exhibited a large roll of
bills in one of the variety theaters. A few minutes afterward he
started for his room; on turning the first corner, in a crowded
thoroughfare with the lights from saloons making the locality as
light as day, he received a blow from a bludgeon, and two hours
later awoke to consciousness, lying in a gutter in which he had
fallen, and discovered that his gold watch and a thousand dollars
of his own and his company's money had been taken from him.
The next day he was sent to his Eastern home in disgrace . . .
The charge was frequently made that the police were in league
with the robbers, and many circumstances seemed to give color
to the charge."

The speculation in real estate and profiteering in food and
other commodities were intense and unconscionable. Lots on the
principal thoroughfares, bought a few months earlier for $10,
were selling for $4,000 to $5,000. One visitor claimed that
Leadville rents were higher than New York City's. Flour, bacon,
coffee, and other staples were selling for three or four times what
they cost in Denver, some of the markup being justified by the
fact that all supplies had to be freighted in over tortuous
mountain roads.

Leadville was laid out, almost as if by prearrangement, to sieve
the dollars out of everyone's pocket. Chestnut and Harrison
streets were lined with the banks and respectable businesses, and
decent women could walk down them without being harassed.
State Street, one block above Chestnut, was devoted entirely to
saloons, gambling houses, and dance halls. One block above
State was Main Street, where the more elegant parlor houses
were located.

Anyone with a talent for dealing cards or swindling a fellow citizen, anyone bold and tough enough to jump a claim or hold squatter's rights on a piece of local real estate, any female of passable looks willing to sell her favors, prospered quickly in Leadville. Certainly, gambling was the prime local industry. The slap of cards and the click of wheels and the rattle of chips almost drowned out the sounds of new buildings being constructed. "The town is full of oldtime sports," wrote one Leadville gambler to a colleague back in one of the Eastern states. "There are eight to ten public saloons with all kinds of games, and all are making money. This is a good place for a small man to operate in. It is a gay place and there is plenty of money around. One old sport arrived here a few months ago with $3 and is now owner of a frame house, for which he refused $600 a month rent. Today he received $25,000 for a fourth interest in a mine. You can't imagine the excitement going on here."

One of the most successful of the Leadville gamblers was a twenty-five-year-old Arkansan named Luke Short. He was a tiny fellow with an outsize talent with the six-shooter, which won him the sobriquet of the Undertaker's Joy. Shortly before the Leadville boom began, Short had been the proprietor of a trading post in Nebraska at which Indians were supplied, illegally, with whiskey. The cavalry raided his post and Short was placed on a train with two guards. Short escaped through a men's room window and made his way to Leadville, where his mild appearance, his look of helplessness, attracted the attention of the local cardsharps.

The idea of bullying Little Luke had occurred to a number of the local bravos. They were discouraged in that sport one day when Short was dealing a game of stud and a loudmouthed character named Brown—he didn't last long enough on the local scene for anyone to learn his first name—kept jogging his elbow and trying to bait him. "Go away, mister," said Luke in his whispery voice, "and don't bother me while I'm working. It ain't regarded as genteel." Mr. Brown persisted in annoying Little Luke, who finally, and with the speed of a rattlesnake, drew his revolver and drilled Mr. Brown neatly between the eyes. After that Luke was given a wide berth by the Leadville hardcases and was allowed to accumulate a sizable stake. He then moved on to Dodge City and Tombstone, where his stature as a gunfighter increased and he was regarded as a peer of Bat Masterson and other experts in that line.

The most celebrated of Western dentists, Doc Holliday, whose drill was more likely to be a six-shooter than the kind used to repair molars, was also attracted to Leadville. He was a transient type, but soon made Leadville his headquarters for the last nine years of his life. A good dentist, like an undertaker, was always in demand in a boomtown, but Holliday was more interested in faro than in his old profession. Holliday was tubercular, and the two-mile-high mining camp was good for his health; he left it only when he scented an opportunity on the plains below. Once it was to work an elaborate con game on a Midwest banker selected as the "mark" by a confederate. Holliday sold him gold bricks bearing the government seal and therefore supposedly stolen property, for $20,000. When the banker reached Chicago with his fake gold bricks, he was arrested by two other Holliday confederates claiming to be United States marshals and released only after paying them a $15,000 bribe.

Holliday left Leadville again when Tombstone, Arizona, heated up and his services were required by the Earp brothers in their controversy with the Clanton family. After the gunsmoke over the O.K. Corral had drifted away, Doc returned to Leadville, his cough worse than ever, likewise his temper. In 1884 he was forced to deal harshly with two members of the Leadville constabulary. He merely pinked Bill Allen in his gun arm but he killed an officer named Kelly, who thereby earned the distinction of being the last name on Holliday's lengthy list of unsuccessful opponents. In the spring of 1887 Holliday bought himself a one-way ticket to Glenwood Springs, the spa which claimed so many cures, and died there before the year was out. . . .

Leadville was a classic example of frontier materialism running out of control as it would in the Klondike and all future

mining or oil-drilling boomtowns; one more place where a man
could collapse of hunger and be trodden underfoot by throngs of
revelers. The local newspaper called attention to the fact that
there were losers as well as winners in the race for riches and
published an editorial under the heading FEED THE MINERS!
which reported that "All up and down the mountainsides for
miles and miles around Leadville are thousands and thousands of
diggers after happiness and homes. It is a fact that many of these
industrious delvers are destitute of food this afternoon. They have
used their last nickel; they know they will have to go down but
ten feet more; they do not like to give up or give away their
competence for a few mouthfuls of bread. Few of these fellows
will beg. Neither will they steal anything beyond what is
required for the immediate sustenance of life."

The response of Leadville's city fathers to that appeal for
compassion was to pass stricter laws against anyone walking into
a local restaurant without being able to pay for his meal.
Murderers got off with a "tut-tut" from the local judiciary, but a
man who tried to walk out of a restaurant without paying the
check was committing a crime against property and would
languish in jail for months.

To enforce the laws against offenses which property owners
deemed the most heinous, Mayor Tabor imported an experienced town-tamer named Mart Duggan and born in County
Limerick, Ireland, as city marshal. Duggan was of only middling
size, but his ferocity was unquestioned. He had already notched
the butt of his revolver seven times as a memorial to seven souls
dispatched for recklessly challenging his authority. No desperado
lasted long in Leadville unless he bowed politely to Marshal
Duggan and kept his gun holstered. His method of quelling any
suggestion of a challenge to his right to administer the law as he
saw fit was the quick and brutal assault—and he didn't care
whether the challenger was a drunken prospector or one of the
local nabobs. Even Mayor Tabor's pals weren't safe from
Marshal Duggan's touchy disposition.

One night Duggan accepted the offer of August Rische, then

still Tabor's partner in the Little Pittsburgh mine, to have a
drink with him. After hoisting a few, Duggan took offense at
something Rische said and announced that Rische would be
spending the rest of the night in jail. Rische offered resistance,
upon which Duggan knocked him down and dragged him to the
jailhouse.

Mayor Tabor hastened to the one-cell calaboose to rescue his
partner, but found Duggan in a truculent mood. "Shut your
trap, Tabor, or I'll run you in, too," the marshal told him.

Tabor took the advice and went away quietly.

Duggan's career ended as violently as any frontier historian
would have predicted. Shortly after retiring in 1880 to operate a
livery stable, he was driving a sleigh in response to a call from
Madam Minnie Purdy when he almost ran down a citizen
named Louis Lamb. The two men quarreled, drew their Colts,
but only Duggan got a chance to fire. Lamb was killed instantly.
Duggan was acquitted on a plea of self-defense, a verdict
unsatisfactory to Lamb's widow, who swore she would wear
widow's weeds until her husband's death was avenged.

Mrs. Lamb was forced to wear her widow's weeds until they
had turned green and ragged. The vengeance she yearned for did
not come for another seven years. Meanwhile Duggan's livery
stable went bankrupt and the ex-marshal tended bar for a time
in Douglass City until the boom ended there and he had to
return to Leadville and work at various short-term jobs. In 1887
he signed on with the police force as an ordinary patrolman.
Duggan with a gun on his hip was a man looking for trouble.
Soon after pinning on the badge he was embroiled in a feud with
Bailey Youngson, the proprietor of the Texas House gambling
joint. On April 9, 1887, he started a row at the Texas House and
dared Youngson to come out on the street with his gun strapped
on. Some of Duggan's friends persuaded him to leave. He didn't
get very far before someone shot him behind the right ear. Next
morning he died, his last words a refusal to tell his fellow police
who shot him. Mrs. Louis Lamb promptly delivered her ragged
widow's weeds to Mrs. Mart Duggan with her compliments.

What Leadville had become under the influence of sudden prosperity, and what Horace Tabor was becoming under the impact of quickly acquired wealth distressed his wife. Plain living was her style, decency and modesty her standards. The headlines in the local *Chronicle* told her what sort of place Hod Tabor and his fellow "Carbonate Kings" were reigning over: DANCEHALL GIRL TRIES TO ARSENIC HER WAY FROM LEADVILLE . . . STREETS FULL OF PERIL . . . BULLETS AT THE BON TON . . . BRAWL IN A STATE STREET BEER HALL, ONE DEAD . . . PARSON DECRIES IMMORALITY. . . .

And Horace's hat size was swelling with every honor that came his way, with every imprint he left on Leadville. He threw a huge party for himself when he retired as mayor, and announced the sponsorship of a pretentious, pseudo-military outfit called the Tabor Light Cavalry, which supposedly would serve as an auxiliary police force.

At an estimated cost of $10,000 Tabor made himself a "general" and commander of the Tabor Light Cavalry and costumed it as brilliantly as any Hussar regiment west of Vienna. Tabor and his troopers wore uniforms consisting of bright blue coats, red trousers, and brass helmets resembling the German *Pickelhauben.* For whatever operations they might undertake, they were supplied with three line officers and five staff officers, with only fifty men in the ranks. The proportion of officers to enlisted men was about that of the Mexican army. This doughty squadron was housed in an armory which included stables, club rooms, and a sizable bar, and most of its maneuvers consisted of waltzing some of the town's shadier ladies at the annual grand ball.

Augusta could only cringe when she read about Horace's military venture in the *Chronicle,* which emphasized the sheer gorgeousness of the Tabor Light Cavalry in satiric detail: "The staff officers, including General Tabor, wear black felt hats with a black plume and gold cord, and flashing steel scabbards on belts mounted with gold, and having gold buckles with the monogram of the company. The General's belt is of Russian

leather, embroidered in gold by hand. The price of this article is
$50. The sword is a straight one. The blade bears on one side the
inscription, *General H. A. W. Tabor, C.N.A.,* and on the other,
Tabor Light Cavalry. The General's epaulets are mounted with a
silver star and ornamented with three-ply genuine gold fringe.
The spurs of the privates are plainly formed of brass with steel
wheels, while those of the officers are plated with gold. Their
pants are of light cloth, with broad gold stripes running down the
legs. . . ."

It was generally conjectured that if and when that splendidly
costumed squadron ran up against a determined enemy—a
group of drunken miners, say, hurling empty beer bottles—it
would make a picturesque picture in panicky retreat.

And Augusta could only shake her head at the way Horace
was spreading his money in all directions and starting up
enterprises of dubious merit. William H. Bush, former manager
of the Teller House in Central City and now presiding over the
Clarendon in Leadville, had become Tabor's boon companion,
factotum, and fellow schemer. Billy Bush was a handsome,
plausible fellow and encouraged Tabor to found Tabor City on
the Ten Mile Road, organize the Pueblo, Canon City &
Leadville Railroad, establish water and gas companies, and a
dozen other enterprises.

Tabor and Bush met nightly in the Clarendon bar to discuss
the further glorification of Horace Tabor while Mrs. Tabor
brooded in the rather modest cottage next door to the Clarendon,
which she preferred to any mansion Horace proposed building.

One scheme that came to fruition before 1879 passed was the
Tabor Opera House, which occupied the second and third floors
of the Tabor and Bush Building on Harrison Avenue. It was
advertised as the most splendidly appointed and elegantly
furnished structure in Leadville, "the most inspiring edifice in
the city," as a local historian wrote, "and conceded by all to be
the finest theater west of the Mississippi."

Tabor appointed himself as its impresario—he had always
been an undiscriminating enthusiast for all things theatrical—

while Billy Bush served as manager. The stage and orchestra seats were on the second floor of the building, the dress circle and the gallery on the third. All seats were upholstered in plush, and the ceiling was frescoed. Seventy-two gas jets provided the lighting. The Number 1 box allotted to Tabor was carpeted, mirrored, and upholstered.

The grand opening on the night of November 20, 1879, was attended by the beauty and chivalry of the mining camp, or at least those boasting enough culture to absent themselves from a rival attraction with even greater dramatic appeal—a double lynching. A footpad named Stewart, and the leader of a lot-jumping gang named Frodsham (Leadville real estate was so entangled that many lots had as many as fourteen claimants, and possession was more often settled by force than due process), were taken from the Lake County jail by the local vigilante organization and outfitted with hemp neckties. The bodies were left hanging from the rafters which projected from the roof of the new jail as an object lesson to "thieves, bunco steerers, footpads and chronic bondsmen for the same" in the words of a placard pinned to one of the victims.

Thus, it was less than a full house that attended the opening performance at the Tabor Opera House, only those who considered that the Forrester Dramatic Company's production of *The Rough Diamond* had greater aesthetic appeal than a well-run lynching. Those attending the premiere, however, were impressed by the luxury of the 880-seat theater. Housed in the same building were Phil Goulding's Cabinet Saloon and two large apartments which served as headquarters for Tabor and Bush. The opera house was connected by a bridge to the adjoining Clarendon Hotel.

On opening night Tabor occupied Box Number 1 with Augusta and their son Maxcy, now twenty-one years old and serving his apprenticeship in business as one of his father's assistants. Augusta gasped at the splendor of her surroundings and demanded what it had cost. "Sixty thousand," Horace blandly replied, pointing out that the total cost was about

$40,000 less than his mines were earning every month. Worth every penny of it, Tabor believed later in the evening, when he listened to the toasts offered by his fellow bigwigs of Leadville at the after-theater party and when he read the Leadville *Herald* editorial which praised him for bringing Eastern culture to the Rockies.

Many celebrated actors and singers appeared on the stage of the Tabor Opera House, but undoubtedly the greatest sensation was the appearance of Oscar Wilde who, with a sunflower or lily pinned on his lapel and a languid manner designed to outrage American audiences, was on a lecture tour of the hinterland. When that playful aesthete's engagement to speak on the stage of the Tabor Opera House was announced—his topic to be "The Practical Application of the Aesthetic Theory to Exterior and Interior House Decoration, with Observations on Dress and Personal Adornment"—plans were afoot to acquaint Mr. Wilde with the rough manliness of the Westerners he was presuming to instruct. The Leadville *Democrat* felt compelled to caution that whatever the "value of Wilde's peculiar views, it is certain that he is a gentleman and as such entitled to ordinary courtesy."

As it turned out, Wilde's appearance did not bring out the vigilantes; he was greeted with greater courtesy than he had received at Harvard, and his audience listened attentively though uncomprehendingly. The poet, aside from his costuming, was something of a disappointment to the *Democrat* reporter, who recorded that "Wilde stumbled on with a stride more becoming a giant backwoodsman than an aesthete, dressed in a suit of very elegant black velvet, which included a cutaway coat cut in circular form, knee breeches, low shoes, and black stockings. At his neck was a Byron collar with a flossy white neckerchief, while from his snow-white shirt front glittered a cluster of diamonds. His hair was very long, falling in a dark mass over his shoulders . . . Without much introduction he proceeded at once to business, pitching his voice at about middle C and inflecting only when tired nature asserted itself . . . There was not a comma or a period in the whole hour, save when he came to a stop to take an unaesthetic drink."

Wilde capped his appearance in Leadville with a demonstration of his alcoholic capacity, one quality which everyone could admire. He toddled into Pop Wyman's Great Saloon, outdrank all challengers, and then departed with hardly a curl out of place.

By the end of 1879, with his mines netting him more than a million dollars a year, Horace Tabor was becoming restless with new ambitions. He had been elected lieutenant governor, a largely ceremonial post except when he had to preside over the state senate, and the governorship seemed to be within his grasp. He was one of the financial mainstays of the state Republican Party, after all, and on completion of a term as governor he could look forward to election as a United States Senator. Every Western magnifico aspired to a seat in the Senate, which was respectfully referred to as the "millionaires' club." He could also solemnly agree with Billy Bush and other confederates and drinking companions that it was entirely possible that within the next decade he would occupy the White House. Meanwhile he had plans, and was setting them afoot, to take over Denver as he had Leadville.

If only Augusta could be persuaded to be more outgoing, to take her place as consort of one of the wealthiest and most influential men in the West, to loosen up a bit and stop staring disapprovingly through her pince-nez. Why couldn't she grow into her role as Mrs. Governor Tabor? She may not have been a beauty, and nothing could be done about that, but she could add a touch of distinction, even elegance, to his own blossoming persona.

It was only with great difficulty that he managed to ease her out of the rather humble cottage and into a plush suite at the Clarendon, newly furnished with six wagonloads of ornate furniture hauled up the mountain roads from Denver. She frowned upon, as he gloried in, the tables inlaid with onyx, the bronze-framed mirrors, the two-foot-high deer made of solid silver and riveted to a block of ebony, the massive walnut bed with its canopy of pink silk and white lace, the writing table of mahogany inlaid with mother of pearl.

The more splendid his life became as the foremost of the silver magnates, the more glittering his political and financial prospects, the chillier and more foreboding was Augusta's response. She openly yearned for the days when they kept a store and together carried bullion over the dangerous mountain roads. Her Yankee soul seemed to need struggle and privation, and her pale flesh visibly shrank from the silk and velvet gowns he insisted on buying for her. Hers was the Biblical view of wealth, and he did not doubt that she would rejoice if he gave away his millions.

Augusta had shared two decades of hardship in the desolate mining camps without complaint, and now she could not adapt herself to the fact that they had struck it rich. He was beginning almost to hate her for casting doubt on his triumphs, for greeting each success and honor with a vinegary and down-putting remark.

He was becoming convinced that she would never prove herself a worthy marital partner of the Honorable Horace Tabor.

His consolation was that if Mrs. Tabor refused to enjoy herself, he could still quaff champagne by the magnum as he had once downed four fingers of red-eye, build more enterprises to the greater glory of his name, deck himself in the finest tailoring available, and emblazon his shirtfront, cuffs, and pinkies with outsized diamonds. And he could and would spend as little time in Augusta's withering presence as possible.

For some months, according to later accounts, he had been straying from his own fireside and looking for livelier company than Augusta offered. For all the wealth that caused journalists to dub him "The Croesus of the Rockies," he apparently cut a poor figure with the available girls; even in a throng of hardrock miners he was distinguished only for his awkwardness and a high degree of intoxication. More than half a century later a part-time

on his arm. In Baby's scrapbook may be found several invitations to balls, addressed to "J. Sands and Lady."

On the evidence of the scrapbook she was playing the field during her first weeks in Leadville. There was a letter from one T. B. Corrigan, sent from Chicago, which read, "I know of your domestic trouble, and to be brief, would simply ask you to sit down and write me as you would to the best friend you have. If I should have the pleasure to hear from you and you desire it, I may write you a more interesting letter." And there was another admirer who sent her a scrap of homemade verse and for discreet reasons of his own signed it simply "A Friend." It was dedicated to "B.D." and read:

> Like the morning sun in Summer
> Gilding bright the ocean wide,
> Like the gentle rain, in Summer
> Cooling green, the mountain's side,
> So your presence here among us,
> Fills our hearts with sweet delight.

And all the time Baby was compiling a sort of mental dossier on Lieutenant Governor Horace Tabor. Occasionally she caught a glimpse of him, while out on the town with Jake or another admirer, as he strode into Pop Wyman's or the Clarendon bar, shouting greetings, slapping backs, buying drinks for everyone in the house. Jake, of course, knew him but Baby didn't suggest an introduction. She would manage that on her own, under circumstances of her own choosing.

The rumor in briskest circulation around town was that Tabor and his wife weren't getting along. Augusta had returned from several months in Maine, but the separation hadn't improved her disposition. Nor had it made her appearance any more palatable. Her visit back home seemed to have only added more native granite to her character, and more tartness to her tongue. A number of clergymen called on Augusta at the Tabor suite in the Clarendon to present arguments on behalf of their various faiths and thereby solicit contributions to their churches. Augusta listened impatiently, then acidly commented, "I suppose Mr. Tabor's soul and mine are of more value now than they were a year ago."

Augusta now wore blue-tinted glasses to protect her weak eyes from glare, and they gave her a more forbidding appearance than ever. She bluntly refused to listen to Tabor's renewed arguments that she must live up to their new position in life. She rejected all suggestions that she play the great lady. She regarded with contempt Tabor's ambitions to play the host, refused to act as his hostess, and referred to his friends as parasites.

Not long after she returned from Maine, Horace removed her from Leadville to Denver on the grounds that his duties as lieutenant governor and his Denver building plans required the new residence.

Certainly Augusta couldn't complain of the style in which Horace uprooted her from Leadville. A long caravan of stage-coaches was engaged to transport their furniture and other possessions from the Clarendon suite down the mountain roads to Denver. Horace had already bought a four-story, mansard-roofed mansion with seventeen rooms in the capital. Formerly it had been the home of Henry C. Brown, the real estate promoter who developed what was then known as Brown's Bluff and is now Capitol Hill; it was a red-brick structure at Seventeenth Street and Broadway which dominated the surrounding homes of other magnates.

No doubt Horace was relieved to have Augusta's frowning, angular presence removed from Leadville. A mere stripling of fifty, he was footloose and feckless, though a certain amount of discretion was required because his son Maxcy was still posted in Leadville and his sympathies had always been with his mother. Otherwise his position as Number 2 man in the state government, multimillionaire, commanding general of the Tabor Light Cavalry, etc., did not weigh heavily upon him.

Then came the fateful evening Baby Doe tracked him down. That night Jake Sands was off on one of his gambling sprees, and Baby decided to place herself in Tabor's path. She knew that he and a friend or two usually dropped into the Saddle Rock Café for supper after the performance at the Tabor Opera House. When she entered the Saddle Rock, Tabor was seated at a table with Billy Bush. She took a table nearby and ordered oysters.

Now every gesture counted. She couldn't appear to be too brazen; she was a divorcee, a curious and tantalizing position for a beautiful young blonde in 1880, and that brought her close enough to the borders of the demimonde. She tilted her head away from the Tabor table and pretended to ignore the two men. That spring-heeled opportunist Billy Bush, of course, knew her well—perhaps too well—from the Central City days, and he wasn't going to risk sharing his influence over Horace Tabor with a female. Though they were sitting not more than ten feet apart, Bush ignored her and obviously hoped Tabor would do likewise. If any move was made, it was up to Tabor.

She could almost feel Tabor's penetrating blue eyes fastened on her, unless her imagination was hyperactive, but couldn't risk confirming it. She could hear Tabor murmuring to Bush, and was certain that she was the subject. Then she could hear Bush replying; no doubt he was filling in Mr. Tabor with details of her slightly lurid background. She risked a glance at the other table. Tabor was staring at her with a consuming interest.

A few minutes later a waiter was summoned to the Tabor table while Bush scrawled on the back of a theater program.

Baby's heart was pounding. Tabor evidently had overruled any demurrers Bush may have offered to introducing them. Presumably Bush had reported on her association with Jake, but that had only whetted Tabor's interest.

The waiter brought the note over to Baby's table.

"Won't you join us at our table?" it read. It was signed William H. Bush.

The scarlet thread running through Baby Doe's reputation hadn't frightened off Horace Tabor. He had been discreet about entanglements with the dancehall girls and other readily availa-

ble women, because he prided himself on having a touch of class.
Baby Doe might be a little "fast" but there was something almost
virginal—ignoring a rather bold glint in her large blue eyes—
about her childishly round face, her golden curls, her magnolia-
petal complexion. "Untouched" was the word for it. This was
definitely no soiled dove.

Horace called for champagne, declaring that "this is an
auspicious occasion."

He and Bush talked business but all the while Tabor's eyes
were fixed on Baby Doe. Bush took the hint. He muttered
something about having to confer with the manager of the opera
house and took his departure.

Tabor leaned closer to Baby and suggested that she tell him
about herself. Candor was the best policy. It would take Tabor
half a day to find out all about her background, even if Bush
hadn't provided him with a vivid sketch of the details. So she
spilled her brief biography, her respectable upbringing, her
unhappy marriage, the death of her baby, her relationship with
Jake Sands. She indicated that she was eager to break off her
association with Jake, but that she owed him money, which he
had advanced her from time to time when Harvey was proving
himself a poor provider.

"But you don't want to marry this fellow Sands?" Tabor asked
her.

She shook her head.

"Tell you what," Tabor said. "I've got more money than I
know what to do with. Let me pay him what you owe him."

"I couldn't do that," Baby replied.

"Look on it as a grubstake. I've backed more men than I can
remember. Hundreds of 'em. I wouldn't be sitting here in the
Saddle Rock tonight if I hadn't taken a chance on a couple of
fellows named Hook and Rische."

Tabor ordered another bottle of champagne. He and Baby
stayed at the restaurant until it closed just before dawn. They
discussed Baby's future—a girl alone in a tough mining town—
but probably not the fact that Tabor had a son older than she.

They were both romantics to a large degree, but they were practical about money and the pleasurable uses to which it should be put. Without any false sense of delicacy they struck a bargain at their first meeting. Baby would accept a check for $5,000 to pay off Jake and buy herself a suitable wardrobe; she would move out of the rooming house and into a suite at the Clarendon.

It was all very businesslike. Next morning Billy Bush went to Jake Sands with a note from Baby terminating their relationship and enclosing what she owed him plus a thousand dollars.

Some might say Horace had bought himself a concubine, but nobody could say Baby Doe had ever been up for sale. She had been smitten by the idea of Horace Tabor—if not the man himself, the legendary type he represented—long before she had ever heard of him. Since adolescence she had been determined to marry Tabor's sort of man; not merely because he was rich, but because he was bold, authoritative, had the courage to take what he wanted. Then she had zeroed in on Tabor because he was an exact representation of what she had in mind. Morality as imparted by the priests in her childhood was no hindrance. What Baby wanted was more important than what God was said to want for her. Still regarding herself as a faithful daughter of the Church, she was certain that God would forgive any little discrepancies between the divine scheme and her own desires.

She became Horace Tabor's mistress overnight, and in 1880, nine long decades before such actions were permissible, that was a plunge into the depths of degradation. She took the plunge with open eyes and the spirit of an adventuress.

A mistress, after all, could become a wife.

As it happened, Tabor had to spend most of his time in Leadville that spring because of a growing threat of labor trouble. With food and housing costs as high as they were in the boomtown, the silver miners were expected to get along on wages of $3 a day. For that they worked twelve hours a day, six days a week, deep underground in cold wet tunnels where many contracted pneumonia. It did seem that mines which produced almost 9,000,000 ounces of silver in 1880 could afford to pay their workers a more decent wage.

About that time a fire broke out in the Chrysolite mine and it took days for the Tabor Hose Company to bring it under control. Some said it had been started by arsonists hired by New York speculators who wanted to depress the price of Chrysolite stock so they could buy up a large block cheap; others that disgruntled workers might have been responsible.

Almost a year earlier the miners had started talking about unionizing themselves. They wanted their wages increased to $3.75 a day. They asked for greater mine safety. Many of the mines, despite the fact they produced immense profits, were inadequately shored up by timbers, and miners were injured by falling rock. They also suggested establishment of a hospital for treatment of miners ill from lead poisoning, since there was a large lead content in the carbonate ore.

Most of the owners, like Tabor himself, had recently risen from their ranks, but they were outraged by the miners' demands. Unionization, they warned, would be met by force. None was more indignant than Tabor, who had spent his youth cutting granite and part of his manhood in bashing away at hard rock. Few of the owners had the excuse of not knowing how hard and dangerous were the conditions under which their employees labored. Horace might snort that he had once fed his family on less than $3 a *week*, but that wasn't in a boomtown.

The owners' response was to alert the bloodthirsty vigilantes and organize more militia companies, including the Carbonate Rifles and the Tabor Tigers, along the lines of the Tabor Light Cavalry. Further, they held a meeting at the Clarendon and resolved to lower wages to $2.75 a day if the miners didn't fall back into line. There was a sizable pool of the unemployed in town. Since the railroads reached Leadville, including the Denver & Rio Grande as well as the Denver & South Park, every train unloaded men attracted by tales of easy money to be found in Leadville and soon reduced to begging for employment. Two men especially prominent in trying to organize a union were picked up by the vigilantes, accused of being Molly Maguires, and told they would be killed if they didn't leave town.

Until then, Tabor had been "Good Old Hod" to his work force. He had courted popularity among his miners because, after all, they had the vote and he had ambitions to be elected governor and later Senator. With his capitalist blood boiling, however, he forgot all about those political ambitions. It was an indiscretion he would pay for in future frustration. Unlike more adept politicians, he forgot there were more miners than mineowners in the Colorado electorate. When delegations came to him pleading for reconsideration of his refusal to increase wages slightly and improve safety conditions in his mines, he turned them away with harsh and arrogant words. "Do your damnedest," summed up his attitude.

A pronunciamento from Tabor brought on a dangerous confrontation, the first of many strikes in the Western mining regions which brought on the Western Federation of Miners and the even more radical and violent IWW (Industrial Workers of the World). That was his contribution to labor history, one which his fellow moguls would regret for decades to come.

Tabor late in May ordered that anyone found smoking or talking down in the workings of the Chrysolite mine was to be fired. Even the shift bosses quit rather than try to enforce that order. The Chrysolite miners elected Michael Mooney as their leader and spokesman and walked off the job. Then they marched up and down the gulch calling for a strike against all the other silver mines around Leadville. Most of the properties were closed down. The strikers tried to picket the Chrysolite but were driven away by the Tabor Light Cavalry (while Horace, like any good and sensible general, stayed at headquarters).

The chips were down now. Tabor could have persuaded his fellow owners to back off their obdurate refusal to bargain with their employees; perhaps he would have if Augusta, instead of

Baby Doe, had been at his side. Instead they began telegraphing
for mine guards, actually licensed thugs from the cities, and
arming every citizen who opposed the miners' demands.

It looked as though any day the "Magic City" would become
more widely known as "Bloody Leadville." The striking miners
held a mass meeting on Carbonate Hill and voted to seek a
$4-a-day wage and an eight-hour working day. Then, 4,000 of
them arrayed in a column of fours, led by Mike Mooney on
horseback, they marched in ominous silence through Leadville
and out to Fryer's Hill. Another meeting was held on Fryer's Hill
at which the Miners Cooperative Union was formed and
Mooney urged that no violence be offered the mine guards who
were then fortifying themselves around the Little Pittsburgh, the
Chrysolite, the Little Chief, and other properties. Workers at the
nearby smelters walked out in sympathy and now there were
almost 10,000 men on strike.

One minister, who felt that God was naturally on the side of
those blessed with the most worldly goods, appealed to the
strikers with an impassioned address. "Look across the ocean to
poor starving Ireland, to the workingmen of England, to the
downtrodden of Russia; and I ask you, are you justified in
the course you have taken?" The reply they roared back at the
Reverend was forthrightly blasphemous and obscene.

The mineowners and leading members of the community were
called to a meeting at Tabor's rooms in the Tabor Opera House
to organize a Committee of Safety, "patterned after the famous
San Francisco Vigilance Committee," as it was stated. A whole
regiment of amateur soldiers would be organized to smash the
strike, it was decided. Every store in Leadville was ordered to be
closed, and their owners and employees enrolled in the militia
companies which would reinforce the Tabor Light Cavalry and
others already in existence. C. C. Davis, the editor of the
Leadville *Chronicle*, having already distinguished himself in
action for his editorial broadsides against the strike, was elected
commander. Tabor, having received certain cautionaries from
Denver, was chary of any further military honors. A lieutenant

governor leading a charge against men striking against his properties made himself a controversial figure. Such considerations, however, did not prevent Tabor from delivering an impassioned address to the assembled regiment from the balcony of his opera house.

A show of strength had been decided upon. The newly organized regiment, largely composed of trembling clerks and counterjumpers, did parade down Harrison Street with their rifles, shotguns, and ax handles. Many in the crowds watching the demonstration booed. Further meetings of the Committee of Safety were held, with Editor Davis using a pistol as a gavel. It was resolved to send the several leaders of the strike, who had been identified by the Pinkerton detectives earlier hired to ferret them out, a warning that if they didn't leave town by the next day they would be seized and summarily executed. As champions of "law and order," the Committee of Safety further resolved that the strike leaders would be hanged from the rafters of the courthouse to make it look as official, if extralegal, as possible.

During those hectic days and nights, Horace Tabor hurried from various meetings, demonstrations, and parades of military force to seek comfort and reassurance from Baby Doe in her suite at the Clarendon. Occasionally they flitted down the block for dinner at the Saddle Rock.

Baby always appeared on his arm wearing a heavy veil suspended from her hat. No one, it appears, recognized Baby as the mystery lady; the relationship was still more or less a secret. Awkward though it might be to sip consommé through fabric, Baby would become accustomed to that veil in the next year or two, as the clandestine relationship continued. It would become irksome to hide herself, to slip around corners for a rendezvous, to live a sort of underground or back-street life, but at the moment it was tremendously exciting to be Horace's confidante during the hours of crisis. There was an almost narcotic exhilaration about having a small hidden role at the side of a shaper of events, to observe the workings of brute power.

At last she had found herself a real man, even if he were a little grizzled around the edges. Sooner or later, she was certain, she would be able to discard that veil and displace the dour Yankee woman who was holding Horace down and preventing him from realizing his ambitions.

And what a comfort it was for Horace to have at his side, during those hours when Leadville trembled on the precipice of anarchy, the uncritically adoring Baby Doe, who agreed with everything he said, instead of that desiccated humanitarian Augusta with her doubts and her warnings against the dangers of overweening pride.

Thus inspired, Tabor was a whirlwind of forceful action during the June days. Five days after the formation of the Committee of Safety he managed to persuade Governor Frederick R. Pitkin to proclaim martial law in Leadville and send several companies of state militia. The sheriff issued a proclamation of dubious legality ordering the miners to disband their union and go back to work, imposing a 10 P.M. curfew and closing all the saloons. All persons unable to show they were then employed were to be rounded up as vagrants, and more than 400, including several union leaders, were jailed.

Governor Pitkin, who knew his proclamation would be as unpopular elsewhere as it was popular with the mineowners of Leadville, wasn't going to let the lieutenant governor make any more rash moves, however. He sent David J. Cook, major general commanding the state militia, to take charge in the embattled mining town. Cook was a forceful man who had cleaned out the outlaw bands during the early years of the territory, had served as city marshal of Denver, and wasn't about to be overawed by Tabor or his colleagues.

In his memoir, General Cook recalled that when he arrived Leadville was about to explode. The miners and the owners were at the point of collision and there was a sizable third force, the underworld of Leadville, waiting to plunder when the situation got out of hand.

Cook was a fair and honorable man and he wasn't about to serve as the mineowners' chief strikebreaker. Nor was he going to allow the Committee of Safety to behave like a Central American junta; Leadville was still part of Colorado and the United States, and Horace Tabor was subject to laws other than those he promulgated *pro tem*. Even the conservative forces in the state, Cook knew, were appalled at the arrogance of the Carbonate Kings. A Denver newspaper hitherto unsympathetic to any sort of liberal cause had observed in an editorial that "The bonanza kings of the Carbonate Camp seem to believe that laborers have no rights; that if they assert any, they ought to be hanged by the Vigilance Committee."

Cook saw that if mass violence were to be averted he would have to interpose himself between the Committee of Safety and its extralegal armed forces and the strikers, who were equally belligerent and somewhat more desperate. He had brought several members of the Rocky Mountain Detective Association, including Lieutenant Matthew Hickman, to help him feel out the situation. Shortly after his arrival in Leadville on June 13, Cook learned from Hickman, who had been mingling with various elements on the mining camp's streets, that the flashpoint was close at hand.

"I ran into a man who really seemed to know something," Hickman told General Cook, "and when I let him think I was working direct with the committee he spilled a lot. It seems you and the soldiers came at just the wrong time. The Committee of Safety is hundred-percent against the miners and for a week they've been cooking up a scheme to settle the miners' hash by killing Mooney and five other strike leaders."

"Kill them?" Cook said. "How?"

"They were just about ready to go when martial law went into effect, so they have to change their plans in a hurry. Mike Mooney and the others are supposed to be arrested on charges of disturbing the peace and causing riots. Since the town's in charge of the troops now, of course, the six of them would have to be turned over to the soldiers. That's where the catch comes in. The idea is to grab Mooney and his pals and hand them over to a squad of soldiers who are on the committee's side. Then there's going to be a mob. It's going to spring up all at once and charge the guards who have Mooney and the others in tow. Of course the friendly soldiers are going to put on a good show and pretend to fight, but they'll give up soon enough."

"You mean this has been fixed up with some of our men?" Cook demanded. "When is all this supposed to happen?"

"Tonight," Hickman replied. "Sometime between ten o'clock and midnight."

General Cook ordered Hickman and his fellow undercover operatives to learn the names of everyone on the supposedly secret Committee of Safety. Then he summoned his second-in-command and his adjutant to the headquarters tent and ordered them to supply him with the muster rolls of his 600-militia force. Those who sympathized with the mineowners, and might be willing to involve themselves in a lynching plot, had to be weeded out immediately.

By ten o'clock that night Cook had been supplied with the names of about a hundred of the 115 members of the Committee of Safety and had identified those of his militiamen who sympathized with the mineowners. The potential troublemakers were pinpointed. At the same time Cook decided to take over Tabor's militia companies; those who opposed lynching were enrolled in his own force, the others were ordered to disband. One of his new recruits was Captain James Murphy of the Tabor Tigers. "On being questioned as to whether their men could be trusted to round up 'stranglers' or not," Cook recalled in his memoir, "Murphy replied, 'Now you're shoutin'. If there's anything in the world these boys are dead set on, it's stranglers.' "

"All right," Cook replied, as he recalled in his autobiography, "I'm going to give you the chance. Divide your company into small squads and go through this town like a fine-tooth comb. I want you to arrest every group of three or more people they find. If you find any of 'em hiding in cellars or any other place, arrest 'em. I want every bunch mopped up, and that goes whether they're in uniform or not. And you don't have to be too gentle about it either."

By his swift action General Cook saved Leadville from a multiple lynching and the mass disorders which inevitably would have followed. By using Tabor's own private army, he rounded up more than 200 troublemakers that night, all of them placed under detention, some of them members of his state militia. By 2 A.M. the streets were quiet and by dawn the tension of the past several weeks had been drained away.

During the ensuing three days, Cook kept a tight rein on Leadville, under the provisions of martial law. The Committee of Safety was ordered to disband. Tabor was deprived of his private army, and treated with little of the respect due a lieutenant governor.

At the end of the three days Governor Pitkin considered the situation past the crisis point and announced that he was about to revoke the martial law decree. Most of Leadville, however, had had enough of Tabor's adventurism; the citizenry had peered over the brink of anarchy and been appalled by what they saw or sensed. In repudiation of Tabor in his new guise, in revulsion from his proposals to smash the miners' strike at any cost, more than a hundred of the city's leading men telegraphed Governor Pitkin imploring him to let General Cook run the city until the strike was settled. Four officials of the Miners Union, all of whom had been nominated for the lynch rope, also wired Governor Pitkin asking that martial law be retained.

Several days later General Cook arranged for a peace conference between the union leaders and the mineowners. It didn't take the miners long to learn that their sacrifices had been in vain. Tabor and his fellow magnates were not prepared to bargain, to yield on any point, and there was no legal machinery in those days to force them to be reasonable.

The union leaders proposed that the miners return to work at the old $3-a-day scale but that the working day be reduced from twelve to eight hours.

No dice, replied Tabor and his group.

With a hauteur that American capitalism would learn to regret, they informed the union that "our right to regulate the affairs of our mines is absolute and we will not submit to any dictation as to hours of labor or rates of wages from any person or association."

The strike ended in failure, with the miners going back to work, risking injury, pneumonia, and lead poisoning for twenty-five cents an hour . . . and with the days of the dynamiters and more radical agitators than Mike Mooney just around the corner. The Carbonate Kings were triumphant, but their days, too, were numbered. The mines around Leadville had been so hastily and recklessly exploited that their silver-bearing carbonate lodes were rapidly being exhausted. That was particularly true of Tabor's Chrysolite and Little Pittsburgh. Leadville's peak of production would be reached two years later, when the mines sent out $17,000,000 in bullion, but it was apparent to the experts that Leadville would soon be played out. A local newspaper mourned late in the year that 1880 "has been a year of mingled prosperity and melancholy" marked by "an incessant struggle with adversity, with widespread distrust, with undeserved obloquy and loss of confidence."

Yet the biggest splurge in the city's short history was in the offing that summer.

It was a hoedown none of its participants ever forgot when ex-President Ulysses S. Grant came to Leadville at the invitation of the builders of the Denver & Rio Grande. Naturally Hod Tabor took charge of the festivities, and no one was so indelicate as to recall that Tabor had worked for the Denver & Rio Grande's rival, the Santa Fe, several years earlier when he contracted to cut timber to facilitate the latter's race for the Royal Gorge route.

General Grant had taken a trip around the world after leaving the White House and while in Japan (it was said) had heard of the miraculous flood of silver that came tumbling down the mountains from Leadville. Grant had always been fascinated by stories of great and sudden wealth, partly, perhaps, because of the grubbiness of his own origins, and he loved to rub shoulders with men who struck it rich. Whether even his egalitarian tendencies could survive acquaintance with Hod Tabor's back-slapping camaraderie was an open question.

According to plan, Governor Pitkin would welcome Grant to Denver, Lieutenant Governor Tabor to Leadville. The ex-President would then be shown how a conquering hero should be greeted. The result was something between a Roman triumph and a mining-camp riot.

When Grant's party arrived at the Leadville station he was greeted by a roaring (and in some cases, roaring drunk) crowd of 30,000 waving flags or whiskey bottles according to their dispositions. As the bearded little general dismounted from the train and proceeded toward the open barouche which would bear him to the Clarendon Hotel, he felt someone slap him on the back and shout, "How are yuh, General?" It was Tabor, who could not wait to be formally introduced.

With Tabor at his side, Grant was conveyed down Harrison Street in the carriage drawn by four black horses whose backs had been sprinkled with gold dust.

That night he was honored at a banquet in the Clarendon. The gathering was not notable for its sobriety, but then neither was General Grant. He was presented with a copy of the Leadville *Chronicle* printed on white satin as a souvenir of the occasion, which he later left to the Smithsonian Institution, where it may still be found.

Tabor of course sat at the head table beside Grant, pouring confidences into the ex-Presidential ear until Grant began to wonder whether he was being affected by the altitude.

Baby, too, attended the banquet but she had to sit down among the common folk, far from her rightful place (as she saw it) on the dais occupied by her protector and his fellow magnificoes. She could only visualize herself sitting among the mighty, her blond hair and creamy bosom glittering with diamonds, charming General Grant and adding to Tabor's glory.

After the banquet ended and the fallen were helped from the

hall, Tabor came to her suite with comforting words. He
understood how it must have galled her, he said, to have to be
separated a discreet distance from the head table.

"I know the President wanted to meet you," he added, "more
than anyone else in Leadville. I saw him look at you several
times—you're always the most beautiful woman in any gathering. But you know this mining camp and how it talks. We've got
to be careful."

During the next two days, Grant was taken on tours of the
mines and smelters, the eroded gulches, the scarred hillsides
where so many fortunes had been made. Everywhere he went
Tabor was at his side, pouring a torrent of words into his ear.
The ex-President was growing exceedingly weary of the Tabor
biography and the history of Leadville as interpreted by his host.
There was another banquet the final night of Grant's visit;
Tabor was still as adhesive as a mustard plaster. After the
feasting, Grant was hauled into Tabor's office in the adjoining
opera house for yet another tête-à-tête that threatened to last
until dawn. Tabor's loquacity only increased with every bottle of
champagne he uncorked. Finally Grant simply got up and fled
for his own suite in the hotel next door. He was certain that
Tabor had bored his way to a fabulous treasure in the
surrounding mountainsides by an overpowering stream of hot air.

Shortly after the Grant visit, Tabor decided to shift his
headquarters to Denver. There was nothing left to conquer, he
felt, around Leadville. His mines would continue to produce
millions indefinitely (he didn't believe the warnings of metallur-
gists and geologists) and they could be run by his managers.
Greater glory awaited him in Denver and Washington. Baby
Doe of course would make the move with him—his future
triumphs would be empty without her. Still, they had to keep
their love affair hidden from censorious eyes; Baby understood
that, though a restive look might cloud her pretty face from time
to time. So they traveled separate routes to the capital, Tabor by

stagecoach to South Park and then to Denver in David Moffat's private car, heavily veiled Baby (like the heroine of a daring contemporary novel) on the Denver & Rio Grande direct to Denver.

5. *Career of a Veiled Lady*

JUST then Denver wasn't the wisest choice of cities for a prominent public figure who wanted to keep a young mistress and yet maintain a façade of righteousness. Respectability had gained the upper hand for the moment and sins of the flesh were rigorously proscribed, or at least made more difficult to transact. It was a ticklish spot for a man who aspired to higher office and greater public esteem.

For years after it was a tent city acting as supply base for various gold rushes in the Colorado mountains, Denver had been a wide-open town profitably catering to the tastes of lusty fellows who came down from the mining camps ready to spend all they had gained. Now circumspection had replaced the old laissez-faire attitude toward moral issues. Prunefaced dowagers and grim female reformers seemingly had taken over and established a neo-vigilante rule symbolized by the reticule and the rolling pin rather than the lynch rope, tar, and feathers. They had set up a shadow government through various organizations which threatened social and communal, if not legal reprisals against those who defied their standards of conduct.

The cleanup was more apparent than real. Prostitution was allowed to continue but in a more circumspect guise. The red-light district was now confined to three blocks of Holladay (later Market) Street, which were lined with cribs containing an estimated 3,000 prostitutes. A whiff of burning opium came from the Chinese rookeries in Hop Alley just behind Holladay Street, and two blocks away were the big gambling houses on Blake Street. Also tolerated was a sizable underworld, efficiently organized, on a friendly footing with city hall and the police department. The Denver underworld was so potent a factor in civic affairs that its "czar," a bulb-nosed and affable French-Canadian named Lou Blonger, was as powerful as any city official. His wealth and influence were based on a dozen policy shops operating throughout the city. ("Policy" is better known in the East as the "numbers game.") Denver was also the Western headquarters of the infamous Louisiana Lottery, an enterprise which proved that criminal syndicalism was well advanced long before the Mafia appeared on our shores. And nowhere in the nation did the various bunco rackets flourish more openly and profitably than in Denver. Blonger reigned in Denver from the eighties to the 1920's, and established branches of his various rackets in Cuba, Florida, and California. Until a crusading district attorney sent him to prison in 1922, he virtually controlled the police department and its governing body, the fire and police commission. He maintained his dominance largely through heavy contributions to the campaign funds of both political parties—a fair measure of the actual state of morality in the city and state at a time when Horace Tabor's peccadilloes were viewed with mounting horror by the Capitol Hill establishment.

Tabor would have a hard time adjusting to the difference between mining-camp mores and the hypocrisies of a more settled community; between being the kingpin of Leadville and being just one more financially successful and politically promising man down in Denver. A sense of discretion, a talent for dissembling, an ability to play a two-faced role, would have helped; but Tabor was too bluff and forthright, and perhaps too assured of the efficacy of his wealth, to lead a double life.

He might, however, have taken warning from the storm signals

flying all over town that it would take more than his considerable
fortune and his political influence to achieve respectability while
indulging himself in a clandestine romance with Baby Doe.

The Denver Protective Association was campaigning against
"tight lacing"—of corsets, that is, which produced the currently
fashionable, wasp-waisted, hourglass figure—allegedly to "prevent ladies from killing themselves." This crusade undoubtedly
was inspired by middle-aged ladies unable to achieve a waspish
waist even with the aid of whalebone. The group also cam-
paigned for an ordinance to prevent girls from the Holladay
Street establishments from parading themselves on Exposition
Road on Sundays.

A law and order association demanded that the saloons be
closed on Sundays, ignoring the fact that was the only day
workingmen had to enjoy themselves. Such sturdy local institutions as the gambling house run by ex-gunfighter Bat Masterson
and the Palace, Ed Chase's gambling saloon and variety theater,
were threatened with closure or severe regulation. There was also
a vigorous anti-tobacco movement led by ladies who for years
had been disgusted by the brown juice dribbling from their
husbands' chins. Eugene Field satirized the crusaders against
alcohol and tobacco: "This is a bottle. What is in the bottle?
Very bad whiskey. It has been sent to the City Editor. He did not
buy it. If he had bought it, the whiskey would have been poorer
than it is . . . What is this nasty looking object? It is a chew of
tobacco. Oh, how naughty it is to use the Filthy Weed. Go quick
and throw the horrid stuff away. Put it in the ice-cream freezer or
in the coffee pot where nobody can see it. Little girls, you should
never chew tobacco."

Even the redoubtable Field could not prevail against the
crusaders, though elsewhere his shafts had punctured some very
tough hides. They were in the saddle and riding down everyone
who fancied his life and tastes were his own business. Even
wealth and influence could not armor a man against their
assaults. A man like Tabor, who formerly could have kept a
mistress for every day of the week, was now expected to Set an

Example for the lower orders, and devote his surplus energy to the furtherance of Culture and Elevated Thought.

Tabor might just have bent to the prevailing winds if Augusta had proved a little more flexible herself, if she had not taken every occasion to bruise his ego and slash away at his pretensions. It could easily enough have happened that Billy Bush, bearing a sizable check, appeared at Baby Doe's door one day and sent her back to Oshkosh. But the moment that Horace appeared at their new mansion, having stashed Baby in a luxurious suite at the Windsor Hotel, he found Augusta's disposition as corrosive as ever. He found Augusta quartered, not in the master bedroom, but down in one of the servants' rooms just off the kitchen. It was plenty good enough for her, she explained with asperity, since her head had not been turned by sudden wealth.

Horace had hardly set foot in his new house before Augusta began condemning him for his activities as chief strikebreaker in Leadville. "You're a fool, I've always known that, but I thought you had enough sense not to call a common lynching gang the Committee of Safety. And getting mixed up with that egotistical rooster, Davis, and letting him use a six-shooter for a gavel. And insisting that Governor Pitkin proclaim martial law. Mark you, Horace, you've lost all the popularity you've been trying to buy. You've made enemies from one end of the state to the other."

She knew him too well, they had been married for more than thirty years, and she was not devious enough to conceal her opinions. She did not hesitate to disclose her belief that it was more dumb luck than brains which had made him a multimillionaire. Nothing he did seemed to please her. If he came down hard on striking employees, he was being mean and brutish. If he gave money away—such as when he bought the land at Sixteenth and Arapahoe and gave it to the city of Denver as the site for a new post office—he was trying to "buy popularity." .

His official home with Augusta—as opposed to the secret nest he was maintaining for Baby at the Windsor—had become a courtroom in which he was daily arraigned for his misdeeds.

With Baby he found not only a sexual reawakening in middle

age but equally important, perhaps, soft words, encouragement,
balm for his lacerated ego. Yet Baby knew that her relationship
with Horace was not completely secure. She was still more a
sexual plaything than a person, less real and established in his
life than his carping wife. She realized how shaky her standing
was, how Billy Bush plotted against her as a threat to his own
position with Tabor, and how some of his other friends might
persuade him that Baby could be unbearably costly. Denver
wasn't Leadville, and the old free and easy attitudes of the
frontier, of the shifting populations of mining camps and
boomtowns, were being replaced by the stuffy moralizing of a
more settled society. The old biddies had conquered the West
and were turning it into an annex of the Epworth League.

She also knew that her hold on Horace wasn't necessarily
exclusive, that some other female might catch his eye and she
would be relegated to the same back-shelf status as his wife. Proof
that Horace was not completely enslaved came shortly after they
had made the move down to Denver.

City life was becoming irksome for Horace and he took off on a
junket back to Leadville without asking her to come along.

Billy Bush, posing as best friend of both parties, filled her in on
the details of Horace's excursion. With loving malice, Bush
revealed that Horace had borrowed David Moffat's private car
to attend a ball in Leadville. It was an affair at which the
demimonde of the mining camp annually indulged in a licen-
tious rout, a gathering of the big spenders and the fancier whores.
And Horace had told Baby that he was going up to Leadville on
"business."

The charmer on Horace's arm, according to Bush, wore a
spangled gown which a few days before had been on display in
the window of Daniels, Fisher & Smith's drygoods store in
Denver. Bush intimated that the girl he escorted to the ball was
definitely Baby's rival. And Horace had made a fool of himself,
considering that he was supposed to be lieutenant governor of
Colorado. After the ball, the surviving celebrants adjourned to
the Odeon Variety Theater, where a special show was staged.

With a cigar in one hand and a bottle of champagne in the other, Horace sat in a box with a girl on each knee. Every time a performer pleased him, he would put down his bottle and throw gold and silver coins onto the stage. As Bush told it, Horace's holiday up in Leadville had turned into an "orgy."

When Horace returned to Denver, pale and somewhat shaky, Baby was too intelligent to upbraid him. That job was reserved for Augusta. But Baby knew that she would have to move Horace toward a divorce, and toward seeing her as more than a plaything, or she'd lose him to another woman.

One way of tightening her hold on his esteem was to share in his somewhat grandiose plans, to encourage him in his daily expanding ambitions, as Augusta refused to do. If his wife persisted in cutting him down to sensible size, in opening the valve on his ego, his mistress would reinflate him. And which woman was he likely to prize the more?

Certainly Tabor's head was buzzing with schemes, late in 1880 and early in 1881, for laying the groundwork of various enterprises which would leave a lasting indentation on the city's architecture and cultural history. His first essay in that direction was the relatively modest one of completing the Windsor Hotel. With a group of British investors he took over the debt-plagued hotel before its interior decoration had been completed.

In a Medici-like mood, he insisted that the Windsor outshine the American House in every way possible. The huge inside doors were fashioned from black walnut, with hand-tooled and engraved, solid-brass hinges. The ceilings were twenty feet above the hardwood floors. Frescoes of cupids and ornate plaster moldings decorated the public rooms. The lobby was a red-plush extravaganza reflected in full-length, diamond-dust mirrors. The hotel's grand ballroom, in which the Empire Builders of the Rockies twirled their ladies through the square dance and the waltz, was fitted with parquet flooring and crystal chandeliers as weightily impressive as those of a European palace.

Naturally he superintended the liquor-dispensing facilities with special care. On the first floor alone there were two barrooms, one off the lobby, the other off the billiard room. The main bar, with from six to twelve bartenders on duty and such celebrated boozehounds as John L. Sullivan, Buffalo Bill Cody and General Grant among its occasional patrons, became a nationally famous watering hole. A notable career, too, began behind the Windsor's main bar, that of Harry H. Tammen, who rose from barkeep to co-publisher of the Denver *Post* partly on capital acquired from the Windsor's till. "I got my first real capital at the Windsor," Tammen once told the late Gene Fowler, his biographer. "You see we had no cash registers. I used to toss a dollar to the ceiling. If it stuck there, it belonged to the house. If it fell, it was mine."

And for those who indulged themselves too freely in that pleasure dome, the Windsor provided Russian and Turkish baths, the decor alone of which should have aided recuperation from an outraged liver. "These oriental ablutionary parlors," as Tabor's advertising proclaimed, "are elegantly fitted up and handsomely furnished throughout in white marble."

When the Windsor was completed to Tabor's satisfaction, he installed his son Maxcy and Billy Bush as co-managers.

And that was only the beginning of his building spree. Every day in Baby's suite at the Windsor he expanded on his plans to turn Denver from a red-brick replica of an eastern American city into something new and more vivid, a mountaintop Paris or Budapest. Baby didn't laugh at him or ridicule his pretensions as Augusta would. She made her own suggestions but in an oblique manner that convinced Horace they were his own.

Certainly this collaboration brought them closer together than any mere physical intimacies. It made Horace respect her mind as he admired her pocket-Venus figure. She was always ready to listen, to sympathize with problems as they developed. Soon enough she regained her confidence that one day she would legitimately share the throne of the Silver King.

His first project was the $325,000 Tabor Block at Sixteenth and Larimer streets, for which he tore down the old Broadwell Hotel. Colorado granite wasn't elegant enough, so cut and polished stone was imported from Ohio quarries. Emissaries were sent eastward to buy black walnut for the doors, frames, and sashes, marble for the stairs, special flaggings for the sidewalks produced in Illinois. The six-story structure, as his advertising agents proclaimed, was "reared like Solomon's Temple . . . ornate but tasteful." Over the capstone was inscribed *Dies Faustus*, along with the symbols of his good luck, a miner's pick, a shovel, a prospecting pan, and a windlass. It was almost as beautiful a building as Tabor believed it was, but too much money had been spent on decoration to make rental of its office suites profitable and it was soon known as Tabor's Folly.

Meanwhile he was startling the populace with plans for the Tabor Grand Opera House, to be constructed at an estimated cost of one million dollars on Sixteenth Street between Curtis and Arapahoe. It would be a five-story building of red brick with white stone trimming. The architects, W. J. Edbrooke and F. P. Burnham, were commanded to design a structure which would outdo in sheer magnificence anything in New York or Europe. He peeled off a series of thousand-dollar notes and handed them to Edbrooke with orders to tour Europe and study the construction of opera houses in London, Paris, Berlin, and Vienna.

"Don't pattern my place after those chicken coops," he instructed Edbrooke without ever having visited Covent Garden or the Vienna State Opera, "but pick up any good ideas they've got laying around."

Edbrooke dutifully set out on his grand tour without telling Tabor that he and Burnham already had complete plans for the Tabor Grand Opera House drawn and locked in their safe.

Other agents were dispatched to find the costliest materials for enhancing the interior, one man to Brussels to buy acres of carpeting from Belgian looms, another to France for tapestries and brocades, another to Japan to buy cherry wood for the interior woodwork, another to Honduras for mahogany. Italian marble was imported for pilasters and lintels. Heavy silk was bought in France to line the three tiers of boxes.

The auditorium, Tabor's agents announced, was "designed

upon the selected features of the Covent Garden Theater, London, and the Academy of Music, Paris, and combines the beauties and excellencies of both." Eugene Field, who devoted much of his Denver journalistic period to his duties as a self-appointed Tabor-watcher, commented that the style of the building under construction was "modified Egyptian Moresque."

No doubt that for a time the Tabor Grand was the gaudiest showplace west of Chicago. Under a large dome of cathedral glass was suspended an immense crystal chandelier lit by hundreds of gas jets. The proscenium arch was supported by two huge cherry-wood columns.

The curtain itself was a work of art on the heroic scale. Painted by Elliot Daingerfield, it depicted the ruins of a Roman city, with an ancient temple tumbling into rubble and lions crouching among the shattered pillars. There was something a touch Freudian about that conception—and definitely something premonitory about the fate of Tabor's works. Below it, Tabor ordered, was to be inscribed the verse composed by Charles Kingsley:

> So fleet the works of man,
> Back to earth again;
> Ancient and holy things
> Fade like a dream.

His rather ominous choice of verse suggests that Horace Tabor was a more complex man than the rough-hewn outlines of his character would indicate. Or that he was unconsciously trumpeting the forebodings of his wife Augusta. The English clergyman-poet had visited Colorado in 1874 and briefly occupied the pulpit of the Grace Episcopal Church in Colorado Springs. Tabor met Canon Kingsley after listening to one of his sermons and was presented with a volume of his poems. When he got around to building the Tabor Grand a half-dozen years later, Tabor read through the Kingsley verses and selected not only the inscription for his curtain but, unwittingly, his own epitaph.

It was the old, authentic, rough-diamond Hod Tabor, however, who one day strolled into the lobby of his opera house as it was approaching completion. On his way to inspect his impresario's quarters on a floor above the auditorium—which were furnished with a mahogany sideboard with silver trimmings and gold decanters, a mahogany desk inlaid with ivory and mother of pearl, and a solid gold inkstand—he paused to look over a painting which had just been hung.

"Who's that feller up there?" he demanded, pointing at the portrait.

"Why, sir, that is William Shakespeare, the Bard of Avon."

"What the hell did he ever do for Denver?" Tabor snorted. "Paint him out and put my face on that picture."

The Shakespearian portrait went back to the studio and the playwright's face was replaced by Horace Tabor's homelier features, and to hell with cultural piety.

His attention to every detail of the Grand Opera House's construction and operation even extended to the newsboy given the privilege of hawking his papers on the sidewalk outside the house. Naturally Horace chose one O. J. Owens, who had attained a local celebrity by crying his wares in rhyme. Owens had been crippled by polio in his boyhood and could barely shuffle along on warped limbs, but had an agile and inventive mind. He and Eugene Field often stood in front of Tabor's theater and competed in rhyming contests, and a local historian years later described him as "the best-known street figure in Denver."

When he wasn't playing Lorenzo the Magnificent or sequestering himself with Baby Doe in the suite at the Windsor, Tabor concerned himself, in the somewhat haphazard and offhand style of cow-country legislators, with affairs of state. He was serving his second term as lieutenant governor, an office he regarded as a mere way station en route to the governor's mansion, the Senate cloakroom in Washington and, ultimately (as his sycophants assured him), the White House.

Never mind that the image he projected was more picturesque than was usually required of a nineteenth-century statesman.

One oddity of his appearance, aside from a diamond display that outglittered the richest madam on Holladay Street, was a curious splashed look to his apparel. Tabor would readily explain it. On rising in the morning, he would dress himself and then proceed to shave. Naturally he splattered shaving soap all over his Prince Albert, but he regarded it as a pardonable foible.

In the years before the capitol building was completed, the state legislature was supposed to convene formally in the Barclay Block on Larimer Street. The real center of legislative affairs, however, was a nearby barroom, where deliberations were opened, not by a chaplain's invocation over bowed heads, but by the bartender's cheerful call of "What'll you have, boys?"

Those sessions would become much drabber and less fun-filled when they were confined to the new capitol's chambers, but no one could deny that Lieutenant Governor Horace A. W. Tabor cut a princely figure as presiding officer of the Senate in its less formal manifestation. With a flurry of outriders, he would enter the bar shouting greetings, slapping backs, ordering the first round of drinks and most of those that followed. The real business was transacted there, with the Barclay Block offices used mainly for sleeping off hangovers and receiving the soberer types of constituents. The lower house of the legislature met at the Denver House or the Planters Hotel, but without a presiding officer willing to spring for the drinks. A lot of the fun went out of lawmaking when the process was confined to the chambers of the new capitol.

The opening of the Tabor Grand Opera House on the night of September 5, 1881, was a cultural landmark even for those newly risen citizens who were stuffed into evening dress by their wives and who considered operatic singing a lot of screeching in a foreign tongue. Eugene Field memorialized the event with a scrap of verse:

> The opera house—a union grand
> Of capital and labor,
> Long will the structure stand
> A monument to Tabor.

The opening night had been preceded by a long and rancorous controversy over whether a "fulldress swallowtail affair" was truly democratic, whether boiled shirts and silk hats really were necessary to dignify the occasion. Horace made a lot of enemies among his fellow males by insisting—though only a few years before he had considered a red flannel undershirt suitable for most occasions—that evening dress was *de rigueur*; he made it plain that this was not just another mining-camp hoedown, and anyone who didn't want to pay proper tribute to the million dollars he had spent on his temple to the arts could damn well stay away.

Eugene Field, for once, supported him, though with sly humor. "Mr. Tabor's demand does not furnish grounds for assault. The wearing of a dress coat has never been regarded as a crime, even in Colorado. A man who will not wear a dress coat on a dress occasion is a snob. When Tabor is before the public as a politician, he is a legitimate subject for criticism. When he is before it as an enterprising citizen, he is not."

Every nabob in Colorado, plus everyone else who could buy a ticket, crowded the opera house that night to hear Emma Abbott's English Opera Company present the light opera, *Maritana*. Baby Doe attended in a diamond-decked turquoise gown, but she had to sit down in the orchestra seats. She could stare up at the Tabor enclave, Box A, and only wonder how long it would be before she took her rightful place on one of its white satin chairs. It was Baby's idea that the Tabor box be enhanced with a silver plate, the lettering in raised gold letters, fashioned from a block of silver two feet long and six inches thick smelted from ores taken from the Matchless mine.

No one occupied Box A, which was empty except for a huge horseshoe of red roses resting on a chair. The question Where is

Augusta Tabor? buzzed around the auditorium, almost distract-
ing attention from the magnificence of the decor and the
brilliance of the ladies' costumes, "cloaks of snowy plush," as a
society reporter wrote, over "heavily embroidered silken crepes
and exquisite combinations of cashmere and swan's down,
satin-lined."

Those who knew of Horace's dalliance and Augusta's neglect
were certain Mrs. Tabor's absence signaled domestic storms. And
they were right. Augusta had learned of the affair, refused to
participate in Horace's night of triumph even for the sake of
appearance, and was spending the night in her lonely brownstone mansion. Their son Maxcy and his fiancée, Luella
Babcock, were seated in Box H and seemed to be unaware of the
buzz of comment about the emptiness of Box A.

The program opened with Emma Abbott alone on the vast
stage before a backdrop. She sang the set piece from *Lucia di
Lammermoor* to thunderous applause. After that curtain raiser, the
master of ceremonies read a poem dedicated to Tabor (so inept
that Eugene Field had to be restrained by companions in Box F
from hurling a chair at the stage) and presented a solid-gold
watch fob designed to express the gratitude of Denver's citizenry.
"I wish to say," the MC explained, "that upon this fob is
engraved the history of Lieutenant Governor Tabor. This
represents an ore bucket. It is filled with nuggets of gold. From
the handle of the bucket is suspended a spade, a shovel, and a
pick, woven into the monogram of Governor Tabor. Then follows
the picture of a mule. That mule, let me say, stands in front of a
beautiful engraving of the old store where the governor passed so
many years. Here are the steps of a gold ladder, *Labor omnia vincit*,
'labor conquers all.' Upon this ladder, Mr. Tabor began to
climb. Next to this is the Tabor Block. Then there is another
climb, and at the top is a beautiful engraving of the magnificent
edifice in which we are tonight."

There must have been many in the audience who reflected
that, though only a Byzantine craftsman could have crowded
more symbolism on the surface of a watch fob, the biography left

out certain interesting details. What about a lace garter to symbolize Baby Doe? What about a shotgun superimposed on a noose to signify his suppression of the Leadville miners' strike? What about a steaming plate of sauerkraut in memory of Messrs. Hook and Rische, the real authors of his fortune? But perhaps this wasn't the time and place to bring up such matters. Most of his peers in the audience had large sections of their lives equally better concealed from public scrutiny.

Tabor stumbled through a reply in which he recalled having "looked Denver over carefully with its people, and here I found a town at the base of the Rocky Mountains—a city of thirty thousand or forty thousand inhabitants, the finest city, I think, of its population on the American continent. I said if Denver is to have an opera house, it should be one worthy of the city. Here is the opera house. I shall leave it to your judgment if I have done my duty in this respect."

Then the curtain dropped and a few moments later was raised on the opening scene of the night's performance.

One thing that Horace shared with Baby was a love of the theater in all its forms. During the worrisome months ahead, in which he had to disentangle himself from Augusta without arousing too much public indignation, the Tabor Grand Opera House was his prime distraction. Every night he held court in Box A, surrounded by visiting celebrities and the more sportive of his friends. Champagne was served continuously through the performance, and the performers, no matter how considerable their stature, were often distracted by loud conversation and the pop of corks from the Tabor box. Horace's love of the theater was genuine enough, but it extended to the superfluities of the theatrical ambience as much as the play or opera being performed.

Sir Henry Irving, Ellen Terry, Eleonora Duse, Sarah Bernhardt, Adelina Patti, Richard Mansfield, Mary Anderson, Maurice Barrymore, Lawrence Barrett, and many other luminaries appeared on the stage of the Tabor Grand, were jovially greeted in the green room backstage by their impresario, but cavalierly treated when onstage as they struggled through scenes punctuated by guffaws and exploding champagne bottles from Box A.

Tabor believed that he could do as he pleased in his own theater. Actors and singers (like hardrock miners) were only hirelings who were supposed to do their job as long as they got their pay envelopes.

Only occasionally would some artistic ego flare up and challenge Tabor's boorish behavior. The great Italian tragedian Salvini, for instance, who brought his *Othello* to the Tabor Grand. Tabor had a grudge against Shakespeare ever since it had been necessary to replace him with Tabor's face on the portrait in the lobby. He and his friends were especially uproarious during Salvini's opening performance.

Outraged, the Italian star sent a note to Tabor's box during the intermission following Act I threatening to ring down the curtain if Box A didn't quiet down.

"What?" Tabor bellowed when he read the note. "Tell that Eyetalian I am worth ten million dollars and I own this theater. We're gonna keep on having some fun. My theater is a playhouse, as much for the audience as the actors. If that Eyetalian wants to pray, let him go to church."

Salvini could only reflect on the barbaric condition of the American West and continue his performance against the competition of Tabor and his companions.

Undoubtedly Tabor in that period was suffering from a toxic condition of the ego. His money was piling up faster than he could invest, spend, or give it away. It seemed that anything was buyable. His expanding political prospects, his reputation as a local benefactor, the constant flattery of people who wanted something from him, all combined to persuade him that he was impregnable; that public opinion didn't count when you'd reached his dizzying height of affluence and success. He could literally squash anyone who got in his way.

Except, somebody wiser should have told him, an embittered and betrayed female with the stored-up resentments of more than thirty years of marriage.

With construction of the Tabor Grand finished, it was time to move on his next objective: divorce and remarriage. Baby made no secret of the fact that she expected him to marry her. She came of a respectable and pious Catholic family, she emphasized, and it was becoming more and more difficult to explain in her letters home just what her relationship with Tabor was. There would be more than enough family opposition, not to mention the hurling of Irish curses, when she got around to marrying a divorced man. The Church would not countenance the marriage of a divorced woman to a divorced man—and that was something else Tabor's millions would have to swing their weight against. Something had to be done quickly to legitimize their relationship or . . . Baby did not have to mention the alternative.

Horace reluctantly undertook his maneuvers to extricate himself from Augusta. Apparently he let Augusta know directly that he wanted a divorce—a quiet one, issued in the obscurity of some distant county court where the newspapers wouldn't pick up the story. Except for an occasional visit, he no longer spent any time in the brownstone mansion he had bought for Augusta. In a belated bow to discretion, he moved Baby out of the Windsor and into a suite at the American House, while he stayed on at the Windsor, so no one could say he and Baby were actually living together.

He was convinced that Augusta would shortly succumb to pressure for divorce, which was largely exerted by his smooth-talking aide-de-camp Billy Bush. The last time he called on Augusta, Tabor had packed some of his few remaining possessions in the house he had shared with her for only a few months. As he was leaving with his suitcases, she broke down and wept. "Oh, Pappy," she cried out, "don't leave me. You know it will be your ruin." Cassandra to the last.

The next move, in surprising and distressing form, came from

Augusta. She did not file for divorce, but for a property settlement. She saw no advantage in divorce, as Tabor read it, but every advantage in tying up part of his money as a hedge against any bad luck that might come his way.

Horace was even more infuriated when he learned that Augusta, in pressing her claim, was charging him with nonsupport. She was making it as hard on him as possible without giving him what he wanted most—a divorce. The whole state was scandalized by Augusta's charges that Tabor had contributed nothing to her support for two years, had deserted her a year earlier, and forced her to keep body and soul together by "renting rooms in her place of abode and by keeping boarders."

That charge was nonsense, but there were all too many people willing to believe it, even more to sympathize with Augusta as an abandoned wife and condemn Horace for leaving her so soon after he got rich. Women particularly were outraged. If that sort of thing were allowed to happen, few of them were safe from the moment their husbands made money. A divorce fever would streak over Capitol Hill like wildfire. Political bigwigs were warned that no matter how much money Hod Tabor contributed to party war chests he must not be rewarded for his transgressions.

Tabor was becoming desperate; divorce and remarriage had to be accomplished before the end of the year (1882) because he wanted either the governor's office or a seat in the U.S. Senate no later than the following year. First there was Augusta's disgraceful suit to be dealt with. She was demanding that he settle $50,000 a year on her and turn over the Denver mansion to her. In support of those demands she listed holdings estimated at more than $9,000,000. They included a valuation of $800,000 on the Tabor Grand ($200,000 less than he claimed it had cost), $500,000 in Denver National Bank stock, the Matchless Mine estimated at $1,000,000, a part interest in a group of other mines totaling $3,000,000, $200,000 worth of government bonds, jewelry worth $100,000, and various real estate parcels. She added that his income came to $100,000 a month.

Augusta's suit, however, was dismissed on the curious grounds that the court had no jurisdiction. It was apparent that if she wanted a property settlement she would have to give Horace a divorce, but she remained obdurate and the domestic war of nerves continued.

By midsummer, 1882, with Horace's lawyers getting nowhere with Augusta's lawyers (the latter had informed the former that Mrs. Tabor might consider agreeing to a divorce in return for half of everything Tabor owned), Horace took a step of breathtaking audacity, not to mention criminality. This was urged on him, not only by Baby Doe's presumed importunities, but by the ripening political situation. With the assassination of President James A. Garfield the previous year, Chester A. Arthur, formerly a member of the malodorous New York political ring, had succeeded to the Presidency. He intended to appoint U.S. Senator H. M. Teller as his Secretary of the Interior, which would open up one of Colorado's Senate seats. Senators were then elected by the state legislature, and Horace was confident (recalling all the liquor he had bought during the past three and a half years to sluice down legislative throats) that he could win a Senatorial seat if only his domestic situation could be pacified. How often he must have reflected on the beauties of the Moslem method of divorce.

His solution was a drastic one. Emissaries were dispatched to Durango, the La Plata county seat, in the southwestern corner of Colorado. Connections were made with a sympathetic Durango judge. Tabor owned mining properties down there, and with his Midas touch might make the region flourish.

Without having papers served on Augusta, Horace quickly obtained a divorce, garlanded with fraud and perjury though it was. He and Baby then journeyed secretly to St. Louis, where they were married by a justice of the peace. Technically, they were now living not in sin but in a state of bigamy. He promised that they would be married in a Catholic ceremony once the legal obstacles were cleared.

Baby was pacified for the moment—at least she had a

marriage certificate to fondle—but a secret marriage was almost
as unsatisfactory as the previous arrangement. She was getting
awfully tired of wearing that heavy veil whenever she and
Horace ventured into public view; of tripping over curbstones
and blundering into lampposts. Furthermore the disguise wasn't
fooling people anymore.

Finally, in January of 1883, just before the state legislature
convened to take up the matter of the Senatorial election,
Augusta was persuaded to yield, largely because she dreaded
scandal and because she was convinced Horace would never
return to her. The possibility of a scandal which would damage
her son as well as Horace arose when a new clerk of court was
elected in Durango. The newly elected clerk discovered that two
pages of the court records had been pasted together by his
predecessor, the ones recording Tabor's secret divorce. He
informed Augusta of the illegal divorce. Now she had a choice of
setting out to ruin Horace, as a lesser woman might, or avoiding
the scandal of bigamy and giving him his way.

So she tidied up the situation as she had so often straightened
out his haphazard bookkeeping when they were struggling
storekeepers, and agreed to the divorce. In those days before
alimony became an established institution, the settlement she
received was decidedly a modest one considering the size of
Tabor's holdings. She accepted the mansion she had been
occupying with her son Maxcy and his new bride plus a cash
settlement of $250,000—and it was one of the more biting ironies
of their sundered marriage that, in the end, the shrewd and
conservative Augusta made a lot more of her quarter-million
than Horace did with his much larger share.

Augusta did leave an avidly curious public with one dramatic
sequence before she walked out of Horace's life, one which made
a significant impression on the electorate and prejudiced Denver
society, which Horace hoped would accept Baby Doe and grant
her fervent desire to become one of the queens of Capitol Hill.

When Judge Benjamin F. Harrington granted the divorce,
Augusta, in a manner curiously at variance with her distaste for

scenes of any kind, for displaying her emotions in public, dramatically demanded of the judge: "What is my name?"

"Your name," he assured her, "is Tabor. It is yours by all legal rights."

"I will keep it until I die," Augusta proclaimed. "It was good enough for me to take. It is good enough for me to keep. I thought to thank you for what you have done, but I cannot. I am not thankful. But it was the only thing left for me to do. I ask you to put it on the record, *Not willingly asked for.*"

Augusta left the courtroom sobbing.

That night her ex-husband and his wife-to-be somewhat moodily celebrated the occasion. The path was clear—or was it?—for a legal marriage, for political triumphs in Washington and social dominance in Denver. Yet they were aware that Augusta, with her final words in court, like the sting in the tail of a dying scorpion, had left them with something to remember her by.

Within weeks of the divorce, Augusta began reflecting publicly on its circumstances. She left no doubt, in newspaper interviews, that she believed she had been submitted to relentless pressures from both her own and Tabor's counsel; that she considered it significant that her attorney, County Judge Amos Steck, had been the one who granted Baby Doe's divorce from Harvey Doe, a fact she had apparently been unaware of when she engaged his services. Steck, as a Denver historian noted, "brought pressure on her by telling her it was hopeless to try to wage a court fight against a man worth so many millions, that a man of Tabor's character would blast her reputation through purchased testimony, sue for and win the divorce itself, and she would get nothing."

Also indicative of her attitude were the clippings of newspaper commentary on the divorce which she pasted in her scrapbook. "A bonanza king can purchase anything that he wishes, even a divorce in four hours," reported a Denver journal. "Tabor's

friends are probably as glad as Tabor to have an affair speedily
and quietly concluded, which if sifted thoroughly by daylight,
might prove dangerous to the lofty aspirations of the lieutenant
governor. Mrs. Tabor probably has it in her power to tell some
very ugly truths about her ex-spouse, but as Judge Steck says, 'If
the truth were known, it would be enough to ruin him forever.
She loves him and that settles it. She will not say a word.' "

Out-of-town papers were even harsher in their judgment of the
Tabor divorce. "Denver is morally rotten," a Washington *Evening
Star* editorial declared. "There is a low tone to Denver society.
Most of the bonanza kings are shockingly open in their liaisons.
The air is full of scandal and tales of intrigue constantly heard.
Things are tolerated in Denver which would not be permitted in
any northern or eastern city . . . O, ye wicked men and women
of Denver!"

If Washington could moralize at Denver's expense, so could
not entirely spotless Chicago, where one of the newspapers
seethed with indignation over "the Colorado magnate who threw
his wife over for the embraces and smiles of tawdry, painted
courtesans . . . Vulgarly flaunting his shame in the face of
respectability, he aspires to the highest place in the gift of the
people of Colorado . . . He runs the race of a conscienceless
millionaire—coarse, corrupt and ambitious. He publicly disports
diamond cufflinks and embroidered nightshirts. They call him
'Senator.' His name is Tabor."

In a bitterness that would intensify during the coming months,
Augusta Tabor would brood over plans to nullify the divorce,
even if that wouldn't bring Horace back to her side.

6. The Nuptials of Senator Nightshirt

UNDOUBTEDLY Baby Doe would have agreed with the Somerset Maugham dictum that "Money is the sixth sense that enables you to enjoy the other five." But there was more to her determination to become the second Mrs. Horace Tabor than simple greed. Although she reveled in the furs and jewels and silks that Tabor's money could provide, and frankly agreed that beauty deserved a proper setting, she was fascinated by the man himself; she later said she was half in love with him, or his legend, before she ever met him. She had always seen herself as the helpmate of a man who did things in a big way, not only because of what those things could provide, but for the excitement of sharing in large projects, of exercising power, of taking sizable risks. Ever since the childhood hours spent in her father's store, she had looked up to men who exuded self-confidence, which to her was the essence of masculinity. To share in the life of a man determined to leave his mark on the world, she was willing to sacrifice much of herself, as she had proved in Central City when, to wide disapproval, she took up hardrock mining herself. Certainly an overview of her life would show that her dedication to Horace Tabor was more than a matter of the things he could buy her.

The influential people of Colorado, however, did not view her in that light. She was simply an adventuress to them. By then rumors of the scandal attending her first marriage, particularly her association with Jake Sandelowsky, had followed her to Denver. It didn't help when word got around that she had conspired with Tabor to arrange his illegal and secret divorce in Durango. Nor that she always held her head high, looked down her short, tilted nose at anyone who insinuated that she was a kept woman, and failed to show the slightest penitence for all the trouble she was causing.

The more tolerant were willing to forgive Tabor's involvement on the Victorian grounds that male behavior was apt to be a bit brutish on occasion and you couldn't blame a man too much because he had been ensnared by a designing female.

Few, however, were willing to forgive Tabor to the extent that he should be hoisted into the United States Senate. The weatherbeaten, pioneer wives of legislators, who would have found Baby Doe's petal-like complexion alone unforgivable, may not have been enfranchised in 1883, but they could exercise enough domestic influence over husbands in the state legislature to prevent Tabor's nomination. It was apparent that his divorce from Augusta, coming within days of the Senatorial contest, might well cost him the object he then gave the highest of priorities.

Aside from the scandalous complications, the situation was a tangle of conflicting ambitions. The prim and proper Governor Pitkin, who epitomized the change in the sociological climate from that of the mining camp to that of the settled community, had his own ambitions fixed on the Senatorial vacancy created when H. M. Teller was appointed Secretary of the Interior in mid-1882 after President Garfield was assassinated and replaced by Vice President Arthur. To keep that seat warm for him, Governor Pitkin had appointed a lusterless party hack named George M. Chilcott to serve to the end of 1882. Then the state legislature would convene late in January, 1883, to elect one man to serve for thirty days, another to serve the regular six-year term. Besides Pitkin and Tabor there was another prominent

Republican—much craftier than either of them—with Senatorial ambitions. He was Tom Bowen, another mining magnate, with a career as politically checkered as Tabor's was personally tainted. Before striking a fortune of several millions with the Little Ida gold mine in the San Juan Valley, Bowen had joined the carpetbagger rush to the defeated South just after Appomattox and had served on the Arkansas supreme court. Later, President Grant appointed him governor of the Idaho Territory. On acquiring his fortune in Colorado gold, Bowen began plotting a revival of his political career. He couldn't pour as much money into the Republican Party's coffers as Tabor, and he couldn't match Pitkin's claim on superior morality, but he was suaver and trickier than either of his rivals.

Horace and Baby Doe had to endure much in the way of public opprobrium and private innuendo during those days when Tabor's Senatorial ambitions hung in the balance. An editorial in one Denver newspaper asserted that Tabor was "a disgrace to Colorado" and should be "driven from the state" instead of receiving its highest honor. The *Rocky Mountain News*, published by a supporter of Senator Hill, who was bitterly anti-Tabor, called him a "shambling, illiterate boor . . . If both of Tabor's wives should take the stump, what a red hot canvass they would make!" Tabor promptly filed a $30,000 libel suit against the *News*, but another journal upped the ante and claimed Tabor had *four* wives.

"There is not a person in the State who sincerely believes that Mr. Tabor would make a good Senator or that he ought to be elected," fulminated a periodical called the *Inter-Ocean*. "This, no matter what they may say in print or conversation. Such a state of public sentiment is not necessarily uncomplimentary to Mr. Tabor." The *Inter-Ocean* went on to explain, "The republic has not grown old enough for acquiescence in the domination of rich families; and yet we have passed beyond the period which distinguished Rome, when Rufinius was expelled from the Senate because he was the owner of silver plate of the value of ten pounds."

Even his fellow statesmen, those not personally beholden to
Tabor, were making rude noises about his candidacy. It galled
Teller, in his eminence as a Cabinet member, to think of Tabor's
rump planted in the Senatorial chair he once occupied. When
Tabor asked for his support, Teller replied with unnecessary
candor, considering how much Tabor money had been siphoned
into Republican campaign funds, that "You are mistaken in
supposing that I could elect you if I wished. I could not do so if I
wished, I would not if I could. I know you are not fitted by
education, temperament or personal equipment for that office."

Tabor remained serenely confident that the money he had
contributed to the Republican treasury would win him the
Senatorial seat as it had brought him the lieutenant governorship. For several years most of the Republican members of the
state legislature had been drinking on his tab. How could they
deny him what he wanted most? "Tabor is going to have the
senatorship," commented the Denver *Tribune*, "or know why
money has lost its potency. He has more of that excellent
senatorial qualification than any one or two of the balance of the
Republican crowd." It noted, however, that Tom Bowen was
spreading his money around the legislature and "his gold is a
very nightmare to other aspirants."

Tabor himself was more concerned about Governor Pitkin's
pious attitude than Bowen's gold reserve. "Pitkin," he complained, "knows I'm not such a scalawag as some fellows try to
make me appear." In his increasingly concerned search for
support he turned to Jerome N. Chaffee, who had become
notorious for his speculative activities and was suspected of
having plotted the Wall Street maneuvers against the Little
Pittsburgh mine. Chaffee was known to be more dangerous to his
friends than his enemies. To Eugene Field, who believed that
poetry could be applied even to politics, Tabor was a fleecy lamb
about to be sheared by the unscrupulous Chaffee:

> Chaffee had a little lamb
> Who wore a fierce mustache,

> And people wondered how that lamb
> On Chaffee made a mash.

> What makes Chaffee love the lamb?
> Incessantly they cried.
> The lamb has got a golden fleece,
> The knowing ones replied.

Political insiders whispered that Tabor was "riding for a fall," and many of them, including those who had long accepted his favors, welcomed the prospect of his downfall. "It will be worth a great deal of money for Mr. Tabor to tumble himself," as a statehouse correspondent observed, "even if it is necessary for the grand opera house to fall on him to bring about the desired result." But Horace remained confident of the power of his millions, and touchingly gullible about the durability of political loyalties. He had reportedly distributed $200,000 around Capitol Hill to insure those loyalties. Regarding Governor Pitkin as his most dangerous rival, he had made a deal with slippery Tom Bowen for the latter to support him on the first 6 ballots. If he didn't win the nomination by the sixth ballot, he would throw his support to Bowen.

It was evident from the first meeting of the Republican caucus that Tabor was going to have a hard time winning the nomination. On the first ballot Tabor received only 10 votes to Pitkin's 25 and Bowen's 5. Tabor rallied his forces, reopened his purse. On succeeding ballots Tabor began overtaking Pitkin. He got his vote as high as 24 on one ballot, but 3 still held out for Bowen. Those 3 votes would have provided him with the necessary majority. Tabor now charged Bowen with bad faith, with having withheld just enough votes to keep him from getting the nomination. Bowen responded in like terms. The Republican caucus then decided that further balloting would be by voice vote instead of secret ballot. The contest would not be out in the open, and as the Denver *Tribune*'s political correspondent noted, "Pitkin's followers were now open to seduction." Chaffee, for all his promises to deliver the nomination to Tabor, simply opted for the candidate whose methods, more subtle than Tabor's, matched his own and whose tenure in Washington for the full six-year term would serve his ends better.

On the ninety-seventh ballot the Republican caucus voted for Bowen as the Senatorial nominee. Since the Republicans held a majority in the legislature, his selection was a foregone conclusion. But that left Horace Tabor out in the cold and might deprive the party of his much-valued financial support. A sop had to be thrown in his direction. The bosses, on January 27, assuming their most placatory manner, appeared as a delegation in Tabor's office suite in the opera house. Hod mustn't be upset by his rejection. The Grand Old Party was grateful for all his services and would reward him with the temporary appointment; that meant the Honorable Horace Tabor would be the United States Senator from Colorado for thirty days until Bowen took over the seat. Tabor was silent for a long while, then agreed to accept the sop to his vanity. "It is not always that one who goes in for a big prize is put off with one seventy-second part of it," he told the delegation, "but I am thankful and satisfied."

That night there was what one survivor called a "Wild West celebration" in Tom Bowen's suite at the Windsor. Champagne flooded the suite like the sluiceways from which came the gold to pay for cases of the bubbly (and the Senatorial nomination).

Tabor came in from his own suite across the hall, congratulated Bowen, and then slipped back to the consolations offered by Baby Doe. At least they would be married in Washington, and a President would dance at their wedding, and all the prunefaced dowagers in Denver could turn puce with outrage and envy.

Six days later, in considerable style, Tabor left Denver to take up his duties in Washington, while Baby prepared for her wedding in less than a month. He engaged a private train, at a cost of $5,000, to take him to the national capital.

A reporter who met the train in Washington interviewed the

porter and got himself a story which was widely reprinted and caused violent guffaws in Denver and the mining camps where Tabor had once cut so homely a figure. According to the *National Intelligencer*, Tabor had ordered the porter to make up his berth early the first night of the journey, and then broke out a magnificent silk and lace nightshirt with gold buttons which had cost $1,000 and was more suitable for Napoleon Bonaparte on his bridal night than Hod Tabor in a Pullman. "A gorgeous velvet cap, elaborately decorated, was first produced and hung on a hook for all to see," the newspaper recounted. "Next followed a magnificent ruffled nightshirt, half smothered with costly point lace of the finest quality." The lace alone, Tabor boasted, had cost $250.

The reports of his elegant negligee did Tabor as much damage among the menfolk of Colorado as his divorce did among their women. From then on Eugene Field usually referred to him as "Senator Nightshirt." One touch of sybaritism—a sneaking fondness for French cuisine was bad enough—was sufficient to doom any political career; a man could wallow in whiskey and wild women if he did so without calling too much attention to himself, but wearing lace next to the skin was so epicene as to border on degeneracy. Whatever hopes Horace had of making a political comeback once the scandal over his divorce and remarriage died down were null and void.

The hubbub over his nightshirt did not deter Horace from taking himself seriously as a statesman. Immediately after checking into his ten-room suite at the Willard and unpacking his nine suitcases and thirteen trunks, he was sworn in by the presiding officer of the Senate. "Great God!" one of his fellow legislators was heard to exclaim as Tabor appeared in a blaze of diamonds. The gentleman from Colorado wore a large diamond solitaire on each hand, square cuff buttons of diamond and onyx the size of postage stamps, and a diamond with the glitter of a small headlight on his shirtfront. The Senate was not so dazzled as to appoint him to the Foreign Relations Committee but relegated him, as a thirty-day wonder, to a standing committee on pensions and claims and a subcommittee studying epidemic diseases.

Eugene Field had to observe his Senatorial career from afar, but that did not inhibit him from passing sardonic judgment on the quality of Tabor's statesmanship. Field did allow that Tabor was doing "at least as well as Chilcott who won golden opinions by his silence and promptitude in voting as directed by his party. But he must shoot that diamond ring. If any burleque actress should happen around, it might get him into trouble. It did once before as will be remembered."

What Field lacked in solid information about Tabor's Senatorial career he supplied from his Western journalist's stock of hyperbole. The Denver *Tribune*'s poet-columnist pictured Tabor, mindful of his silver mines, introducing a bill calling for the suspension of gold coinage:

"Tabor, having obtained the floor, kept the whole Senate at bay for three hours, delivering the most powerful address in the Senate since the great French Arms debate. He analyzed the bill to the dregs and was at times ferociously satirical."

He also imagined Senator-*pro tem* Tabor being summoned to a Cabinet meeting by President Arthur, who promised to "hold up all appointments until Senator Tabor gives the word to go ahead," and Tabor rising on the Senate floor to raise a question of privilege. "He said his attention had been called to a late copy of the *West Mountain Pilot* in which occurred a paragraph designating him as an *anomaly*. He had determined when he started out on his political career to pay no heed to the utterances of his enemies. But here was an instance where the libel was so unprovoked, so wanton, the slander so malicious and the charge so appalling that he felt impelled to notice it. How and at what time had he committed the offense? Who was his accessory to the deed? Honorable Senators would observe absolutely no qualifications; why had his slanderers neglected to draw up a bill of particulars? He would tell the Senators why; the charge was unqualifiedly and ignominiously false. (Applause.)" The joke within a joke was that most of the *Tribune*'s readership would have been as confounded as Tabor by the meaning of "anomaly."

Tabor, in any case, was too busy enjoying his brief Senatorial career and arranging for his wedding to be wounded by Field's comments. As he understood it, the art of politics leaned heavily on the number of drinks a successful practitioner was willing to buy. Every hour or so he charged into the Senate cloakroom and rounded up a quorum of his colleagues for a sortie to the nearest barroom. One of the prissier members of the Senate rejoiced that Tabor was serving only a thirty-day term, "otherwise the Senate would never do any business."

In politer society than a Capitol Hill barroom, however, Tabor was declared, according to Eugene Field, a total liability. From a few shreds of fact Field reconstructed a weekend Tabor spent in New York as the guest of the lordly Senator Roscoe Conkling, an occasion on which his portrayal of what the newspapers were calling "the Wild Western Senator" did not endear him to effete Easterners. As Field reported to his readers:

"Tabor spent Sunday in New York as the guest of the Honorable Roscoe Conkling. 'Tabor,' remarked Conkling, 'is a charming fellow. He is full of anecdotes and bon mots, and quicker at repartee than any man I know. As we sat at table this afternoon, Vanderbilt, who is something of a wag, was inclined to banter Tabor for cracking nuts between his teeth instead of using the silver instrument provided for the purpose. What have become of your crackers, Horace? said he. Quick as a flash, Tabor retorted, I ate them in my soup an hour ago. Ha! ha! ha! a merry fellow—full of jest and song and mirth when the occasion demands.' "

A much less tolerant view of the seat-warmer from Colorado was taken by Senator John J. Ingalls, who fumed over the depreciation of Senatorial dignity in a letter to his wife. "The Colorado millionaire, Tabor, took his seat last week. A fouler beast was never depicted. He is of the Harvey type [apparently a reference to William H. Harvey, a publicist of violent disposition], but indescribably lower and coarser. Such a vulgar, ruffianly boor you never beheld; uncouth, awkward, shambling, dirty hands and big feet turned inward; a huge solitaire diamond on a sooty, bony blacksmith hand; piratical features, unkempt, frowsy and unclean, blotched with disease, he looks the brute he is. He was stared at with curious but undisguised abhorrence."

Tabor was blissfully unaware that the jovial, backslapping, belly-up-to-the-bar-boys style which went down well enough in Colorado political circles wasn't suitable for the more rarefied atmosphere of Washington, on which some of the Eastern Seaboard manner had rubbed off. He was exuberantly writing Baby of his plans for a dinner party and assuring her that his obsessive love had not diminished with the approach of their wedding date:

"Everything is working all right. I have quite a grand dinner party tomorrow night, in fact the best that has been held here for a long time and I do not know that it has ever been excelled. I will have to it the President, Senators Sherman, Morrill and a lot of the best—there will be twenty altogether.

"You watch the Associated Press dispatches Sunday morning and you will see an account of the dinner. The room will be decorated luxuriantly with flowers and all will be lovely.

"I shall write you no more for you will not get it, for you will start Tuesday night I presume by the Limited on the Pennsylvania route that will get you here Wednesday night and I shall meet you at the train.

"You must wire me from Pittsburgh or have Pete [her brother] do it, and wire me just before you start. I may write you again tomorrow for I have something particular to tell you. I love you to death and we will be so happy. Nothing shall mar our happiness for you are all my very own. I am yours from hair to toes and back again. We are at the present time having quite a time in the Senate—there is not a quorum and there is lots of filibustering. It is 8:15 P.M. and we may stay all night. Write me all the news, that is, how you are getting along. I love you I love you Kiss Kiss forever and ever Love Love Love Love Kiss Kiss

Kiss Kiss Love Love Love Love Love Kiss Kiss Kiss Kiss Kiss Kiss. . . ."

Tabor was so delirious over his coming wedding and what he believed was his acceptance by his Senatorial colleagues that he probably didn't read a more realistic appraisal of his social standing in a Washington dispatch to a New York newspaper. The dinner party, it noted, was being given to "the few people who have been polite to him."

Such quibbling over the quality of his acceptance would not have dismayed Horace. He was content that forevermore he would be called Senator.

Brief though his Senatorial career might be, Tabor was determined to leave his benchmark on the legislative annals. He won his place in the *Congressional Record* by introducing a bill appropriating $100,000 for the establishment of an army post in western Colorado for the preservation of the Western forests, not because he was an ardent conservationist but because otherwise "I don't see where railroad ties will come from."

His colleagues could only applaud his reason for voting aye on a tariff bill which exempted jute from the payment of import duties.

"I want 'em to have enough hemp in Colorado," he declared, "to hang those fellers who wouldn't elect me to this club for six more years."

Back in Denver, Baby Doe was daily thrilled by bulletins from Horace detailing his preparations for the wedding on March 1. It had been a hectic six years since she left Oshkosh as a bride to seek her fortune in the Colorado mountains, but now all her dreams were coming true.

They had agreed before Horace left Denver that a proper Catholic ceremony would be arranged. Horace would find a priest, offer him a large fee, and hope that he wouldn't inquire too closely into their backgrounds.

Everything about the ceremony would be tip-top in elegance, Horace was assuring her. The wedding invitations would have

quarter-inch silver margins and be engraved with a silver ink.
Horace had visited the White House and secured President
Arthur's promise to attend. His Number 1 wedding present
would be a $90,000 diamond necklace bought in New York. And
there would be other trinkets of greater intrinsic value. Months
before, Horace had learned that the jewels Queen Isabella had
sold to finance Columbus's voyage to America could be located
in various Madrid and Lisbon pawnshops. Horace sent two men
to buy some of the jewels for Baby, without bothering to
investigate the authenticity of the reports. His agents had
returned, supposedly from the Iberian peninsula, with a rope of
pearls and other jewels. Actually Horace's emissaries had
traveled no farther than New York, where they bought the
trinkets in New York pawnshops, and made a tidy profit on the
deal. Neither he nor Baby would ever hear of suggestions that
Queen Isabella's genuine jewelry might not actually be gracing
her.

But that was only one of the illusions they embraced with the
vigor of uninhibited romantics. Both were certain that the
splendor of the wedding would dazzle everyone into accepting
Baby as a future social leader, as an ornament of cotillions and a
respectable member of "high" society. They confidently sent
invitations to members of the Colorado Congressional delegation
and their wives and other prominent political figures.

Baby was determined to make the most of her wedding. On
her way to Washington in a private train, she stopped off in
Oshkosh to visit her family and, incidentally, to flaunt her most
elegant furs and silks before the hometown folk who had gossiped
about her, before and after the wreckage of her marriage to
Harvey Doe, and said she'd wind up in a parlor house. She was
also able to reconcile her family to the second marriage. She had
always been her father's favorite, and he was unhappy over the
idea of a decently reared Irish Catholic girl marrying for a
second time, but he was finally appeased by the fact she would be
married by a priest. Any resentments in the McCourt family
were further assuaged by Tabor's generosity; the new son-in-law

might be thirty years older than his bride but he was able to provide the McCourts with a fine new residence and settle enough money on McCourt Senior ($150,000) to keep them in comfort. So little Elizabeth had, after all, perhaps in an unconventional manner, revived the family fortunes by trekking out to Colorado.

The McCourts—including her mother and father, her favorite brother, the handsome Peter, Jr., and another brother, Philip, and her sister Claudia, along with other relatives—followed her to Washington. She arrived a few days before the March 1 wedding day, just in time to receive her first rebuff from one of her social peers.

She had sent her liveried coachman, in the victoria Tabor had rented for his Washington stay, with a wedding invitation to the home of Senator and Mrs. Nathaniel P. Hill.

The coachman returned with the envelope and told Baby, "Mrs. Hill said to give you this."

Inside was the silver-bordered wedding invitation, torn in half.

And that wasn't the only rebuff: all the Congressmen and politicians—Secretary of the Interior Teller, Senator-elect Bowen, Representative James Belford, Jerome Chaffee, Senator Hill, and other bigwigs—signified their intention of attending the wedding. Their wives, however, could not be bullied into doing likewise. The trade union of Respectable Wives and Mothers Amalgamated closed ranks against her.

No matter, it was still a triumphant occasion. Even the disapproving had to concede that Washington had never seen a more beautiful bride. Her white satin gown had cost $7,500, with a daring décolletage to which Baby's lush contours did ample justice. There may have been something more knowledgeable than virginal in the bride's big blue eyes, but nobody could deny the impact she made on the witnesses to that occasion. President Arthur himself, a high-living bachelor who had been a connoisseur of such things in his profitable years as collector of the Port of New York, was suffering from an illness which would soon be fatal, but he could still summon up a gallant response to her beauty. "I have never seen a more beautiful bride," he told her. "May I not beg a rose from your bouquet?" While all her family and friends from Oshkosh watched, homely Irish faces beaming, little Elizabeth stood on tiptoe to fasten a rose to the lapel of the President of the United States. The American dream could not have been more fully realized than in that instant.

The wedding party had assembled just before 9 P.M. in the parlors of the Willard Hotel. An odd hour for a wedding, but as the Washington *Post* commented, "The bold originality of the method and hour of celebrating his marriage and the splendor of its surroundings are exciting much comment, and none that is not favorable to the Senator's taste and independence. Those who have met him personally have learned to appreciate his amiable and frank character united to a clear, quick mind."

The ceremony was an abbreviation of the usual nuptial mass, performed by the Reverend P. L. Chapelle of St. Matthew's Roman Catholic Church, innocently unaware that he was marrying two divorced persons, one of them a member of his own faith. The bridal couple stood in front of a massive table draped in cardinal red and holding a candelabra with ten lighted tapers.

At the conclusion of the brief ceremony, according to a newspaper account, "the bride was fittingly congratulated by the President, her husband and family and attending friends. The party then proceeded through the folding doors to the collation chamber where, after the bride had cut her cake, the viands were partaken of.

"The table upon which the collation was served was in the first parlor nearest to F Street. The setting was beautifully and profusely aided in effect by flowers. In the center was a massive wedding bell of white roses, surmounted by a Cupid's bow, with arrow on the string, tipped with a heart of violets, the rest being composed of various hued roses. Below this structure was a basin or bed of flowers. At each plate was a boutonniere of artistic design. Flowers relieved each dish of dainty viands. . . . The wedding cake rested upon a table devoted to its sole support, and decorated with appropriate and beautiful blossoms. Above this was a canopy of flowers with trailing foliage. The cake itself was chaste in design, though the short notice at which it had been prepared precluded great elaboration of detail.

"The bride is a veritable beauty—blonde, with face and form alike almost ideal in their lovely proportions. She is medium height and well rounded in figure and of charming manner, with vivacious and entertaining conversational power. The bridal toilette was of white satin. The waist was low in the neck and edged with a ruching of tulle, and the white gloves reached above the elbow. The bouquet was of white roses.

"The collation ended, the party engaged in general conversation, the President paying particular attention to the bride. . . ."

That was a clipping Baby pasted in her scrapbook.

Everything considered—including the fact that many of the witnesses were uneasily aware of the fact that Father Chapelle had been duped into performing a ceremony which was not entirely licit by rules of his faith—the wedding and reception were a success. In Denver newspaper offices, too. The moment Father Chapelle pronounced them man and wife, a telegram by prearrangement was sent to Denver and cases of champagne were hauled into each of the Denver city rooms. Hod's champagne, of course, would not inhibit Eugene Field from continuing his satirical assaults.

Everyone carefully avoided remarking on the fact that there were no Congressional wives present, nor any members of Tabor's family.

The President was the first to leave, about two hours after he arrived, his departure possibly speeded by the overly hearty manners of the bridegroom, who now proceeded to slap his second Presidential back (ex-President Grant's having been the first). President Arthur was taken aback by the familiarity; once he had been one of the boys in the back room but, like most men who attain that office, he had come to believe in the respect and dignity which should enclose the Presidency—even from tycoons recently liberated by their millions from the exuberant democracy of the mining camps.

"Well, Mr. President," Horace boomed, "are yuh having a nice time? How about you and me having a little drink on the side?"

While Horace was reaching for a fresh pair of goblets, the President beckoned to his military and naval aides and hastened away to the White House.

At midnight the rest of the guests dispersed and Baby and Horace were left to enjoy, at long last, the legitimate pleasures of the marriage bed.

Hardly had the roses in Baby's bridal bouquet wilted before there was a fresh outbreak of scandal. By noon the following day someone—possibly a newspaper reporter—informed Father Chapelle that he had been tricked into marrying two divorced persons. He was outraged, returned the $200 wedding fee to Tabor, and announced he would refuse to sign the marriage certificate. He was writing a letter of explanation to his archbishop. Furthermore, in an interview published by the Washington *Post* he recalled, "When I asked the bride's father if he knew of any impediment to the marriage, he clearly answered he did not," and added, "To say all in a few words, I was shamefully deceived by the McCourt family."

Senator Tabor denied there had been any deception. "There is evidently some mistake," he told reporters in the Senate cloakroom. "Father Chapelle did not ask either Miss McCourt or myself about it. If he had, we should have had no hesitancy in telling him the facts. Regarding myself, I supposed everybody understood that I had been divorced, and as to Miss McCourt, I am certain there would have been no concealment on the part of herself or her father had the question been asked."

Father Chapelle calmed down, possibly on the advice of his clerical superiors, and registered the marriage.

The day after he had exploded in wrath, however, there was

an even greater sensation aroused by the investigations of scandal-scenting journalists. They had come up with the fact that, three months before he was legally divorced from Augusta, he and Baby had been secretly married. Somewhat lamely, they both tried to dismiss the St. Louis marriage as a mere sentimental gesture, a sort of down payment on the official ceremony. It was necessary to obfuscate the issue, as Baby later explained, because Horace still had high hopes of pursuing political advancement. He was, in fact, envisioning himself as President of the United States and would soon encourage a boomlet which he hoped would surge into a cresting wave of popular demand and deposit him on the threshold of 1600 Pennsylvania Avenue.

If Chet Arthur, the ex-boodleman, could make it to the White House, why not Hardrock Horace?

The scandal would die down soon enough. Nit-picking journalists could be bribed to take a more constructive approach to his activities. His self-intoxication with the idea of attaining the Presidency readily communicated itself to the new Mrs. Tabor, who was enthralled by the possibility of snooting Mrs. Senator Hill and all the other old hens who stayed away from her wedding.

If only the scandalmongering journalists could be horse-whipped into refraining from making such malicious and inaccurate comments. Soon enough she received a clipping from the free-swinging Dave Day's mining-camp journal, the *Solid Muldoon* of Ouray, Colorado. In his account of the wedding, Day had written, "President Arthur gave the bride away in the presence of many senators and members of Congress, any of whom was better qualified to give her away than the President."

BOOK II

Silver Queen

7. *Not Quite the First Lady of Colorado*

BABY was a stylish and glittering figure in the ladies' gallery the day Senator Tabor marched beside Senator-elect Bowen to present his successor to the presiding officer and made his last appearance on the Senate floor. Not that Horace had given up all hopes of making it back to Washington as one of Colorado's representatives. His hopes had been buoyed by an editorial in Denver's *Rocky Mountain News* which reminded its readership, "There are twenty-six men in the United States' Senate because they are millionaires. Why should Tabor be barred because of his millions?"

Senator Tabor had just sent a quiver of apprehension through the more sedate quarters of Washington society by announcing that he was planning to build a house in the capital, as the New York *Tribune* correspondent reported, gratuitously adding that "There has been nothing so picturesquely vulgar as this gorgeous hotel wedding of a pair married months already." Horace Greeley's man in Washington considered that a fellow of Tabor's temperament and proclivities would be well advised to avoid politics and look elsewhere for ego-satisfaction. "If he wants to marry a wife, and Mrs. Teller and Mrs. Belford refuse to come to the wedding, he can get on just the same. Still, it is sure to be mentioned. When a man steps out into the public square and has a band play behind him, he must expect people to look and listen. The man who insists upon Tabor's sort of a good time must take it and be content without honors or office."

Content without honors? Not Horace Tabor, as anyone could see for himself when Tabor jovially occupied the Senatorial spotlight for the last time on the afternoon of March 3.

Occasionally he glanced up to exchange prideful looks with Baby, who was attracting even more attention in the ladies' gallery. She wore a form-fitting brown silk dress that clung to her exuberant curves, along with her $90,000 diamond necklace and an even flashier ornament, a jeweled waist girdle in the shape of a serpent with diamonds for eyes, a ruby tongue, and an emerald tail. Her brown costume showed up nicely against a background of green faces belonging to the other Congressional wives.

That was Horace Tabor's last bow on the national political scene, and naturally it did not pass without sarcastic notice from Eugene Field, who wrote a long column in the Denver *Tribune* imagining how Washington must be plunged into mourning over Tabor's departure.

"The flags were hung at half-mast," Field wrote, tongue in cheek, "and in many a shop window appeared the portrait of the retiring statesman trimmed with crepe and immortelles." Tabor entered the Senate chamber "bearing a new patent leather gripsack and wearing a superb trousseau of broadcloth and diamonds. The vast crowd became hushed as the grave. It was generally remarked as the Senator passed down the aisle, looking pale and calm, that his appearance bore a striking resemblance to the popular steel engraving of Mary, Queen of Scots, going to her execution. He proceeded at once to his own place, from which he had thundered out those utterances which shook the world, and will live in all history as the grandest monuments to his genius. Opening his gripsack, he proceeded to stow away in it the countless pamphlets, volumes and papers that had accumulated during his long term. It was a touching spectacle. Strong men wept like babies, and several ladies, notably the wife of the

Spanish Ambassador, were borne out of the gallery in a swooning condition. . . .

"The Senator rose to speak. There were tears in his eyes and his voice was very tremulous. It were [sic] impossible to describe the delicate beauty of his remarks and the intensity of the scene that transpired during his delivery. As he proceeded to recount his services, his love of country and devotion to the public weal, the men groaned and sobbed in speechless agony. . . .

"At night there was a torchlight procession in Ex-Senator Tabor's honor. It was an imposing affair, numbering twelve thousand persons in line and the entire American navy on wheels and gorgeously illuminated.

"Tabor, accompanied by President Arthur and members of the foreign legations and their wives, viewed the pageant from the front stoop of the Ebbitt House. A charming feature of the procession was a huge papier mache yacht, representing the Ship of State, and manned by forty-one beautiful young girls representing the States and Territories, *all of them from Oshkosh.*"

Field's japery may have amused his readers in Denver, but Tabor's political associates in Washington could hardly conceal their relief at the departure of Horace and Baby. His unpredictability was a constant cause of concern among his colleagues. They liked Hod well enough personally but his lack of inhibition, his garrulity in the presence of journalists, his unabashed delight in displaying his wealth—all were serious handicaps so far as careerist politicians were concerned. In a mere thirty days, they reckoned, Tabor had done as much damage to the Congressional image as anything since the Crédit Mobilier affair.

Secretary of Interior Teller wrote a friend back in Colorado that Tabor's departure was the best thing that had happened to Washington since the British sacked the capital in 1812. "I thank God," Teller wrote, "that he was not elected for six years. Thirty days nearly killed us. I humiliated myself to attend his wedding because he was senator from Colorado—but Mrs. Teller would not. . . ."

"Tabor is an honest man in money matters, and I believe he is truthful, but he made a great fool of himself with reference to that woman, and he ought now to retire and attend to his private affairs."

But retirement was the last thing Horace would have considered. He had determined on a comeback, to restore himself as a man to be taken seriously by the political managers and the electorate. It grated on Horace and Baby, when they returned to Denver, that he would not be given his due in the city for which he had done so much, for which he had built a temple of the arts and donated the land for the new post office. That so many people were eager to sneer at his aspirations. That a mere gypsy journalist like Gene Field could get away with mocking him, and worse yet be applauded for it. The ungrateful populace of Denver was even ready to believe the report that he and his bride had slept in the White House so they could become familiar with their prospective residence.

Horace and Baby were, in fact, rather optimistic about Horace's Presidential possibilities. They returned to Denver and a suite at the Windsor, which they would occupy until suitably resplendent permanent quarters could be built, riding the crest of his Presidential boomlet. On the editorial page of the Bayonne *New Jersey Statesman*, a journal hitherto more concerned with shipping in New York Harbor than the blossoming of Western politicians, there had just appeared a banner proclaiming FOR PRESIDENT OF THE UNITED STATES, HORACE TABOR, and beneath it banked headlines conveying the sense of the editorial proposing Tabor's candidacy:

Silver King of the Pacific Coast,
Colorado's Citizen, Banker
and Senator of Sterling
Merit and Purity

AN INDEPENDENT STATESMAN UPHOLDING
THE CONSTITUTION AND UNION

A Foe to Monopoly and Centralization of the Money Powers
Endangering Liberty, Favoring a Gold and Silver
Currency and Protection to the Manufacturing
of the Country. Champion of the Working
Man from the Ranks of the People.

There were widespread suspicions that the Bayonne editorial
had been "planted" by Billy Bush, who was still (but not for
long) Tabor's paymaster, factotum, and drumbeater. They were
hardly dissipated when Tabor imported 500 copies of the *New
Jersey Statesman* for distribution in Colorado and paid $200 to
become a lifelong subscriber; years later the paper would be
mailed to him when his aspirations were no higher than putting
meat on the table that night.

The now-friendly *Rocky Mountain News* was persuaded to
reprint the editorial and comment favorably upon its argument,
but it was taken seriously only by Horace and Baby, and those
beholden to them. There was no doubt of his advocacy of silver
coinage but Tabor as "champion of the working man" was hard
to swallow for any who remembered him smashing the miners'
strike in Leadville.

Although the first three months of 1883 had been crammed
with material for those who liked to masticate their scandal with
relish, Horace and Baby had returned to Denver with all the
flash and filigree of returning conquerors. They would put down
the slanders by behaving as though the rest of the nation held
them in the highest regard; they would go over the heads of
small-minded, tongue-wagging Coloradans and seek a wider
constituency. And Horace could always pay the tab for those
who were willing to praise and cheer him.

Shortly after they had established themselves in a suite at the
Windsor, the German Athletic Societies came to serenade them
with a medley of beer-garden melodies and bear them off to a
banquet at which Tabor was extolled as being one of the first
non-German Americans to support the *Turnverein* movement
which aimed to "educate our youth, not only in physical but in

moral development." Horace listened approvingly to the speakers listing him among the moral standard-bearers of his time, and picked up the bill for all the wurst and Würzburger beer consumed during a long, bibulous, and morally uplifting evening.

He also seized the opportunity to associate his name with a national luminary when General William T. Sherman announced plans to visit Leadville with his staff. Both he and Baby loved celebrities, aside from the fact that linking his name to the eminent increased his own importance.

Horace made the most of the occasion. He and Baby traveled to Leadville in David Moffat's private car, which was loaded with six cases of champagne to see them through the journey. The Tabor Light Cavalry and the Tabor Hose Company turned out in full force and resplendent uniforms to greet them and escort them to a suite at the Clarendon. Later that day the Tabors met Sherman and took him on a tour of the mines, entertained the general at dinner and later at the Tabor Opera House, where the performance was punctuated by the popping of champagne corks in the Tabor box.

On the way back to Denver, Tabor was still exhilarated by the experience of entertaining the general-in-chief of the United States Army. In their private car he confided to Baby that they were on their way to the top. The gossip about them would soon be drowned by applause for his achievements. Capitol Hill society would open its doors, and Baby would be accorded her rightful place among the cotillion leaders and reigning dowagers. The politicians would resume their obeisances; there was a national election coming up next year and Horace's money would be needed for the Republican war chest. His political career would resume its upward trajectory.

"First lady of Colorado, hell!" he told Baby. "You'll be the first lady of the land."

Baby could only agree, certain their star was in the ascendant. Like most Irish she fervently believed in the "power of the word." Saying something, and believing it, could make it come true. It

Baby Doe Tabor shortly after her marriage to Horace Tabor.

Harvey Doe, Baby's first husband.

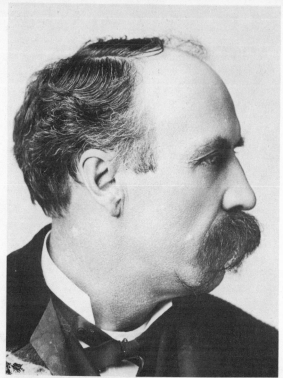

Horace Tabor.

Augusta Tabor.

Baby Doe in her famous ermine opera cloak.

The Tabor Mansion in Denver, where "a hundred live peacocks strutted on the lawn."

Horace Tabor working as a slagman in Leadville after he lost his fortune.

Exterior of the Matchless Mine (Baby Doe's cabin is on the right).

Silver Dollar Tabor, Baby Doe's ill-fated daughter, greeting Theodore Roosevelt during his visit to Denver, August 29, 1910.

Baby Doe leaving her cabin on an autumn day in 1933.

Baby Doe on a Denver street in 1931.

Interior of Baby Doe's cabin as she left it at her death.

Baby Doe's cabin after its restoration in 1953.

BABY DOE DIES AT HER POSTGUARDING MATCHLESS MINE

One-Time Queen of Colorado's Silver Empire Faithful to Last to Horace Tabor's Parting Injunction

News 3-8-35

CLAD IN RAGS OF FORMER FINERY, $2 IS LEFT OF $11,000,000 FORTUNE

Woman Once Sought for Beauty, Power and Wealth Lies Alone Two Weeks on Bleak Leadville Hilltop, a Frozen Corpse

BY ROBERT L. CHASE

They found the body of the faithful Baby Doe Tabor in her Leadville miner's shanty yesterday.

Her lonely vigil at the Matchless Mine is ended. But, to the death, the proud Elizabeth McCourt Tabor, one-time queen of a silver empire, had kept the deathbed trust of her late husband, Senator H. A. W. Tabor, to "guard the Matchless."

Two neighbors, Tom French, a miner, and Sue Bonney, broke into the crude board shanty on Fryer Hill yesterday afternoon to learn why Mrs. Tabor had not been about for several days.

They found her on the floor of the one-room shanty, frozen to death.

Coroner James Corbett said she probably had died about Feb. 20. Biographers of the Tabor family give her age as 73; her brother said she was 81.

Tattered remnants of a wardrobe which once made her the best-dressed woman in the West covered her body.

A small cache of food and a few sticks of firewood were found in the shanty. Of the once great Tabor fortune—estimated at some $11,000,000 when Baby Doe and the silver king were married before President Chester A. Arthur, cabinet members and senators—only two wrinkled dollar bills and a few small coins were found among her modest possessions.

Mrs. Tabor's last visit to Leadville, a mile and a half from her home, was on Feb. 20. On that day, she trudged thru the streets of the two-mile-high mining town, a gunny-sack slung over her shoulder, to get a supply of provisions.

Probably Had Pneumonia

It was the first time since Thanksgiving that Mrs. Tabor had been to town. Deep snow covered the ground and, for the 300 yards from her cabin to the highway, there was not even a trail.

Several times Mrs. Tabor slipped and fell in the cruel hike and her clothes were covered with mud and water when she reached town.

The trip back must have been worse, too much for even the strong heart of Baby Doe. She took cold, possibly was stricken with pneumonia.

Coroner Corbett surmised she had attempted to treat herself rather than summon the aid she always had scorned. Her condition growing worse, she probably found herself unable to replenish her fire and lay calmly down to await death.

See Body Thru Window

J. R. Dewar, assistant postmaster at Leadville, who was accustomed to pay a weekly visit to Mrs. Tabor and often to take her provisions, was prevented by inclement weather from making his customary trip. Consequently, it was not until the two neighbors went to the shack yesterday that her death was discovered.

French and Miss Bonney found the door locked from inside, but peering thru a window, they saw her body. They broke the window, attempted to revive Mrs. Tabor, and then called the coroner.

Baby Doe lay on her back, near the rickety rocking chair in which she had spent many lonely hours with her brilliant memories.

There was a small bruise on her nose, possibly made when she fell while trying to get to the woodpile. She apparently had gone to bed, but tried to get up when the biting cold crept in thru the rough board walls.

A brother, Willard McCourt, retired salesman, of 1568 Harrison st., was on the way to Leadville last night to take charge of the body and complete funeral arrangements. Two other brothers, Philip McCourt of Denver and Marx McCourt of Oakland, Calif., also survive.

Funeral in Leadville

A daughter, Rose May Echo—Silver Dollar Tabor—whose name is reputed to have been chosen by the late William Jennings Bryan—died more than a decade ago in a fire in a cheap rooming house in Chicago.

Mrs. Lillian Tabor Last of Milwaukee, Wis., believed by friends to have been a second daughter of Baby Doe, denied that relationship and told the Associated Press last night that she is a daughter of John Tabor, a brother of the Colorado senator.

Tentative plans are for funeral services and burial in Leadville.

From the *Rocky Mountain News*, March 8, 1935.

was a way of conning fate. She was able to propagandize herself into picturing Mrs. Horace A. W. Tabor as the doyenne of Capitol Hill, the governor's lady, the chatelaine of the White House. Ever since childhood she had propelled herself forward on the belief that she was born for better things, and that psychic fuel-supply had seen her through the rigors of her first marriage, the humiliations of Central City and Leadville, her many months as the "veiled lady" lurking in the background of Tabor's life. She could endure all those vicissitudes, not because she was insensitive or "hard," as other people believed, but because she believed that she was following a predestined path more wonderful and hazardous than other people could imagine for themselves. She was as tough-fibered as circumstances would demand, as gentle and considerate as they would allow.

The fate to which she devoted herself with an almost Arabic intensity to the last melodramatic day of her life insisted, however, on constantly testing her devotion. She and Horace returned from Leadville confident that their path would be smoother, but a large and jagged obstacle to their acceptance soon presented itself.

Unwisely, considering how many backroom deals he had engineered, how many sordid missions he had undertaken for Tabor, Billy Bush was summarily discharged from Tabor's employ. It came about because Baby had always wanted to see her favorite brother, the handsome and dashing Peter McCourt, rise in the world. So she persuaded Horace to remove Bush as manager of the Tabor Grand Opera House and install Peter as his successor. Billy Bush, who liked swanking about the green room of the theater with famous actresses, fiercely resented his removal. A public quarrel with Tabor followed.

Then, even more unwisely, Tabor brought suit against Bush and charged him with having embezzled $2,000. Bush responded with a counter-suit claiming Tabor owed him $100,000 for clandestine services rendered but never adequately compensated.

Once again the public was to be treated to a festival of Tabor scandal, and as always it was avid for the last grimy detail. And

once again Tabor's private life, exposed as it would not have
been in the case of a man of greater discretion, damaged his
prospects for political advancement. The political bosses could
only shake their heads over his tendency to wash dirty linen in
public. Certainly it was evident to them that much of his trouble
stemmed from obeying Baby's whims. Perhaps Baby, too,
realized now that her willfulness was causing her new husband a
lot of trouble. If she had been less demanding, the divorce from
Augusta could have been arranged without the scandal attending the "secret" divorce in Durango and the illegal marriage in
St. Louis. If she had not been so intent on a spectacular
Washington wedding, there wouldn't have been that brouhaha
over Father Chapelle's deception. And now her insistence that
brother Peter be given a cushy job had resulted in a public
falling-out with Billy Bush, who could spill more dirt about
Horace than anyone else. Baby, it seemed, kept tripping over her
vaulting ambition, and bringing Horace down with her in
ungainly public sprawls.

Certainly both Tabor and Bush marched into court determined to squash each other. First it was Horace's turn. His
charge of "embezzlement" proved to be a misnomer by any legal
definition. He testified that he had backed Bush's play in poker
games in Clifton Bell's gambling house located in the Tabor
Grand Opera House, but that Bush had failed to repay the
money Tabor advanced him. His suit was quickly thrown out of
court.

Billy Bush, in a vengeful mood, had a lot more ammunition to
fire at his ex-employer. Among the sums he demanded were
$5,000 for "helping Tabor emerge from the obscurity of Califor-
nia Gulch into the realms of statesmanship." That is, as Tabor's
fixer, bagman, and publicist. The public, eagerly following the
testimony, was more interested in Bush's demand for $10,000 for
aiding Tabor in "effecting a marriage with the said Mrs. Doe,
commonly called Baby Doe." Bush testified, with even more
damaging effect, that Tabor had asked him to manufacture
evidence that Augusta—the utterly straitlaced—had been an

unfit wife. He also claimed that he had persuaded Augusta, finally, to agree to a divorce. Bush in addition asked for $1,547 he had advanced out of his own pocket to bribe legislators during Tabor's recent campaign for the Senatorial seat. Tabor was pictured in the suit as a cheapskate of an employer. Demanding additional compensation for his services as manager of the opera house, Bush summoned expert witnesses on his behalf. The New York theatrical producer Charles Frohman testified that $75 a week was adequate but the celebrated actor Lawrence Barrett declared on the witness stand that Bush should have been paid twice that much.

Naturally the public was deliciously shocked by all the squalid testimony, but the court dismissed Bush's suit as "indecent and irrelevant." The repercussions, however, were more damaging to Tabor than to Bush. For one thing Tabor's only son Maxcy had sided with Bush, and father and son were permanently estranged. Maxcy formed a partnership with Bush to lease the Brown Palace Hotel; later he and his wife lived for a time with his mother when Augusta moved out to California.* Horace could withstand the loss of his son's affection—they had never been very close—but it was harder to bear the resultant blemishes on his political prospects. The Bush trial and its revelations disgusted just about everyone. Senator Hill, the smelter magnate and a highly self-satisfied totem of the state Republican Party, knew that the time to kick a rival was when he was down; he issued a statement to the newspapers declaring that Tabor was a disgrace to the GOP and should be placed in political Coventry. The Denver *Tribune* which, aside from Eugene Field's satirical columns, had always viewed Tabor with amiability now attacked him in a savage editorial:

"Tabor," it said, "is an utter disgrace to the State; he disgraced it in private life; he disgraced it as a public officer; he

---

* Augusta Tabor died February 1, 1895, leaving a $1,500,000 estate built up fivefold, largely through shrewd investments in downtown Denver real estate, from her divorce settlement. Half of the estate went to her son, the other half was divided among her seven brothers and sisters.

made it the jeer of the country during his brief but petty career in the Senate. Essentially a vulgarian of doubtful antecedents, he strove to buy his way into political position. To a small extent he succeeded. He bought the cheap creatures of the legislature for the first place in its gift, but did not buy them in sufficient number, and when this failed, he begged his way into the second position. Society in Denver gave its verdict on his course when it recognized the kindly old lady whom, in his gulch ignorance, he put aside. He is a social and political outcast in all senses of the word."

The savagery of the *Tribune*'s attack inevitably brought Tabor a measure of sympathy. After all, there was too much "gulch ignorance" around to be sneered at from the *Tribune*'s ivory tower. Then, too, the *Tribune* underestimated the cumulative power of those millions which continued to accrue to Tabor no matter how wayward and reckless his disposition. Despite the diatribes from Senator Hill and the newspaper, the state Republican bosses were not ready to write off Horace as a contributor to campaign funds. In return, it was willing to humor his ambitions for higher office.

Horace might have been willing to withdraw from the political arena, drawing the somewhat tattered toga of a temporary Senator around him and waiting for a better day, but Baby wouldn't hear of it. The experiences of her young life had taught her that it was always best to brazen it out, to double your bets, in adverse times. And Horace didn't need too much encouragement; the rubbery quality of his self-esteem was a wonder, and a delight, to the Republican leaders. They persuaded him that both his talents and his money were valuable to the cause. He was flattered when they elected him chairman of the Republican State Central Committee—and thereupon poured in fresh funds for the state and national elections of 1884.

That so encouraged him that he announced his candidacy for nomination as the party's choice for governor. His hopes were quickly deflated by the state convention at Colorado Springs, despite the noisy demonstrations on his behalf by the pro-Tabor delegation from Leadville and other mining towns. Three rival candidates combined to throw the nomination to a formerly obscure politician named Ben Eaton. That was evidence enough of the disfavor with which the rank and file of his party, as opposed to the party treasurer, viewed his political aspirations. He would make no more forays into electoral politics.

But there were still Baby's hopes of social prominence to be considered. An imposing residence, they were certain, would attract the best people to the dinner parties, teas, balls, and garden parties they planned. Meanwhile Baby would have to languish in their suite at the Windsor with only an occasional poker party attended by Horace's gallus-snapping cronies at which to display her untapped talents as a gracious hostess.

Except for shopping trips and going out to dinner occasionally at one of the fancier restaurants, she found few opportunities to enjoy the "position" she had coveted. The newspapers had started calling her the Silver Queen, and there was some comfort in the fact that sobriquet had never been bestowed on the determinedly unqueenly Augusta. But where were her courtiers, when would the society editors call to ask for the guest list at her forthcoming soiree, where were the calling cards that should have been drifting like snowflakes on her empty silver salver? When would some kindlier recognition than epithets and curious stares come her way?

Undoubtedly she hoped the ice slowly forming around her social aspirations was thawing when a newspaper reporter called to request an interview. She granted him an audience readily enough, but kept him dawdling around the Windsor lobby for an hour before summoning him upstairs. Everything had to be perfectly arranged for the journalist. Through the medium of that interview, she evidently hoped, the trout-faced dowagers and their stuffy husbands would be shown that she was not in the least perturbed by their neglect.

When the reporter was admitted to the parlor of the Tabor Suite, he was dazzled by the expensive aura Baby had created for the occasion. Though it was midafternoon, she had dressed herself in a peachblow satin gown with a long stately train, quite suitable for a presentation at the Court of St. James's. Her fingers were encrusted with precious stones. She was seated at an ornate desk "discovered," as a contemporary dramatist might describe the scene, at work on sheaves of papers.

"I have been flooded with invitations from the very best people of Denver to attend all sorts of affairs," she told the journalist with a world-weary air. "I have decided not to accept any of them so as not to create jealousy among the society leaders of Denver."

The reporter was supposed to believe that the papers on the desk were invitations that Baby would not accept. The bravura of that announcement was so overwhelming the reporter forgot what he had come to ask her about, but at least he had received an inkling of the kind of spirit that had borne Baby Doe from a mining-camp shack to a suite at the Windsor.

8. *A Hundred Peacocks on the Lawn*

BEFORE the birth of their first child, Baby and Horace moved from the Windsor to the Italianate villa on Thirteenth Street, occupying the whole block between Grant and Sherman, which would be their home for almost a decade, the ten years of her life during which Baby had everything money could buy and a lot more besides. Physically, at least, the house dominated Capitol Hill, even if its social attraction proved negligible, and in the sumptuousness of its interior and surroundings it outclassed all its stately neighbors.

Behind the high brownstone wall that completely enclosed the property there was a three-acre front lawn on which a hundred (live) peacocks promenaded among cast-iron dogs and deer. Two driveways coursed around the house to the carriage house at the rear. When the Tabors sallied forth in an equipage, complete with two coachmen and two footmen, people on the street referred to the ducal apparition as "the Tabor circus." The Negro footmen wore scarlet livery. One of their many carriages was a landau painted black with white trim and upholstered in white satin. Another was enameled a dark blue with gold stripes. Baby would order whichever carriage best matched her costume. When she appeared in brown silk, she took the brown victoria with red trim. And the horseflesh back in the stables was worth a small fortune, along with the gold- and silver-mounted harness with which the horses were caparisoned; four blacks with gold harness, four whites with green, matched bays and sorrels to suit Baby's every mood and costume.

Doubtless Baby and her husband were determined to arouse envy, if respect was unobtainable, among their fellow citizens. The house was "probably the finest residence in the state," as a local historian noted, and it was staffed by a dozen servants. There were five different portraits of Baby executed in oils by a painter named Heyde, all of them placed in the rooms down-stairs where they could be viewed by all comers.

Stately and extravagant though its style, ornately furnished and lavishly appointed from basement to attic, the Tabor mansion was shunned by the people it was designed to attract. The only people who came to the door were those who wanted a favor, occasional politicians, Hod's poker companions, members of Baby's family (including her brother Peter, who had been given a well-paid job at the opera house). The society columns never mentioned the Tabor mansion or its occupants. No coachmen rolled up to the door with invitations to balls, dinners, and coming-out parties.

Denver society kept up its guard against the Tabors through-out the decade in which they had the funds to match their aspirations. For a social group so recently formed of such very raw materials it really did seem to have acquired overnight the sclerotic qualities of, say, Belgravia or the minor nobility of Schleswig-Holstein; its whole energy was diverted into keeping out the "wrong" people. Yet, another little Irish girl, also resident on Capitol Hill, demonstrated how to take some of the steam out of the local dragons; the method was simply to seek social acceptance abroad and display proof of it in Denver.

One can only wonder why Baby didn't follow the venturesome course of the former Molly Tobin, a redheaded girl whose finishing school was the Huckleberry Finn sloughs of the Mississippi, but who had married J. J. Brown shortly before he made his millions in the Leadville mines. Mrs. Brown, known to latter-day musical comedy audiences as the "unsinkable Molly Brown" for having survived the *Titanic* in spectacular fashion, had come to Denver along the same route (though without the scandalous bypasses) as Baby Doe.

The Browns built a mansion on Capitol Hill, which the present Denver establishment has turned into a tourist shrine. They invited the *bon ton* to the parties Molly gave, but none of the elect appeared. That did not prevent the spirited Molly from crashing *their* parties until she was bluntly informed that social aspirants did not enter other people's homes without an invitation.

Molly Brown decided that she could become a certified lady without help from the Denver matriarchy. Leaving Mr. Brown behind, since he had experienced no similar desires to achieve gentility, Molly went abroad and spent many years learning five languages, studying singing, making friends with Sarah Bernhardt and other celebrated or titled people. She acquired two genuine French maids, presided over homes in New York, London, and Paris, and became a social figure of considerable prominence. Her Western breeziness made her as popular among the world-weary as her fellow native of Hannibal, Missouri—Mark Twain—who once pulled her naked from a Mississippi mudbank. Occasionally, in regal style but as boisterous as ever, she returned to Denver to stay a few months with her husband. Touring celebrities from the East, and European nobility invariably cast aside invitations from other Denver hostesses and settled in with Mr. and Mrs. J. J. Brown. Her envious peers on Capitol Hill could only seethe and mutter that jaded cosmopolites found her amusing for her gaucheries, as a sort of female counterpart to Buffalo Bill.

Baby Tabor did not elect Molly Brown's course, but settled for domesticity and motherhood instead. Perhaps she had heard of Molly Brown's remark, "Give me the rugged men of the West any time. The men of Europe—why, they're only perfumed, unbathed gallants in France and brandy-soaked old colonels in England!"

One respectable and esteemed lady did come calling several months after Baby was installed in the Italian villa—the last one she would have expected.

The butler entered the drawing room one afternoon with a calling card on his silver salver. Baby could hardly believe her eyes when she read the inscription.

"Mrs. Augusta Tabor," it announced.

Baby, wondering what sort of trouble the first Mrs. Tabor was planning to make, hurried upstairs to change into a new dress with a Chantilly lace collar.

The first Mrs. Tabor sat stiffly on the edge of her chair, refused Baby's offer of tea or a glass of sherry, and did not immediately come to the point. There was an uneasy, faltering conversation for about twenty minutes, the first Mrs. Tabor discussing a recent trip to Maine she had made, the second Mrs. Tabor expanding on the architectural wonders of Washington, D.C.

Just before leaving, Augusta explained the reason for her visit. She had heard that on her account, but without her wishing it so, the Denver elite had placed Horace and his new wife in social quarantine. "I came here with great reluctance," Augusta added, "but it seemed to me that if I called, others might follow." After that first and only meeting with her predecessor, Baby regarded Augusta with a lasting respect; it took a generous soul, she believed, to make that gesture.

Augusta's motive may have been less magnanimous than Baby fancied. It could have been simply curiosity about the woman who displaced her. Certainly she was not overflowing with magnanimity a few months later when she told a Denver reporter: "She [Baby] is a blonde and paints her face. Mr. Tabor has changed a great deal. He used to detest women of that kind. He would never allow me to whitewash my face, however much I desired to.

"She wants his money and will hang onto him as long as he has a nickel. She don't want an old man. He dyes his hair and mustache now. . . .

"I understand she has all her family quartered at his house. I mean all in this country. I understand that a fresh invoice is coming over from Ireland. Is there really seventeen in that McCourt family? That woman will break him. . . ."

The vinegary flavor of that interview was probably indicative of Augusta's real attitude. She had not reconciled herself as yet to her displacement as Horace's wife. About a week later she gave an interview to the Denver *Republican* in which she announced that she was considering legal action to have the divorce set aside. She had been "inveigled into it by my attorney," she said. "I had no rest day or night. Judge Steck told me that Mr. Tabor's evidence against me was overwhelming and that I would be crushed. I wanted a suit for separate maintenance but Mr. Steck wouldn't listen to that. He insisted that I should get a divorce."

It wasn't that she hoped that Horace would come back to her, she added, but "it would be a great deal of satisfaction to me to know that woman would be no more to him than before he gave her his name and mine."

Such public statements could hardly have helped Baby's social advancement, and certainly wiped out whatever good might have come from her formal call at the Tabor mansion. Baby gradually reconciled herself to the failure of her ambition to sparkle at cotillions; she and Horace could still swank it any night they chose in Box A at the Tabor Grand Opera House.

Her shelfful of scrapbooks bore rather touching testimony to a lingering hope of acceptance by her peers. Page after page are covered with clippings from society sections, accounts of dinner parties and balls to which she was not invited, and a sort of serial biography of *the* Mrs. Astor and her reign over New York's Four Hundred. Possibly she found some relief for her lacerated self-esteem from an article published December 6, 1887, in an unidentifiable periodical, the title of which inquired "Should Divorced Women Be Received into Society?" The article's conclusion, daring enough for that late-Victorian period, was that "The reasoning that would keep a divorced woman from society would send to prison the merchant who was robbed by his confidential and trusted cashier."

Much greater consolation for her blighted social ambitions, undoubtedly, was provided her by the 250 letters from Horace invariably beginning "My Dear Darling Wife." They form a record of unwavering devotion, of unquestioning trust. If he ever wrote her in an angry or critical mood, the evidence cannot be found in those letters. Some of them came from as far away as a Mexican mining camp or the headquarters of his Honduras logging operations, but most were sent by messenger from his downtown offices less than a mile away, dispatched in the urgency of his need to be in constant touch with her.

"My darling, darling wife," a typical letter read, "you are near me even when I can't see you. Your love guides me in even the simplest transaction of life. The knowledge of your love for me enables me to carry the heaviest load, as I hope my love for you beautifies your existence."

On a trip to his Chihuahua mining concession, he wrote her that "Pater [presumably her brother Peter McCourt] and I are here at the mine. If only you were here it would be fun. I will tell you about everything when in my arms again you tell me that you love me—and I know that you do . . . My business affairs go well enough but that's unimportant. What seems more important is that I should see you for just a little while. . . . If I could see you for just a few moments—sixty seconds, even—it would make my life more bearable. . . ."

He confided everything in his letters home, including the details of his business dealings, because he regarded Baby as his full partner. One letter told of a quarrel he had with a slippery character who wanted to renege on a deal. "He had the nerve to tell me that his signature on a deed was only a 'good likeness' of the signature . . . but such annoyances do not matter when I receive a letter from you, my darling."

For Baby Doe the sting of social rejection was ameliorated by her participation in every phase of her husband's career. This was rare balm for her ego. None of the matriarchs of Capitol Hill who kept her name off their guest lists could make a similar boast. . . .

Horace's money meanwhile, was not allowed to pile up in bank accounts but was used to expand his interests in all directions. With more enthusiasm than discretion, Horace was making himself a tycoon for all seasons and in all climates when it might have been wiser to hoard his accumulating income as the more conservative silver magnates did. But watching a bank balance grow lacked the excitement Horace looked for; he was a plunger, an adventurer by temperament, not a gouty moneybags, and the charms of compound interest or dividend-clipping escaped him entirely.

The more grandiose a project the more it appealed to Horace Tabor. In 1883 and for half a dozen following years, the income from his mining investments seemed to encourage the notion that he could throw money away with both hands and still his hoard would continue accumulating; the specter of the graduated income tax was still forty years in the offing. Some people estimated his annual income at close to $4,000,000. The Matchless alone netted him about $1,000,000 annually, and he had a part interest in a score of other silver and gold mines around Leadville. If Leadville was soon to be played out, as the experts warned, there was no such indication on his balance sheets. Besides, he was investing in mines elsewhere whose production would take up the slack when the Leadville properties were thinned out. And frequently his nose for profitable veins of ore proved accurate. If you kept enough chips on the board, as he saw it, a certain proportion of the bets were bound to pay off.

Even the more conservative Eastern observers agreed that if his luck held out Horace Tabor would be the richest man in America in another decade. "In fine," commented an Eastern financial journal, "the combined interests, mining and otherwise of Mr. Tabor will make him the richest man in America in ten years. It is almost staggering to hear him talk of millions as glibly and unconcernedly as other men talk of hundreds. Mr. Tabor is far from visionary. He does not look like a man whose head would be easily turned if the course of events should lift him to the highest pinnacle of fame in the councils of the nation or make him the greatest moneyed king of his day."

The dangers of hubris had never been explained to Horace, though Canon Kingsley's lines inscribed on the curtain of his opera house should occasionally have given him pause. The United States was then in a euphoric period, Manifest Destiny was on the wing, and the nation's resources—moral and spiritual as well as physical—appeared to be inexhaustible. There would be no more depressions such as followed the Panic of 1873; the Indians had finally been put in their place (the reservation), and it was time for the United States to start building a steel-hulled navy to carry the blessings of democracy to nations besotted with ignorance and backwardness. There was a Democrat in the White House (Cleveland) but he seemed as solid a man as his massive paunch suggested. And there seemed to be no limit to the dimensions of the American experience.

What did it matter if one or two investments turned out to be variations on the old goldbrick theme? In 1883, for instance, Tabor was gulled into becoming a director of, and sinking hundreds of thousands of dollars into, a paper corporation called the Overland Broadgauge Railroad Company. About its only real assets were a map showing the line extending from New York to San Francisco, in many places paralleling existing routes, and the glib tongues of its promoters. Well, railroads were the big thing in the 1880's, and why shouldn't there be a single transcontinental line? Tabor did not reflect that Jay Gould and several other geniuses in railroad financing spent most of their careers trying to fulfill an ambition which Tabor expected to accomplish overnight. The Overland Broadgauge, in any case, never laid one rail or tie. It did soak up a million of Tabor's dollars, however, before its promoters decided to take a long vacation in Central America.

That venture did not inhibit him from equally risky investments in areas where he had no experience and little expertise.

As one chronicler of the Colorado mining magnates wrote, Tabor expanded his financial horizons almost daily—"As old mines play out, he buys new ones—in Colorado, New Mexico, Arizona and Texas. He buys the Colorado Fire Insurance Company to merge with his own. He buys patent rights to the cyanide process of extracting gold and spends $100,000 to erect a large mill in West Denver. He buys almost a half interest in the prosperous First National Bank of Denver controlled by Chaffee and Moffat. He plots with others to corner the wheat market. He speculates in corn as well. For $1,300,000 he buys a controlling interest in the Calumet and Chicago Canal and Dock Company, which owns a stretch of ground on Lake Michigan some ten miles south of the Chicago River. Tabor plans a great harbor and manufacturing center to rival Chicago itself. . . ." Just one item in his bulging portfolio was the Tabor Investment Company with offices in New York, London, Paris, and Amsterdam to deal in mining properties all over the world. He also bought the grazing rights to a vast tract, 460,000 acres, in southern Colorado.

His vision now became extra-continental in scope, and it was said that for several years he was one of the largest landowners in the world. Whole chunks of territory, with prospects of lucrative development, were acquired by his agents; he could visualize himself as the emperor of vast territories in Latin America, in addition to 175,000 acres of "copper lands" in Texas.

Sight unseen, he ventured into timber and mineral developments in Honduras and Yucatan. It took only the flimsiest evidence of prospective gain to persuade Horace to open his checkbook, and for him to dream of grandiose results. There were rumors that the whole Yucatan peninsula was veined with silver, so he sank hundreds of thousands in buying up concessions there. One day a Tabor City would rise from the jungle. Almost simultaneously he became fascinated with the possibilities of Chihuahua gold. A lawyer had sent him specimens of gold-bearing ore said to have been taken from a mountainside in the Mexican state. That was encouragement enough for Horace to sink more than a million in Chihuahua mineral rights.

But his speculative instincts really ran riot in acquiring mahogany forests in Honduras. He had become interested in that proposition several years before, while building the Tabor Grand Opera House, when he sent an agent to the Central American republic to buy mahogany. Now he aimed to corner the mahogany market; all over America the newly rich were building their mansions, and the dark, heavy, highly polished wood was esteemed for its permanence, its solidity, its sheer richness both for paneling and furniture. Mahogany surroundings virtually certified a man's worth, like the diamond on his pinky and the lavalliere on his wife's bosom.

Tabor bought a vast tract of Honduran forest land, not entirely comprehending, perhaps, that in Central America a forest was really a jungle. A million dollars bought what was described as "four-tenths of 360 square miles." According to an authoritative source (*Appleton's Cyclopedia of American Biography*, 1893), Tabor's concession included a Honduras government grant of alternate sections (640 acres) along a 400-mile stretch of the Patuca River plus a mineral grant comprising 150 square miles in the interior.

Horace "thought big," as a later generation would say. He would need a rail and steamship network to get his mahogany logs out of Honduras, so he built a railroad into the jungle and a fleet of small steamboats to ply the Patuca.

Baby joined in planning the development of his jungle kingdom as she had in the construction of the opera house. She wasn't greatly interested in the details of operating a business, but projects like leveling a vast Honduran forest captured her imagination. When the logging operations got under way, he promised her, he would have enough mahogany hauled to Denver to build a house made entirely of mahogany.

Probably about $2,000,000 disappeared into the maw of the Honduran operation for the timber concession and the railroad-steamship system, but Horace never so much as received a mahogany toothpick out of the deal. It was another paper kingdom, another scheme that benefited only the peddlers of concessions that looked magnificently productive on paper. But what did it matter, with the Matchless alone bringing him almost $100,000 a month? He went on plunging recklessly. A group of Leadville promoters took him for $100,000 they asserted would be used to build the Tabor Grand Hotel—Horace fancied the name—in Leadville. He bought a fourth interest in the Fifth Avenue Hotel in New York, and sank a sizable sum in a worthless gold mine at Boulder, Colorado.

At least the Tabor Grand was built as promised, and a suite was set aside for Horace and Baby on their occasional trips to the source of his wealth and the site of their first meeting, but like his other earthly works it would prove as evanescent as the smoke from a smelter stack.

And all the time, the lawyers, who took over the conquest of the West from the pioneers and adventurers, were enriching themselves at Horace's expense. He was constantly engaged in litigation. Every successful mining operation was beset by claimants who complained that they had been "jumped" somewhere along the line. The boundary lines between mines were somewhat erratically surveyed and recorded. Nuisance suits, too, were popular. A whole phalanx of lawyers battened off the Maid of Erin suit, in which the mine's four owners (including Tabor) battled for part of an adjoining claim and won after three years of litigation. Tabor celebrated that empty triumph in February, 1884. A month later he was suing the owners of the Dolphin mine, adjoining his Matchless, on the claim that their property was part of the Matchless. He lost that argument and had to settle on a counter-suit for $400,000.

It would be impossible to estimate how many legal-eagles, promoters, con men, and other vulpine types, too lazy to go digging into the hills themselves, found their own bonanzas in Tabor's pocket.

Aside from busying himself with schemes to multiply an estimated worth of more than a dozen million, much of it silver profits traded for airy promises and distant concessions, Horace was also producing a family during the first half-dozen years of his second marriage. Two daughters were born to them, but a son (like Baby's firstborn) lived only a few hours.

The first daughter was born July 13, 1884, and a few weeks later was taken to Oshkosh for christening at the altar of St. Peter's Church. Peter McCourt, Sr., had died the year before, but the christening of Elizabeth Bonduel Lillie Tabor called for a family reunion and was a joyous occasion.

Certainly the baby Elizabeth made her debut in style. Her layette had cost $15,000 and included christening robes of lace and hand embroidery fastened with gold and diamond pins. Her booties were handmade. The infant also wore a jeweled necklace with a diamond locket. On her wispy hair was a French felt hat tipped with marabou feathers. Little Elizabeth would never romp around in dirty pinafores, as a contemporary chronicler made clear: "The baby's wardrobe at the present time consists of fifty lace robes and dainty velvet gowns of the richest description. She has a profusion of jewels of rare and unique designs, presented by her father and by friends everywhere, even from Europe; and every pin placed in her clothes is garnished with a diamond."

Immediately after returning from Oshkosh, Baby and Horace had a hundred gold medals struck off with the inscription:

BABY TABOR
July 13
1884

On the reverse side it read, with un-Tabor-like circumlocution, "Compliments of the Tabor Guard."

The medals were sent to the "best people" whom the Tabors had hoped for more than a year to lure into their social orbit. Being pure gold, they would hardly be discarded. Perhaps Horace and Baby hoped that respectable parenthood would invoke the blessings of the Capitol Hill community, that it would serve as a signal to the social lionesses that the Tabors were settling down and becoming worthy of acceptance. If so, they were disappointed. When Baby took her bejeweled infant out for an airing in her black landau behind four black horses, the faces of matrons in passing carriages were still averted, still frozen in disapproval.

When their second daughter, Rose Mary Echo Silver Dollar Tabor, was born on December 17, 1889, her parents did not bother to strike off any more gold medals. By then they knew that medallions the size of dinner plates wouldn't influence anyone.

The Tabor Grand Opera House became the center of their social life. No one could snoot them on part of their home territory. Nor could anyone ignore their presence. Almost nightly they appeared in the white satin-quilted Box A, so close to the stage they were almost part of the performance and as visible to the rest of the audience as the actors themselves. It was impossible to ignore them, because the Tabors held court in their box, opened champagne, and often talked quite loudly if the performance was not sufficiently gripping. Nor could the local aristocracy absent themselves as a sign of disapproval. The Tabor Grand was the premier temple of the arts. No one could risk missing a Bernhardt appearance without being stigmatized as lacking in devotion to Culture. The price they had to pay was watching the Tabors living it up in Box A with whatever raffish friends they had managed to collect.

Thus the Tabor Grand turned out to be a form of revenge on their contemptuous peers—and as such worth every penny it cost.

It was their funhouse, gazebo, and personal cabaret. Box A was always banked with lilies, whose odor of funereal sweetness was wafted over the audience below and mingled with the livelier scent of spilled Piper Heidseck. But its centerpiece was the dashing young Mrs. Tabor, with her figure daringly displayed in gowns with a low-dipping décolletage. Baby took no chances on not being noticed. She always waited until the moment the curtain was rung up and the stage lighting came on full force to make her entrance. Generally she was complimented by a swiveling of opera glasses in the direction of Box A, and they weren't focused on Horace's balding crown or paunchy waist-coat.

Baby lost no opportunity to impress the Tabor Grand's patrons that they were there on sufferance, that they must tolerate her whims or find some other place to amuse themselves.

When her first daughter was only three weeks old, Baby brought the squawling infant, swaddled in lace and diamonds, to the theater and paraded her through the lobby between the acts.

The only person who visibly objected to nursery noises intruding on the sacred hush of a dramatic performance was the great tragedian Edwin Booth. The Tabors appeared a little later than usual that night. Booth was just playing an intensely dramatic scene in Act I of *Richelieu* when the Tabor party made its appearance. First, Baby, glittering in jewelry which blinked in the footlights, then Horace carrying the infant Elizabeth. There was a rustle in the audience as it turned its attention from Booth to the Tabors, who took their time about seating themselves and settling down to pay attention to Booth thundering away only a few yards below them.

Booth glared up at Box A and interrupted the scene long enough to announce in tones that almost corroded the golden velvet ropes draped around the Tabors:

"If anyone in the audience above the intellectual level of Barbary apes is *still* interested, and if I may command no further distractions from the other side of the proscenium, this perform-ance will now proceed."

Tabor was outraged. No hambone actor was going to insult him on his own property. He jumped to his feet, carried baby Elizabeth under one arm like a bag of flour, grabbed Baby, and stalked out of the box, loudly proclaiming that "Booth will never walk this stage again."

Aside from Edwin Booth, the Tabors delighted in the company of players who, at least, were not burdened by social prejudices or an excess of moralistic attitudes. Baby, of course, had always been stagestruck. The socializing with the great names of the theater and the lyrical stage who trouped through Denver almost made up for being ostracized by the mesdames whose names glorified the society columns. She was hostess at champagne suppers for such famous or notorious theatrical blossoms as Lillie Langtry and Lillian Russell, such celebrated figures as Sarah Bernhardt, Madame Modjeska, Augustin Daly, John Drew, Maurice Barrymore, William Gillette, Joseph Jefferson, Forbes-Robertson, Ada Rehan, Richard Mansfield, Christine Nilsson, and the brilliant young Minnie Maddern Fiske. Later she told one of the few confidantes in her life that the theatrical people seemed to like her, and that when she and Horace visited New York on his frequent business trips their Denver hospitality was repaid in full measure. No doubt, aside from the lack of social cachet, the glamour of a Lillian Russell, the charm of a Drew, and the wit of a Barrymore were more stimulating than the queenly approval of, say, Mrs. Senator Teller.

Curiously enough, the most fascinating appearance on the boards of the Tabor Grand to Horace, if not Baby, was that of the once-revered and now notorious Henry Ward Beecher. Once he had been the most compelling preacher in an American pulpit, but his involvement as the interloper in the messily scandalous Theodore Tilton divorce case had indicated a worldliness incompatible with his ministry. Beecher, however, was still in great demand as a lecturer. Now past seventy, his passions displayed themselves in an organ-toned voice.

His Denver audience was slender, but for once Horace Tabor sat through a performance without opening champagne or otherwise creating a disturbance. He and Beecher talked for hours after the lecture. Otherwise more notable for his sensual appetites, Horace had a curious weakness for the more eloquent divines.

Perhaps one irksome part of the Tabors' career as presiding officers over the Tabor Grand's cultural offerings was that they had to share it with the cynical and hypercritical Eugene Field, who assigned himself to serve as dramatic critic as well as city editor and columnist of the Denver *Tribune.* Field had no respect. Regarding one famous trouper at the Tabor Grand, he wrote that the actor played the King in *Hamlet* as though fearful another actor would place the ace. Field even refused to be awed by Sarah Bernhardt, against whom he delivered the one-liner which still has its calefactory place in the annals of the unending conflict between critics and performers: "An empty cab drove up to the stage door of the Tabor Grand last night, from which Mme. Bernhardt alighted."

It was literally a Field Day when Oscar Wilde appeared in Denver on another American lecture tour. No larger or squashier target had come within Field's range than that languid aesthete soulfully sniffing at his odorless sunflower. Well in advance of Wilde's coming to Denver, Field pretended to be worried over whether Denver was civilized enough to accord Wilde the reception he deserved; this was satisfactorily galling to the dignitaries who claimed Denver was a veritable nesting-place for culture. Field pleaded that Wilde be received "if not as a lecturer, then as one who may yet rank with the strong English poets [Wilde was Irish-born], for his first volume certainly holds out such hope . . . He has taught no bad doctrines and advanced no startling innovations. He has simply said that the gentle and beautiful are pleasant in life and worthy of consideration. If aesthetes are fools, it is because they have a higher opinion of our powers of intellectual evolution than they should have."

Field, however, intended to give Wilde a less respectful welcome than those reflections indicated. The prankster in him gaining supremacy over the cultural arbiter, he planned the sort of hoax Oscar himself should appreciate even as its victim.

Days before Wilde's arrival, Field, as foreman of the city desk, began slipping items into the columns of his paper announcing the arrival time of the poet's train as several hours before its scheduled appearance at the Denver station. He also enlisted a plump and stately member of his staff, O. H. Rothacker, as a member of his playful conspiracy.

Unwitting co-conspirators in the Field hoax were the members of Denver's miniscule intellectual community, who were supposed to welcome Wilde in adoring style and escort him in triumph through the streets to his hotel. Instead they were lured to the railroad station hours before the real Wilde's arrival.

And instead of welcoming the languid poet whom Gilbert and Sullivan had depicted as Bunthorne in *Patience*, they greeted Field's nominee for the role, his friend Rothacker disguised as Wilde and wearing a flaxen wig, a costume featuring ruffles and lace cuffs, and a sunflower in his lapel.

Field introduced the fraudulent Wilde to his admirers, then with many obsequious flourishes escorted him to a phaeton rented for the occasion. Rothacker, affecting a bored and listless manner, occasionally bowed to the crowds gathered on the sidewalks and doffed his plumed hat to those who tittered at his exotic tailoring. He flicked a silk handkerchief at unmannerly oafs who whooped or catcalled. No one along the well-advertised route suspected it was not the real Oscar they were gaping or jeering at.

Two hours later the genuine Wilde arrived at the station to find the reception committee he had been promised was long gone. He threw a tantrum and declared he would not fulfill the lecture engagement at the Tabor Grand, thus providing Field with the opportunity for one of his more celebrated puns: "That's what drove Oscar Wilde."

On reflection, however, Wilde decided that no Irishman can afford to be accused of lacking a sense of humor. Reporters told him that he had been the victim of a Eugene Field hoax, sort of an honor in itself, and he gallantly remarked, "What a splendid advertisement for my lecture!"

He was not one of the more successful troupers to appear on the Tabor Grand's boards, with Field accurately commenting that Wilde "never stirs his audience but in the direction of the door."

The Tabors, of course, were in the forefront of those who lionized Wilde during his brief stay in Denver. Field, who may or may not have been present at a small select party the Tabors gave for Wilde, but whose reportage was never inhibited by a lack of firsthand information, reported that Tabor, with a lordly flourish, presented Wilde with a lifetime pass to visit the Matchless mine whenever he felt the urge. "Mr. Wilde," Field told his readers, "expressed himself delighted, saying that of all things that which he desired most was to visit a mine."

9. *The Crash of a House of Cards*

BABY could revel in newspaper headlines calling her the Silver Queen, in stories detailing her beauty and nominating her as the most beautiful of all the rich men's wives on the continent, in journalistic attention whenever she and Horace went to New York, but it never ceased to annoy her that the dull old harridans of Capitol Hill continued to ignore her existence. Perhaps it didn't occur to her that with her rather sensational looks she would have found it difficult to gain their favor even if she had the combined qualities of Clara Barton, Harriet Beecher Stowe, and Mrs. Rutherford B. Hayes (who served lemonade at state dinners in the White House). To the end of her life, she would occasionally and bitterly recall that the Denver society women would focus their opera glasses on Box A at the Tabor Grand Opera House and, though they wouldn't even nod to her on the street, would have their own dressmakers copy her Paris gowns to the last eyelet and furbelow.

Her galled feelings on this score erupted one night in the Tabor mansion when Horace was out of town on business.

Her brother Peter was accustomed to use his sister's house for his weekly poker games. She had come to resent Peter for his status as a popular bachelor, invited to all the stateliest homes, because "everything he had was due to me and it was particu-

larly galling that he should be asked everywhere I was barred."
Perhaps, too, it seemed to her that Peter, out of sibling loyalty,
should have refused to go anywhere his sister wasn't welcome.

Baby was brooding over her resentments upstairs as she heard
Peter ordering the servants to serve a champagne supper for
himself and his guests, Will Macon, Jack Moseby, John Kerr,
Will Townsend, and John Good, all members of the First
Families set, all of whom had mothers or sisters who constantly
snubbed Baby.

Her Irish temper reached the flash point when she heard Peter
and his chums gaily falling upon the wine and food in her dining
room, as they had week after week.

Looking like a Celtic warrior-queen, she suddenly appeared at
the head of the festive board. The sight of their plump,
self-satisfied faces only further enraged her . . . and Peter,
lounging at the other end of the table as genially expansive as
Diamond Jim Brady, urging his friends to stuff themselves at
Horace's expense. . . .

"If I'm not good enough for your mothers and sisters to call on,
how can my food be good enough for you to eat?" she blazed out.

Peter and his friends were dumbfounded—they couldn't be
held accountable for the social prejudices of their womenfolk,
couldn't be expected to rearrange the pecking order on Capitol
Hill, could they?

They dropped their knives and forks and, embarrassed as men
can be by a female's emotional outburst, shuffled out of the
dining room and into the night. Peter apologized at the door and
then returned to confront his sister.

"What do you mean by saying I could have my friends over
and then causing a scene like that?" he demanded. "Do you
want to disgrace me?"

"Disgrace me!" she shrieked at him. "Everything you have in
the world you owe to Horace and me. If you had any gratitude,
you'd have your friends invite me to their parties, not use me to
further your own ends."

Peter stormed out of the house. They made up a short time

later, but things were never quite the same between Baby and her favorite brother. Peter's ingratitude would soon show even sharper edges, and they would be estranged for most of their lives. His easy, blarneying charm would be seen (if only by Baby) as masking a greedy and self-centered bachelor-clubman who lived off his personality.

Occasionally, however, Baby's Irish wit asserted itself in confrontation with the Victorian inhibitions of her time. One day her coachman informed her that the lady of the neighboring mansion, according to below-stairs gossip, was affronted by the naked statuary on the Tabor lawn. The nude figures that horrified her neighbor were those of Psyche, Nimrod, and Diana, which had been cast in the Parisian foundry that turned out Rodin's metal sculptures.

Baby decided to ease the moral pangs suffered by her neighbor. She sent for a dressmaker, ordered her to take the exact measurements of the statues. Nimrod was to be clad in red hunting boots and a black derby, Diana was to be outfitted with a flowing chiffon gown, and Psyche was to be robed in satin. When the costumes were finished, she draped the statues with all the modesty that Mme. Pecksniff next door could expect.

Soon after the extravagant irony of that gesture Baby would be worrying more about clothing her young daughters than providing finery for her statues.

Horace, it would soon be evident, had been painstakingly constructing a house of cards instead of a financial empire. Because of the instability of the silver market, troubled as it was by political controversy, it would have behooved Tabor to stop scattering his chips, buying anything Baby fancied, funding the state Republican cause, channeling money into his more ludicrous "investments"; that he recognize finally the source of his wealth was not inexhaustible.

Late in the decade it was apparent that he had overreached himself. As early as 1886 a Denver newspaper hinted that Tabor was courting insolvency. The Leadville mines were petering out, and even the Matchless was producing only a relative trickle of silver. Other mining ventures were proving fruitless. There was no copper on his vast Texas holdings. His real estate, insurance, theatrical, gas, and water companies were paying smaller dividends just when they should have been producing larger ones. Honduras and Yucatan were proving sinkholes for his ready cash, his agents down there always demanding more money for "development." Chihuahua was proving to be barren of gold, at least on his holdings. Another half-million went down the drain when he tried to revive the Calumet project on Lake Michigan, the dream city he hoped would outrank Chicago. He lost another half-million gambling in the Chicago wheat pit.

If that wasn't bad enough, silver as a legislatively protected commodity was under attack by the New York and London financial overlords, and the price of silver was in constant danger. Neither Baby nor Horace, nor most of their contemporaries, had the intellectual stamina to grasp all the intricacies of the "silver question," only its more emotional aspects. For several decades that problem had agitated American politics to a degree difficult to comprehend by our generation, which accepted without protest a coinage intrinsically on a par with telephone slugs. Now, the trouble is a silver shortage while in the 1880's it was a glut caused by overproduction.

Silver coinage had been the hottest of political issues for almost twenty years, with Republicans generally leaning toward the gold standard and Democrats toward bimetallism. William Jennings Bryan built his career on the issue of "free silver," that is, unlimited coinage, as the debate continued over whether to commit the United States to the gold standard or parity between silver and gold. One of the more violent silver partisans, W. H. "Coin" Harvey, ended his book *Coin's Financial School* by advocating war against Britain as the center of the gold conspiracy: "If it is claimed we must adopt for our money the metal England selects, and can have no independent voice in the matter, let us make the test and find out if it is true. It is not American to give up without trying. If it is true, let us attach England to the

United States and blot her name out from among the nations of the earth. A war with England would be the most popular ever waged on the face of the earth."

Silver was "demonetized" by legislation passed during the Grant Administration, "the crime of '73" as it was known in the silver-producing states. But that was before Tabor and others struck it rich around Leadville. Partly because of their combined political influence, silver was restored to its monetary status during the Hayes Administration under the Bland-Allison bill. Henceforth the Treasury would be required to buy not less than $2,000,000 and not more than $4,000,000 of silver bullion each month.

Free silver, in essence, was inflationary and risked the stability of the American economy. It was supported with emotional fervor by the creditor class, the indebted farmers of the West, and stubbornly opposed by the Eastern financial interests, who wanted the solid, gold-backed dollar.

Unfortunately for the silver magnates and those with mortgaged farms, Grover Cleveland attained the White House in 1884. He was a Gold Democrat, a conservative in fiscal matters, and those with any insight into national politics were certain that he would be influenced to reduce the status of silver.

Intelligent men with silver-mining interests headed for shelter, consolidated their holdings, but this was just the time that Hod Tabor, euphoric over his remarriage, was extending himself all over the map. Instead of investing his money wisely and disposing of his mining interests in the certain knowledge that their value would shortly be depreciated, Tabor doubled his bets. For a time it appeared that Tabor's hunch that silver could not be monetized without creating a near-revolutionary protest might be proven out. Six Western states with a strong pro-silver tendency—Idaho, Montana, North and South Dakota, Washington, and Wyoming—were admitted to the Union and added close to a dozen members to the silver bloc in the Senate. And in the election of 1888, President Cleveland was disavowed by the considerable pro-silver faction in his own party when he ran for reelection against Benjamin Harrison. The Republican platform that year included a plank calling for the use of both gold and silver as a dual standard of monetary value. It appeared that the gold tide was being reversed. Even the Solid South was wavering in its loyalty to the Democratic Party over the silver issue.

Harrison came to Denver on his campaign tour, and naturally Tabor was in the forefront of his greeters. He was still chairman of the Republican State Central Committee and clung to the belief that he was a political power aside from his financial contributions. In 1886 he had made another bid for the Senatorial nomination, and now in 1888 he was running hard for his party's nomination for the governorship, which again would elude his grasp.

Tabor greeted the future President Harrison with a clap on the back and escorted him along the route of the most enthusiastic torchlight procession Denver had ever seen. A few years hence Horace would have been glad of the offer of a janitor's job at the White House, but he would be able to console himself with the thought that he was the only man to have slapped Presidents Grant, Arthur, and Harrison on the back. Candidate Harrison stayed in Denver only overnight, but the moment the parade was over Tabor hauled him to his mansion. Baby, a glittering spectacle in white satin, greeted him at the door of the House of Tabor. Drinks were poured in an effort to thaw out the small, shrewd visitor from Indiana, a Presbyterian elder, but Harrison stood on his dignity even as Horace became more exhilarated and called his guest "Benny" (or so local rumor had it).

Next morning Harrison was escorted up to Leadville—that trip was becoming part of a ritual for any candidate who hoped to gain the favor of the silver states—with Tabor as his voluble guide. Harrison was presented with an eight-pound brick of silver. With Tabor beaming at him and a wildly cheering crowd gathered on the street below, the candidate spoke from the balcony of the Tabor Grand Hotel. He delivered a stem-winder of an oration on the magnificence of the "free American institutions," one of which, his auditors presumed, was free silver.

"We stand here today on the mountaintop," he concluded, "and see what I think is the highest evidence of American pluck to be found in the United States." Tabor, taking that to be a reference to his "pluck" in backing Hook and Rische with a gunnysack full of groceries and a jug of whiskey, was so enraptured that he sent his plug hat sailing into the crowd below.

Silver was sinking in value when President-elect Harrison took the oath of office. The silver bloc in Congress, including about half the Democrats in the House of Representatives, moved to rescue that commodity by pushing for a free-coinage act that would give silver parity with gold as backing for the American dollar; a measure, incidentally, which would have had a disastrous impact on international finance. A long and bitter battle was fought in Congress over how much to yield to the Free Silver cause.

In the middle of that Congressional uproar, William Jennings Bryan of Nebraska, the "boy orator of the Platte," who had nominated himself as the man to save America from being crucified on a "cross of gold" (as his most memorable speech phrased it), came to Denver on an exploratory mission. Naturally he met with Tabor, as the most famous of the silver magnates, to acquaint himself with all aspects of silver mining, of silver's impact on the market economy and its political and economic importance to the Western states which would form the base of Bryan's support. He later professed himself to be disappointed in Tabor from the intellectual standpoint. Horace and Baby entertained him lavishly, but his host did not strike him as a serious man. About all that Horace seemed to know about the momentous silver question was that you extracted silver from ore and got paid a lot of money for it.

Bryan tried to awaken Tabor to the dangers ahead, he would recall, while the latter lounged in his office and drank whiskey. He told Tabor that the "gold bugs" of the East were in a finish fight with the silver forces, and that with all their political influence and economic power they might well succeed in imposing the gold standard. Wall Street, he further warned, would back Cleveland for a second run at the Presidency, and whatever measures the current Congress took to assure parity might be nullified.

Tabor, however, was supremely confident of his position. He reckoned his net worth at close to $100,000,000, but that was pie-in-the-sky reckoning based on a wildly optimistic hope that all his scattered investments would pay off in a big way. His real worth, if any accounting genius had been able to sort out his holdings, was probably not more than a few million in 1890, and only that if he had liquidated his assets immediately.

"Look," he told Bryan, "there's enough silver left in the Rockies to build a wall forty feet high and four feet thick of solid silver around Colorado. Let them gold bugs butt their heads against that wall."

A few months later Tabor's cheeriness seemed to have been justified. The Sherman Silver Purchase Act was adopted by Congress on July 14, 1890. It repealed the Bland-Allison Act and increased the American commitment to silver coinage; the Treasury was directed to buy 4,500,000 ounces of silver bullion a month. It also declared that "the established policy of the United States is to maintain the two metals on a parity with each other upon the present legal ratio (sixteen to one) or such ratio as may be provided by law." And the country, with the exception of Wall Street and some of the more longheaded economists, rejoiced. "Gold monometallism, after all, had been American policy only since the 1870's," as a modern expert on the issue has written, "and it was still possible in the early 1890's for a man to stand for free silver as a return to an old policy rather than a drastic innovation. Free silver inherited the old banners of American monetary inflationism that had been kept waving since the Civil War by the Greenbackers. And while free silver has been much ridiculed, and rightly so, as the single cure-all of the popular thought of the nineties, it is worth remembering that from the debtor's standpoint silver inflation, however inadequate, was not a totally unfitting expedient."

*   *   *

To Baby and Horace Tabor, it would always seem that their fortunes collapsed overnight. One night they were rich, the next morning they were worrying about grocery bills. Baby, of course, was occupied by the cares of motherhood with Elizabeth, then nine, and Silver Dollar (or Honeymaid as her mother called her), four years old. But Horace, who was supposed to be a financial genius, and not only by his own reckoning, adamantly refused to take notice of the economic storm warnings. The price of silver continued to drop despite the artificial support ordained by Congress, partly because the rest of the world refused to prize it as highly as the silver-rich United States.

Despite all the bad omens, Horace continued to spend money in reckless fashion. On a visit to New York he bought a yacht and mothballed it against the day when the children would be old enough to accompany him and Baby on a cruise to Honduras to survey his mahogany forests.

When Silver Dollar celebrated her third birthday, he and Baby not only outfitted the child with a new point-lace dress costing $900, but had a series of fifty photographs taken of her. The pictures were placed in a red plush album with a gold clasp, at a cost of $400 each, and a hundred copies were distributed. And there was that flock of peacocks, a hundred of them eating their heads off, which Horace had bought at Baby's suggestion. Temperamental and ill-tempered as the birds were, they served as family pets. A Tabor offspring could not be expected to play with something so ordinary as a puppy or kitten.

Even as Tabor was being elected president of the Denver Board of Trade as a tribute to his widely proclaimed acumen, the earth was shifting under him and all those who had staked their fortunes on the rigged price of silver.

Two Coloradans named George G. Merrick and Harley B. Morse had appeared at the Philadelphia Mint, bringing with them a silver brick weighing 514.8 ounces, troy, and demanding to see the director. "Coin this silver brick into dollars for us," they demanded of the director. He refused. Merrick and Morse had, of course, known he would refuse and thus provide them with a test case for the highest courts. The United States Supreme Court, however, denied that it had jurisdiction in the matter. That did not discourage the agitation in Colorado, where 220 "silver clubs" had been organized. When both the Republicans and Democrats waffled on the free-silver issue, the Populists nominated David Hansen Waite for governor and saw him elected. The Populist governor promptly made the situation worse by inveighing against those who would demonetize silver, declaring, "I should rather see our men riding through the streets up to the bridle-bits in blood than surrender our liberties to the corporations." Just as promptly, the money managers of the Eastern Seaboard, taking Governor Waite's declaration as a call for revolution, refused to continue investing money in Western projects.

Grover Cleveland had regained the Presidency in the election of 1892, and immediately on moving back to the White House noted that there had been an alarming seepage from the nation's gold reserve, that there was a virtual run on the Treasury by persons holding greenbacks or Treasury notes and demanding that they be redeemed in gold. Under the laws then in force, his Secretary of the Treasury was empowered to redeem such paper in silver, but Cleveland insisted that gold must be paid on demand.

A crisis was in the making the moment Cleveland got his hands on the levers of financial power. He evidently was determined to deflate the U.S. economy. The panic and subsequent depression of 1893 followed his heavy tread into the White House.

By the early summer of 1893 the first shock waves had reached Denver. Ten Denver banks closed their doors during July, thus depriving Tabor and many others of their ready cash. His real estate and other solid assets were already heavily mortgaged. Tabor, unable to meet the mortgage payments, quickly lost them all.

Nor would those banks still open come to his rescue with loans to save some of the collapsing enterprises. "So many of Horace's holdings, which seemed to be so promising when he acquired them, turned out to be worthless paper," as Baby would recall in later years. "He had been swindled by associates and men he called his friends for years without either of us realizing it until it was too late. Some of his real estate was already mortgaged and when the blow first fell he mortgaged the rest. Afterward we learned what a mistake that was. If only we had learned to economize before it was too late. . . ."

Closing his ears to the sound of crumbling façades and crashing roofs, Tabor maintained his optimistic attitude, at least in public. He simply rejected the evidence that day by day his fortune was evaporating, though as an inveterate gambler he should have remembered that every run of luck is broken sooner or later. His own luck, considering his mental capacity, had lasted longer than he had any reason to expect.

To save something from the wreckage Baby proposed that her husband dispose of some of her jewelry. "No," he replied, "the day's coming when you'll wear it again. I've got gold-mine property that only needs development to make us another fortune. Why, down in Boulder County alone. . . ." But Tabor had never had much luck with gold.

By late summer the panic had developed into a severe depression. Silver led the way downward. First the mint of India announced it would accept no more silver for coinage, then other countries followed suit. The price of silver dropped from $1.29 per ounce to $.50. And gold was evaporating from the Treasury. It had always been conventional wisdom that the gold reserve should amount to at least $100 million; now it had fallen to the $70-million level.

In August of 1893, with breadlines lengthening, President Cleveland summoned a special session of Congress to urge the repeal of the Sherman Silver Purchase Act. The measure was rammed through because Congress was warned the economy would collapse unless the United States went back on the gold standard. Silver henceforth would be on a footing with copper and nickel as a metal for coinage, but it would never be equally redeemable with gold. The merchant bankers, who for so long had urged the gold standard, found the situation doubly profitable. Their creditors now had to pay them off in gold-backed dollars. In addition, three of the Titans of Wall Street—the banking houses of Morgan, Belmont, and Rothschild—answered an appeal for help from the White House. President Cleveland asked them to buy 3,500,000 ounces of gold to bolster the Treasury's reserve. They would be paid back, at 4 percent interest, by a government bond issue. The bankers immediately presented their bonds to the U.S. Treasury and took an immediate profit of $7,000,000 for a purely mechanical transaction. Even the Democratic organ in New York, the *Morning World*, found that sort of patriotism indefensible and declared the bankers had made off with their profits without taking the slightest risk. "Is there anything but 'bunco' with which to describe the transaction?" the *World* demanded.

Obviously the silver magnates of Tabor's naïve stripe, for all their economic significance during the eighties, were destined for a wipeout. They were "lucky," but Wall Street was "smart."

One by one Tabor's possessions were stripped from him. The Tabor Block and his Leadville mining properties followed the real estate and other investments down the drain. The Leadville mines were closing down because the market for silver was glutted. Even the Matchless—the diadem, the touchstone of Tabor's fortune—was shut down. The opera house and hotel in Leadville were seized by his creditors.

One hope Horace still clung to. Gold was the thing now, and prospectors were coursing all through the eroded gulches and hillsides high in the Rockies searching for veins that might have been overlooked during previous rushes.

Horace still had what he regarded as an ace in the hole. That was his Eclipse mine in Boulder County, which showed some promise of producing gold if the money could be found to develop its workings.

Just when all his drinking companions and fair-weather

friends, whom Horace had more than his share of, were looking the other way when he came shambling down the street, a man he barely knew came to his rescue. He was Winfield Scott Stratton of Colorado Springs, who had extracted millions from the Cripple Creek gold fields, so lucrative they were known as the "$300,000,000 cow pasture."

Years before, Stratton had worked briefly for Tabor as a carpenter in Leadville. Now Tabor journeyed to Colorado Springs to ask Stratton for a $15,000 loan to develop the Eclipse. Stratton, who had sent $1,000 out of his first earnings to a man who had once lent him a dollar when he was broke, remembered Tabor as a genial employer and listened sympathetically as the latter outlined his plan to develop the Eclipse and use the proceeds to reopen the Matchless.

"You know, Mr. Stratton," Tabor said, "there is still silver in the mine, and I always say to Mrs. Tabor, 'Hang onto the Matchless.' "

"Now, Senator, don't say another word," Stratton replied, reaching for his pen and checkbook. "You don't know how deeply I appreciate this honor. Will this be enough to get started on?"

Before pocketing the $15,000 check, Tabor insisted on giving Stratton a 90-day note for the sum. It would never be repaid. Five years later Stratton returned the note with a tactful letter signed by his secretary: "Mr. W. S. Stratton wishes me to say that he never at any time contemplated the retention of your note and papers as an evidence of indebtedness to him on your part, and in going over his affairs he finds them still on hand contrary to his wishes and intentions. If they remain with him, he must list them with the assessor of taxes and in case of his demise they could not then be returned by his Executors. He therefore directs that they be returned to you at once and asks that you accept them back again as an expression of his best wishes and good will for your future success."

When he accepted Stratton's check that day in late 1893,

Horace, of course, was confident the note would be repaid. Stratton's gesture was an omen. Maybe his luck had taken a change for the better just when his creditors were closing in like redbone hounds on a treed raccoon.

10. *"How Can You Do This to Horace Tabor?"*

THE Tabors never knew what hit them. The whirlwind effects of a panic and depression were something new in their experience. There had been a depression in the seventies, but Horace, struggling away in remote mountain camps, hardly felt its repercussions, and Baby had still been a child. Americans have never been able to believe in the reality of hard times until they are overwhelmed by them; either their grasp of economic history is weak or they are blessed with unretentive memories.

Thus the Tabors were quite unprepared for the ruthless way in which their creditors pounced before the last of their negotiable assets could disappear. Hardheaded realists to a man, they could not share Horace's belief that he had been rich only a few months ago and that, given a breathing space to recover his bearings, he would be able to get back on his feet. Perhaps he would have been able to, but the real powers in Denver, who had dominated the city ever since it was the supply base for the Pike's Peak gold rush, had never shared the rainbow credo of men like Hod Tabor.

Horace and Baby both fought hard to save something from the wreckage. He never let the mortgaged Matchless slip from his grasp entirely, and made a desperate effort to hang onto his next most precious possession, the Tabor Grand Opera House. Baby sold her jewelry so Horace could use the proceeds in a vain and quickly crumbled effort to stave off his creditors.

Baby's Irish spirit rose to the occasion. She did not waste her time on reproaches when Horace's grandiose financial schemes turned out to be a herd of white elephants, but pitched in to use her persuasive powers for their joint benefit.

When they received a notice of foreclosure on the opera house, Baby herself went to Horace Bennett, the young millionaire who was the chief mortgage holder, with a plea for an extension.

"We millionaires must stick together," she told Bennett.

"I am not a millionaire, Mrs. Tabor, and this is a business transaction. I appreciate how you and Mr. Tabor have sentimental feelings about the opera house. But in that case, you shouldn't have mortgaged it."

No doubt it was with considerable satisfaction that the Old Guard of Denver's moneyed class contemplated the removal of Mr. and Mrs. Horace Tabor from Box A.

Baby knew that her brother Peter was in sound financial condition and appealed to him for help in saving the Tabor Grand but—with all the bitter satisfaction of a man naturally resentful of the patronage which had lifted him from a clerk's desk, or what might be called the Uriah Heep Syndrome—Peter was even less sympathetic than Horace Bennett.

Those laughing Irish eyes of brother Peter had turned to casehardened steel, and he answered her appeal by saying, "I haven't the money to spare, and even if I could, you'd only throw it away on some silly extravagance."

That was one turndown Baby never forgave. She and her brother were completely estranged. To Peter McCourt she became a non-person when Horace lost his money. He prospered during the ensuing years and had piled up an estate of $250,000 when he died in 1929. To Baby he left only some stock in a carriage factory which had been worthless ever since the automobile replaced the horse and buggy. Of all the misfortune that would descend on her, Baby often said that Peter was the "worst disappointment" of her life.

Some indication of the desperation with which Horace Tabor tried to extricate himself from the rubble of his fallen house could be detected in the letter he wrote Senator H. M. Teller, a rather chilly and high-minded fellow who had never pretended to be a friend or admirer of Tabor's. Teller, back in the Senate, received a letter from Tabor suggesting that he lean on the Supreme Court in Tabor's behalf. Only a desperate man, or one who completely misread Teller's character, could have expected him to exercise that kind of influence. The near-incoherence of the letter, however, suggests the confused state of its author's mind:

"To fully let you know the status of affairs relative to the blocks [presumably Tabor referred to the Tabor Block and the opera house], I will tell you what Mrs. Smith told me this week. She told me a party told her he had the money in hand to loan her to pay off the North Western [his insurance company] but that he would not talk to her about it until she was in possession. I today tried to get a thirty days option from her and she flatly told me that she would not take less than four hundred thousand dollars, but of course if we can establish it as a mortgage in the upper Court she will have to accept three hundred and thirty thousand dollars, the amount at which she bid it in.

"If she gets possession it will cost me many thousands of dollars on account of her management, therefore we must leave nothing undone to defeat the same. On account of my being such a strong advocate of *Free Coinage* it is at this time impossible for me to make a loan. I feel that the Judges of this silver state should protect me until after the elections for then there will be no trouble to make a loan.

"But now Senator you know that it is exactly the same as in a time of actual war and the Judges have power to issue any order that will protect their own and I feel that I belong to them for my funds were always freely used for the good of the party and country, and if I have it again it will be the same and all I want is to keep what belongs to me and lead a quiet home life.

"And I feel that if you will now go to the supreme court or court of appeals and ask them to issue an order to Judge Johnson restraining him from giving her possession until my time expires for redemption with the North Western which would leave her three months to secure a loan if I failed she being a Judgment creditor I feel Senator that the judges will not refuse you but that they will recognize that there is an actual war. It will not only save me but it will help our silver cause and such an act will be admired by the toiling masses.

"Senator I believe if you ask Judge Johnson to make an order that the assignees stay in possession for both parties the full time of my redemption with the North Western giving Mrs. Smith all the money over and above running expenses because the assignees are economical and trustworthy that he will do it for you and the silver cause. But I feel sure the upper court will do it for you alone. The case comes up before Judge Johnson at ten on Monday next. Trusting in God that something will be done for me. . . ."

That Horace could hope that Senator Teller would descend from his Olympian rectitude to exert a highly unethical, if not illegal pressure on the courts was almost as pathetic as his claim that the "toiling masses" would be cheered by the financial salvation of one of the Bonanza Kings who had oppressed them.

Yet his belief that he had some claim on public and personal gratitude was not so farfetched. He had always been openhanded and generous to people (except to his mine employees) down on their luck. Even a contemporary who did not admire his florid style admitted that "these attributes proved his financial undoing. No man ever went to him for a favor when he had money and came away emptyhanded. No man ever forgave his enemies quite so cheerfully or testified so willingly to the sincerity of his forgiveness by afterwards aiding them . . . He made many mistakes during the days of his prominence and prosperity but, his surroundings and opportunities considered, carried himself as well as any of his contemporaries."

During the ten years of their marriage, he and Baby had managed to squander an estimated twelve million dollars.

Almost overnight they had to learn—again—how to cope with poverty. Horace was sixty-three, Baby thirty years younger, when the cocoon of wealth and privilege, which they had believed as durable and permanent as the carapace of an armadillo, suddenly was stripped away from them.

Baby could have cut her losses and made a run for a fair amount of comfort and security on her own—that is, if her detractors had correctly read her character as a gold-digging, home-wrecking, heartless, frivolous, pleasure-bound blonde.

The betting among the gamblers headquartered on Champa Street was that Baby would desert Horace before New Year's Day 1894, and there were many men, who had eyed her voluptuous body for many years, who waited for that to happen.

She could have taken her jewelry, at least several hundred thousand dollars' worth, including the diamond necklace Horace had paid $90,000 for, the supposed Queen Isabella jewels, and all the other fripperies with which she had been endowed during their marriage, and sold them for a competence to keep her and her daughters in style. It was inconceivable to those with a cynical view of beautiful blondes that she would stick to old Horace, so recently a fellow with a big paunch and a booming voice, now that he had shrunk like a collapsed balloon.

Such small-minded observers had simply failed to take into account the fact that Baby meant it when she said she loved Horace. She may have fallen in love with the Tabor legend before she fell in love with the man, but she wasn't as giddy, as lightminded as she appeared. She was not only dedicated to Horace but she believed that he would make a comeback. The Tabor luck to her was something manifest, as solidly real and durable as Pike's Peak. And her belief in his luck, or destiny, was probably as valuable to Horace as the fact of her fidelity. It would sustain him for a hard half-dozen years.

At first, with a sort of childish flight from the hard edges of reality, they tried to pretend it wasn't happening, that it was all part of a game.

Baby would not acknowledge ruin even when it imposed itself on her in the most visible way. Not even when the Tabor mansion came under the direct fire of their creditors. One day workmen came to shut off the public utilities, gas, light, and water, and Baby flew at them like a mother wren with her nest in danger.

"How can you do this to Horace Tabor, the man who gave Denver its post office and its opera house?" she demanded. "The man who's done more for Denver than it ever deserved. The man who started up the companies that are shutting us off."

The workmen replied that they were only carrying out their orders from the head office.

"Just wait till Congress changes that ridiculous law about silver being worthless and our Matchless is running again!"

At that point, in the winter of 1893–1894, Baby could still believe the fabulous Matchless mine—its timbers rotting, its tunnels caving in, its machinery untended and rusting, its lower depths filling up with water—would again produce high-grade carbonate ore, that the sacred status of silver would be restored. Wasn't William Jennings Bryan's star rising in the West, and with it the promise that the silver-loving West would triumph over the gold-obsessed East? Hadn't President Cleveland's policies brought on a depression that was sending Coxey's Army marching by the thousands (or, more literally, riding in boxcars) to Washington? Why, there'd be a revolution if those gold Democrats didn't realize the mistake they'd made.

So she and Horace pretended that holding off the bailiffs and conning the provision merchants was a sort of charade. Laughingly they carried lighted candles through the dark rooms of their mansion and picnicked with the children in the servantless pantry. It was like that "poverty party" some rich people in New York gave, at which the guests drank out of tin cans and ate off wooden shingles and pretended to be inhabiting a hobo jungle. They drank water from a barrel in the kitchen which was replenished at the old courthouse pump.

That sort of fun ended the day their creditors, having snatched everything else, dispossessed them of the mansion, and moving drays appeared to haul off their furniture, bric-a-brac, statues, silverware, paintings, and so forth to be sold at auction for the creditors' benefit. The horses and carriages went the same route. The hundred peacocks had died in a cloudburst which flooded their lawn.

The few possessions left to them were removed to a cottage on the outskirts of town on a dreary little street in which workingmen and their families lived.

Their neighbors on Capitol Hill, most of whom had been conservative enough not to lose all their holdings as the Tabors did, watched the disappearance of Horace and Baby and their two young daughters without any discernible compassion. None had offered help or even condolences; how could they, since they had never acknowledged the Tabors' existence? The granite features of the Old Guard reflected nothing but grim satisfaction at the final exclusion of the interlopers, at the almost Biblical comeuppance the Tabors had suffered for breaking at least one of the Commandments and flaunting their wealth with such vulgar exuberance.

The Tabors moved into the cottage they rented for thirty dollars a month, from which Horace, for the first several months, sallied forth every morning and walked downtown as though he still had business to transact. Baby learned how to mend her daughters' clothes, how to brew tea three or four times from the same leaves, how to bargain with the butcher for soupbones and stew meat. Plenty of times, she would recall, there was no meat on the table.

Her younger daughter, Silver Dollar, was Baby's greatest comfort. Too young to be aware of the comedown her parents had suffered, she was a bright and affectionate child, she seemed like an echo of her mother's own childhood. Her sister Elizabeth, however, was ten years old and could not understand why she was suddenly deprived of her governess and pony cart, why she

had to go to school with the grubby children of West Denver.
Baby often caught Elizabeth staring at her with questioning eyes.
The bewilderment would soon change to accusation.

For several months Horace would shamble along in the
growing ranks of the unemployed, until he realized that nobody
could take him seriously anymore as the caretaker of a battered
financial empire, until he accepted the fact of his ruin. There
would be no feedback from those millions he had carelessly
diverted to other men's schemes. If he wanted to feed his wife and
daughters, he would have to bestir himself. To Horace, in his
new humility, it was a wonder that Baby hadn't left him,
considering how she feared poverty, how important it was for her
to be surrounded by luxury. She may have come to love him, as
she protested, but there was a litmus test to be applied to such
protestations: would she have married Hod Tabor if he had been
a fifty-year-old storekeeper or day laborer?

At first he couldn't bring himself to take any ordinary job that
might present itself or be offered out of charitable impulse. He
knew Baby would endure anything for the sake of a gamble, for
betting everything on bringing off a coup. She had quit her first
husband not because he was a failure but because he'd given up
trying. She had come to believe more fervently in the Tabor luck
than Horace himself, and that was why—as he believed—she
was handling their comedown so gracefully.

So Horace decided to take another plunge. He had spent the
$15,000 loan from Stratton on paying other men to develop the
Eclipse; perhaps they'd loafed on the job. This time the work
would have to be done with his own hands.

He left Baby and their daughters in the West Denver cottage,
and no sooner had he trudged off to take the Boulder stage than
a series of callers, some of them rather furtive in manner, all of
them male, came knocking at her cottage door. They all had one
thing on their minds, one question in their mouths. Now that
Hod was broke, how about letting them provide Baby with the
pretty things she valued so much? One man, whom Horace had
considered a friend of his, sidled in with an offer to make Baby

his mistress. She recalled for the only confidante of her later years that, in the Irish way, she answered a question with a question: "What kind of wife do you think I am?"

Better yet, she never told Horace about those furtive gentleman callers. As it was, his opinion of humanity had depreciated to the misanthropic level. And besides, the news that his old pals of the barroom and poker table and caucus room were trying to move in on his wife might have brought him rushing back from Boulder.

There Horace was starting all over again, using muscles that hadn't been exercised in twenty years; a penniless prospector again. With pick and shovel he began driving into the flinty hillside of his claim. How had he ever endured this sort of backbreaking labor year after year? People who came by the Eclipse and saw him burrowing away thought he was one of those slightly mad old slammerkins of the prospecting trade, could hardly believe it when they were told that weary, ragged, aging man only a year or two earlier had been known as the Silver King and lived in a mansion on Capitol Hill.

Within a few months he convinced himself that there was no gold on his claim, at least none that could be reached without driving a deeper shaft than one man could dig.

He would go back to Leadville, determined to make enough money by day labor to send Baby and their daughters for their upkeep. He got a job at a smelter pushing a wheelbarrow loaded with slag. It paid three dollars a day. Undoubtedly there were moments of recollection, not only of the times when he spent that much for a handful of cigars, and of when he was the unchallenged overlord of this mining town, with the Tabor Light Cavalry as his palace guard, but of the day when he decided that three dollars a day was too much for an ordinary hardrock miner and lowered the wage scale to $2.75. A memory to make a man feel like crawling away from his own skin.

Tabor spent about a year up in Leadville until wheeling the heavy barrows of slag became too much for him and his health broke down. There was nothing to do but return to the West

Denver cottage and live from hand to mouth. No help came from Peter McCourt, who was well-heeled enough to have taken over the lease and management of the Broadway Theater. When he learned of his father's plight, Maxcy Tabor, with more to forgive, supplied him with funds from time to time.

Horace and Baby were pinning all their hopes on silver making a comeback. The Republicans would nominate William McKinley, an advocate of the gold standard, and though he had been a fiercely loyal Republican all his time, Tabor would turn hopefully to the Democrats. He had spent hundreds of thousands in the Republican cause, and all the Grand Old Party had rewarded him with was the lieutenant governorship and a thirty-day term as U.S. Senator.

Maybe the Democrats would nominate a silver man and quiet the country's fears that its destiny had passed permanently into the hands of Wall Street and what the Populists called the "money power." Silver would be restored to parity and the Western states would recover from the depression that still gripped them.

Those hopes became more fervent, and in the Tabors' case almost delirious, when William Jennings Bryan—whose warnings Horace had ignored several years before—got up on the platform at the Democratic convention in Chicago and delivered the most stirring appeal for the gold/silver standard ever heard.

To the Tabors and many Westerners it seemed that Bryan's words would penetrate the American conscience. The Nebraskan declared war on the "financial magnates" on behalf of "our homes, our families, and posterity." Silver was the panacea for all the nation's economic ills; restore it to parity and the Western mines would reopen and the farmers would be able to pay off their mortgages.

"You come to us and tell us," as Bryan concluded his speech, "that the great cities are in favor of the gold standard. We reply that the great cities rest upon our broad and fertile prairies. Burn down your cities and leave our farms, and your cities would spring up again as if by magic; but destroy our farms, and the grass will grow in the streets of every city in the country . . . If they dare to come out in the open field and defend the gold standard as a good thing, we will fight them to the uttermost. Having behind us the producing masses of this nation and the world, the laboring interests, and the toilers everywhere, we will answer their demand for a gold standard by saying to them: You shall not press down upon the brow of labor this crown of thorns; you shall not crucify mankind upon a cross of gold!"

The Tabors were inspired by accounts of Bryan's speech and took even greater hope from the fact that Bryan was swept to the presidential nomination on his tidal oratory. They could imagine themselves the Silver King and Queen of Colorado again, back on Capitol Hill, back in Box A, and this time they would manage things better. They had learned a bitter lesson about trusting politicians and listening to company promoters. They did not pause to consider that the Matchless was played out, that they had lost the other mining properties, that it would take capital to get back in the game. Just let silver come back as a partner of gold, and everything would be fine.

But Bryan lost the election, and the gold Republicans replaced the gold Democrats in control of the administration. Tabor was now sixty-seven years old and it looked as though his life would end in abject poverty.

Ironically enough, a few months after Tabor had voted Democratic the first time in his life, his old Republican pals finally came to his rescue. It almost seemed there was a reward for disloyalty; certainly there had been none for lifelong fealty.

One day, a shabby and bent figure, he shambled into the lobby of the Brown Palace hoping to make a touch, perhaps, from some old acquaintance. He spotted Winfield Scott Stratton, who had lent him $15,000, the only man to extend a helping hand when he went broke.

Sidling up to Scott as the latter conversed with a group of friends, Tabor tugged at his elbow and asked, "Do you remember me?" Scott shook his head and turned away. Then he asked one of his friends, "Who the hell was that?" "Poor old Horace Tabor," he was told.

Stratton once again nominated himself as Tabor's savior, perhaps motivated by there-but-for-the-grace-of-God feelings, because in many ways his career had paralleled Tabor's. Not least in the fact that Stratton, after striking it rich with the Independence gold mine, had shucked off his old wife and married a young and beautiful girl. Luck more than diligence had also marked his career. Early in the nineties, in Colorado Springs, he was the leading candidate for the title of town drunk; his wife operated a boardinghouse and provided the whiskey money. Then he heard a rumor of a gold strike at Cripple Creek, and for once in his life he experienced a strange pang of ambition. Hurrying over to Cripple Creek, he staked out the Independence claim and rapidly prospered.

And like Tabor, Stratton was capable of gestures other people regarded as either magnificent or outrageous. One night he staged a party at the Brown Palace that grew so noisy the manager evicted him and his friends. Stratton swore he'd get revenge. A short time later, in 1893, the owner Henry C. Brown was caught in the same cashless position as many of his financial peers. Stratton bought the Brown Palace and fired the manager.

Like Tabor, too, he had been an angel of the Republican Party of Colorado. He had engaged the special train which carried Colorado's delegation to the Republican national convention. He had backed McKinley with contributions and his influence in Colorado. Now the Republicans owed Win Stratton a favor, and unlike Tabor, fortunately for Tabor, he would not be fobbed off.

He was determined that Horace, whom he hardly knew, would be taken care of. What about the postmastership of Denver, wasn't that post vacant and on the patronage list? Hadn't Hod Tabor donated the land on which the post office was built? And where the hell did the Republican Party keep its sense of gratitude? Overwhelmed, Senator Edward Wolcott interceded with President McKinley, at Stratton's insistence, and the $3,500-a-year job was given Tabor.

Thanks to a somewhat erratic guardian angel—it almost seemed that an old sinner could look only to his own kind—Horace took over as postmaster of Denver in January of 1898.

Baby, with her mystic belief in the Tabor luck, was certain this was only the first step toward retrieving his fortunes. "It was when you were a postmaster before that you struck it rich," she told her aging husband, whose own optimism could no longer match hers; he was entirely content with enough money to support his family. "This is only the beginning. It's a sign of better times to come." Baby would always believe in signs and portents.

Actually it was only a comfortable interlude. The Tabors moved into a four-room suite at the Windsor and lived within his salary. He performed creditably, it was agreed, as postmaster. No longer did his presence enliven the city's barrooms; the drink-buying days were over, to the regret of a sizable population of barflies. He brought a sandwich with him to the post office and lunched at his desk.

Baby could not persuade him to take her to the Tabor Grand, much as they both loved the theater. It would be too much of a comedown to sit in the orchestra. Someday the Matchless would reopen, perhaps, and they'd sit in Box A again; but he wouldn't settle for less. The only semi-theatrical event they attended, with the children, was that sponsored by the Denver & Pacific, which staged a collision of two of its old locomotives.

There was a quiet, prosaic closing to one of the more remarkable American careers. Tabor served as postmaster for a year and three months. Adversity, perhaps, had taught him something and he would be remembered as a kindly and considerate executive by the postal employees, unlike the workers in his Leadville mines.

On April 3, 1899, he lunched at his desk as usual, then went out for a stroll in the nearby park. A sudden pain knifed through him and he almost collapsed. Somehow he made it back to his office despite the severe abdominal pain. His co-workers sent him home to the Windsor suite in a hack.

Baby called a doctor immediately. At first his ailment was diagnosed as an "inflammation of the bowels"—later known as appendicitis. The doctors were dubious about taking him to a hospital for an operation because he was sixty-nine. And, anyway, the "inflammation" might be reduced. Instead peritonitis developed.

Tabor sank into a coma, and for most of seven days and nights Baby stayed at his bedside.

Occasionally he would regain consciousness for a moment or two and murmur, "Never sell the Matchless, Baby. When silver comes back, it will make millions."

Those words would echo through the rest of his widow's long life, which was as bizarre in its obedience to Tabor's last words as the destiny which raised Tabor from a storekeeper to one of the richest men in America within a year.

On the morning of April 10, the attending physicians insisted that Baby take a sedative and get some sleep. They did not conceal their belief that Tabor would die. A priest had already been summoned by Baby to give him the last sacraments. When she awakened from her drugged sleep later that day, she was told that Horace had died.

BOOK III

Guardian of the Magic Mountain

11. *Prettiest Widow in Colorado*

THROUGH almost four decades of life that remained to her, Baby Tabor would remember the belated tribute the citizenry paid Horace once he was imprisoned in his coffin and it was certain that his robust, extra-glandular personality would never again disturb his more sedate fellows. His death, as she later told her sole confidante, was publicly mourned with "the prestige due a great man." She knew him when he closely resembled a shabby vagrant as well as when he reached the peak of affluence, but she never wavered in her conviction that there was something great, as well as extraordinarily lucky, about Horace Tabor.

Baby had reason to be proud of Horace's sendoff, even if her gratitude for that funereal occasion was laced with bitter reflections that Horace could have used some of that postmortem esteem when he was alive. Hundreds of telegrams arrived to express the condolences of the governor, the mayor, other political figures, and most of the state's civic and fraternal organizations—the list of tributes filled more than a column in the city's newspapers.

Leadville took up a collection for a floral piece six feet high and four feet wide. Other floral tributes and wreaths overflowed from the Windsor suite to the Capitol building, where Horace lay in state while four militiamen guarded his catafalque in the governor's room. There were bundles of telegrams from all over the United States. Odd, she must have thought, how people were reminded of a man only when he was dead; there must be a touch of guilt in such displays.

No doubt Baby was right when she told her daughters that "Papa would have been so proud" of the obsequious way his fellow citizens sent him on his way to the grave.

Indubitably it was the biggest funeral Denver would see until Buffalo Bill Cody, similarly having fallen on hard times, was laid to rest.

The funeral procession included the state militia, police and firemen marching to the dirges of four bands. It moved along Broadway, down Seventeenth Street, and finally to the Sacred Heart Cathedral where four priests officiated at the mass. Then the cortege moved to Calvary Cemetery. It was estimated that 10,000 persons stood with bared heads along the route.

Certainly his death struck an emotional chord; it was more than the passing of a character who had made life livelier, who did not hoard his wealth but spent it with glorious abandon. He had served as a sort of surrogate for all those who would never strike it rich. You might respect a plutocrat who was sensible or greedy enough to hang onto his money and pass it along to his children, but you could love a man, vulgar and boorish though his style might seem at times, who created so much fun, gossip, titillation, and general amusement with his takings. Also, Horace Tabor's death seemed to symbolize something bigger and sadder: the passing of what people already were calling the Old West. He was an adventurer whose antecedents stretched back to the mountain men, and men of his type had succumbed to the businessmen and financial wizards who had taken over the exploitation of the West. The West had been industrialized, systematized; the wildernesses where men like Tabor had wrung out their fortunes now were dominated by the smelter stacks of the Guggenheims and converted into ruthless satrapies of the

Eastern financial establishment, like the Rockefeller-owned Colorado Coal & Iron.

If some people along that funeral route wept, it was at least partly for themselves and the loss of their own expectations.

For Baby and her daughters, the loss was overwhelming, particularly at the moment they began lowering the coffin into the grave. The children cried out, "Mama, Mama, don't let them put Papa down there!" Baby herself had to be led away from the graveside. Others took her children back to town, the mourners departed, and Baby was left at the grave. She knelt and prayed, wept and keened like an old shawlie back in her ancestral island. Finally someone led her away, long after dusk had fallen.

She was still young and pretty enough, with the sexual allure of females half her age, to have remarried as quickly as decently possible. If she had been the voluptuary her contemporaries had considered her, she would have lost no time in replacing Horace with one of those mustache-twirling, portly, and prosperous fellows who had always envied his boldness in making Baby his bride. Prettiest widow in Colorado, everyone (jealous women excepted) said. There would be plenty of offers, and Baby could have justified herself to Horace when they met in Heaven (as she was certain they would) on the grounds that their daughters needed a good provider. That argument never prevailed against her unquenchable loyalty to Horace Tabor's memory. There could never be another man in her life.

Instead of sensibly laying snares for a third husband, she dedicated herself to proving out Horace's conviction that the Matchless could be reopened and its exhausted veins tapped again. She considered the Matchless a legacy of inestimable value. It was the obsession that would grip her for the remaining thirty-six years of her life, and if Baby Doe Tabor is a legend to match Horace Tabor's it is not because of her dazzling beauty but because of her quest, full of loneliness and privation, for that ephemeral fortune under Fryer's Hill. That search, too, symbolized something about the Old West. It wasn't what you found, but the mystique of the search that was important.

She would struggle on through the years with total contempt for those who thought she was crazy for chasing after her own rainbow up in the mountains. Let her clothing fray into rags. Let the soles of her shoes flap like a tramp comedian's. Let people tap their foreheads significantly when she passed them on the street. Let her daughters disappear, one in search of respectability and security, the other frantic for fame and pleasure that wouldn't have to be dug out of mountain rock. The author of *Don Quixote* would have understood her. She would spend almost half her life in dedication to a shared dream called the Matchless.

Horace was able to leave little to his wife and daughters, not even a government pension. Within a few months of his death, Baby and the girls, one fifteen and the other nine, were faced with destitution. They had moved out of the Windsor and into a decaying brick tenement just off Larimer Street.

Daily, after sending her daughters off to school and doing the housework, Baby would put on her best dress and head for the offices on Seventeenth Street occupied by the moneyed men of Denver, mining promoters, bankers, smelter operators, brokers. She cornered them in their offices and delivered her spiel on the possibilities of the Matchless if only someone would supply her with enough capital to pump out the flooded lower levels, shore up the tunnels, install new machinery to bring the ore to the surface.

For years she would haunt the financial district, a "bedraggled fey figure" as one local historian described her, a curiously dogged survivor of a time up-and-coming men would prefer to forget, but a very lively and sharp-tongued ghost.

Finally she found someone who shared, in lesser measure, her belief in the Matchless. He would put up enough money to keep Baby and her daughters going while she tried to raise more capital and resume operations at the Matchless after it had been shut down for almost ten years. Baby must have been a powerful persuader.

With the money advanced her, she told her daughters, they would all move up to Leadville so "we'll be right on the ground and make sure our new partners don't cheat us on how much ore they take out of the Matchless. One thing you'll have to learn is to beware of high-graders."

Elizabeth was a prim and proper young lady who did not fancy the idea of mucking around a mine shaft. She wanted to marry a respectable young man and settle down to a sheltered and comfortable life. Baby would often wonder how she could have given birth to such a thin-blooded, unadventurous, unimaginative child. It was almost as though Elizabeth were Augusta Tabor's daughter instead of her own.

"Nobody but a fool still believes the mine will ever produce again," she told her mother, whose delusions she had long found abhorrent, whose past (or as much of it as she had learned) was purplish with indiscretion. She could forgive her father for the scandal that surrounded her childhood, the way nice little girls refused to play with her or invite her to their homes; and with that merciless perception of her own sex, which always held the female to blame in such situations, resented her mother as the cause of it all.

Her sister, Silver Dollar, on the other hand, was eager for any change of scene, any break with routine, any prospect of adventure. She was a replica of Baby's own childhood, of the girl who bared her pretty legs in a skating contest; and if her fiber lacked some of Baby's toughness and tensile strength, it was not yet apparent.

They moved up to Leadville and occupied rooms at 303 Harrison Avenue, where Jake Sandelowsky had once lived. Baby did not tell her daughters about that affair. No doubt Elizabeth soon learned much of her mother's youthful indiscretions in Leadville and Central City; there are always people maliciously eager to provide such information, and the more wounding the better.

The more she learned about her mother's days as the scandalous Baby Doe, the more withdrawn Elizabeth became. She hated her mother for having passed on that legacy of shame and disrepute. While her younger sister entered eagerly into the juvenile life of Leadville, Elizabeth shut herself in her room and wrote letters to Denver and to her maternal grandmother back in the Middle West. A sort of conspiracy was forming; the respectable faction of the McCourt family would claim one of its own. Baby was dimly aware that the clan back in Oshkosh, lifted out of near-poverty by her husband's money, no longer was awash in gratitude. The letters she received occasionally from her mother were tinged with recrimination. It almost seemed as though she were being held responsible for Horace having lost his fortune, and the people who had sat contentedly under the Tabor money tree were embittered by the fact that the golden fruit no longer dropped from its branches.

Elizabeth became downright rebellious when Baby insisted that the girls accompany her to Fryer's Hill and learn something about practical mining; they would know what a pick and shovel felt like in their tender hands. Silver Dollar eagerly went along with the idea, and put on grimy old miner's clothes she found in the Matchless shaft house.

Baby showed her daughters how to swing a pick and guided them down into the crumbling main shaft of the Matchless, the dark and dripping womb from which the Tabor fortune had emerged and would again, as Baby devoutly believed.

Elizabeth looked at the calluses forming on her palms, surveyed the bleak mountainscape, and shuddered. She could find nothing romantic or challenging about this raped and eroded and slag-heaped desolation. The enthusiasm of her mother and younger sister, their unreasoning hope that they could take a fortune out of that dismal hole in the ground, only convinced her that she was the only sane member of the family.

"You must put on overalls and learn all about mining," her mother told Elizabeth, "so you'll be able to protect yourself when you inherit this mine."

Another bonanza? It was a crazy woman's obsession, as other people in Leadville eagerly agreed.

"No," she told her mother, "I'm not going down in that mine and pretend I'm a miner like Silver. I'm going to run away. I've made all the plans."

Baby then learned that her detested brother Peter had supplied Elizabeth with the train fare to Oshkosh; that her mother, who had sided with Peter when she and her brother quarreled, had invited her to share the home Horace's money had bought. Nothing was said about Baby and her other daughter finding refuge there—not that Baby could have endured the thought of living again in Oshkosh.

So Elizabeth, dry-eyed, packed her few possessions and said good-bye to her mother. The parting was final, and without any expressed regret on the teen-aged girl's part. She marched away to the Leadville station and never looked back.

For Baby the parting was not so easy. At first she raged at the "two traitors" who had stolen her daughter from her. "Good riddance," said Silver Dollar, who had always considered her sister a prissy spoilsport. But it was not so easy to wrench the memory of better and more affectionate days, the years of Elizabeth's infancy when Baby had so proudly displayed the child in her bejeweled swaddling clothes, from her mind.

Once the anger at what she regarded as Elizabeth's desertion had passed, she was overcome by grief. Half-blinded by tears, she stumbled down Seventh Street to the Church of the Annunciation. Still a faithful and adoring daughter of the Church, in extremity, she sought comfort in the beatitude of the Virgin Mary's face as represented in tinted plaster. She drew sustenance from the faith from which she had strayed more than once.

After praying, and vowing to attend mass more regularly, she stopped in at the public library on her way home and took out a book titled *Lives of the Saints*. She reread the book many times during the ordeal of her later years. Nothing else, she would affirm, gave her greater comfort. She would continue to draw solace from her faith even while succumbing to the lure of various forms of mysticism, almost as strong as her belief that a treasure still lay under the pocked surface of Fryer's Hill, which her father-confessors could only deplore as a dangerous leaning toward paganism.

For almost a decade after Horace Tabor's death, her greatest comfort was her youngest daughter. Silver Dollar had inherited her father's dark hair and brown eyes while Elizabeth had her mother's blond hair and blue eyes, but it was Silver Dollar who seemed the true daughter of her flesh and spirit. To Silver Dollar, by some vagary of the genetic laws, had passed her father's willingness to take a chance, her mother's pride and independence.

They were a spirited and attractive pair, more like sisters than parent and child. Baby's parental attitude, under the circumstances, was permissive to a degree. She treated Silver Dollar like a grownup and hoped for the best.

The trouble was that the girl, with a growing sultriness of eye and ripeness of figure, had inherited the reckless passions of both her parents.

Even more than the cold and unfilial Elizabeth, she would make her mother envy Horace for having been the first to die. And she would present her mother with a tragic riddle: which gave the more pain, the unloving daughter who went her own way, or the loving daughter who resembled her so much it seemed like a Biblical vengeance?

12. *The Perils of Motherhood*

JUST how Baby Doe managed to keep the Matchless going as an intermittent mining operation would always be a wonder and a mystery to Coloradans. The story of the Matchless is so ramified with lawsuits, foreclosures, writs and counter-writs that it could be used as a textbook case for the Colorado School of Mines—or possibly for the Harvard Business School.

For more than three decades, sometimes behind a shotgun flourished in the faces of would-be process servers, she kept the property a going concern. With the élan of a rug peddler and the verbal daring of a Baroness Munchausen, she persuaded supposedly hardheaded businessmen and mine promoters that more millions could be extracted from the soggy depths of Fryer's Hill, even talked bankers into adding to the weight of mortgages already pressing on the Matchless. Neither geologists' reports nor assayers' findings on the samples of ore extracted from the mine could convince her that the Matchless was just another played-out property. She was determined to prove that Horace's predictions of the Matchless's continuing worth were well founded; it would be a vindication of his memory.

One might suspect that it was all part of a long-running confidence game, except that Baby devoted all the money she received for leases or in bank loans, and everything else she could lay hands on, to developing the mine. It was not only her obsession, but part of her life with Horace, a monument to his achievements since the statelier ones had fallen into the hands of his creditors. The memory never faded or grew tarnished, commonplace though he may have been to others aside from his phenomenal luck. It was cherished more with each passing year.

For several years after Elizabeth's exit, she and Silver Dollar lived in Leadville during the summers, when they supervised a few workmen at the Matchless, or dug away in one of the new tunnels themselves if there was no money to pay for labor, and in the severe mountain winters went down to Denver to stay in a rooming house.

That period of relative comfort came about when someone, probably Horace's executor, discovered a forgotten safety-deposit box in a Denver bank. Baby had believed that everything went in the crash of the House of Tabor, but Horace had stashed away a few things and then apparently forgotten about them. The discovery occurred just when the holder of the first mortgage on the Matchless was about to foreclose, and the proceeds from the box not only forestalled that calamity but left enough to keep Baby and her daughter going for a few more years.

In the box were various trinkets on which she would have placed no great value during the years when a hundred peacocks strutted on the Tabor lawn. The most valuable was a diamond and sapphire ring. Other items included various gewgaws presented to Horace in honor of his civic-minded projects. There was a huge and ornate watch fob of solid gold, fortunately, which had been presented to Horace at the opening of the Tabor Grand Opera House, when he could not have imagined that years later it would save his widow and daughter from destitution.

With the money left from paying off the most pressing obligations, they decided to save rent money by furnishing and occupying a small dilapidated cabin near the Matchless shaft house.

With more than her share of Baby's romanticism, Silver Dollar willingly shared that lonely existence on the scarred hillside miles from even the rude comforts of woebegone Leadville and all its reminders of her father's overlordship. None was more fascinated by that legend, as transmitted by her mother, than Silver Dollar. She soaked up the lore of Leadville, the legends of "money mountain," and the somewhat glorified facts surrounding her father's role in the exploitation of that country. In the mind of an impressionable and imaginative girl they assumed the shape of myths as remote from reality as those of ancient Greece. Perhaps they turned her head a bit, encouraged her to expect more out of life than could be quickly or easily wrung.

She had begun writing poetry—always a bad sign in an adolescent girl, as any sensible people would warn, when she should have been studying the domestic arts.

Baby only encouraged such tendencies in her daughter, however, recognizing them as part of a maternal legacy. To the extent that it was possible in their reduced circumstances, she spoiled the girl and secretly hoped, perhaps, that she wouldn't take too much after her mother. Silver Dollar was provided with a burro on which she would ride into Leadville, costumed like a cowgirl with a scarf around her throat, a Stetson on her dark-brown hair, and a pistol strapped to her waist. The citizens of Leadville, particularly the males, were enlivened by the spectacle of Silver Dollar whooping as she rode into town and wondered if the place, in its weakened condition, could stand a second Baby Doe.

Baby's hopes for her daughter rose when it appeared that she did harbor a talent that might please other people than her mother. She wrote the lyrics for songs titled "In a Dream I Loved You," "Spirits," and "Love and Lillies," for which the Denver maestro, Professor A. S. Lohmann, usually occupied with drilling silver-cornet bands, supplied the music.

In 1908, President Theodore Roosevelt came to Leadville on a Western tour and the town turned out to supply its usual mining-camp welcome. Silver Dollar rode into town to watch the celebration, but Baby stayed out at their cabin on Fryer's Hill. The Presidential visit only saddened her because Horace couldn't be there to slap another President's back.

Silver Dollar was inspired to write the lyrics for a song, "Our President Roosevelt's Colorado Hunt," music by Professor Lohmann, which was well received in Colorado even if it didn't set Tin Pan Alley on its ear. Baby scraped up the money to have the song published. At the top of the first music sheet was the dedication "In memory of the late U.S. Senator, H. A. W. Tabor." The Denver *Post* published a long article on the budding career of Silver Dollar Tabor, along with a two-column photograph. It displayed an eighteen-year-old girl with smoldering sloe eyes and the kind of contours that had made her mother famous. A provocative-looking female. Born for trouble, people said knowingly. And with her dashing looks went a hoydenish manner. The girl was just about the same age as her mother when the latter appeared in Central City as a bride, and had the same talent for attracting masculine attention.

Perhaps Baby was too busy getting the Matchless back in operation to take note of the storm signals. She had persuaded a bank to loan her $9,000 at the exorbitant interest rate of 8 percent, and was supervising a small crew of workmen as they dug a new tunnel into the flank of Fryer's Hill. And when she was in the grip of her obsession with restoring the Matchless to its former productivity, she tended to ignore more mundane matters.

She was happily unaware of Silver Dollar's involvement with one of the partners in a Leadville livery stable. Silver Dollar had only the burro to ride into town, but the stable operator, eyeing her luscious figure and knowing her passion for riding, often insisted that she ride his big white gelding. The brunette girl and the white horse made a spectacular combination as they galloped up Harrison Avenue. Then, as Baby would learn too late, Silver Dollar began taking a romantic interest in the stable owner as well as his spirited mount. He was a middle-aged man with a swaggering manner who always wore a big white Stetson and acted as though he were the sole authentic relic of the Old West—just the sort that would appeal to a girl steeped in the glamorous falsehoods of the recently departed frontier.

Some kindly soul told Baby about her daughter's affair with the livery stable operator and, as Baby later recalled for her only confidante, she was stunned by the news.* It was only too easy to visualize the sordid scenes in the hayloft of the livery stable. How could the girl have given herself to such a low-class type? How could a man of his years have taken advantage of a girl whom he had known since her childhood, when she trudged into town with a gunnysack over her shoulder?

No one knew better than Baby what an evil place the world could be, and how hard it could be on anyone who stepped out of line. Gossip would make Leadville unbearable for Silver Dollar —she didn't have the toughness of spirit which had enabled her mother to endure, with head held even higher, the malice of a community which found its shaky conventions threatened. Silver Dollar didn't have the inner resources, the independence of spirit, which had always enabled Baby to stand alone, even to glory in her isolation.

Several days went by, with Baby trying to decide how to break up the affair. She knew something about dealing with high-spirited young females, having been one herself. She realized that delicacy was required. Never having played the stern mother, having encouraged a sort of sisterly relationship between them, she couldn't simply lay down the law.

Baby still hadn't made up her mind how to handle the situation that Easter weekend in 1910; it wasn't easy to discipline a girl of twenty even for a woman of fifty-odd, and whatever she said might only make Silver Dollar more defiant.

She didn't try to stop Silver Dollar from attending Leadville's top-drawer social event, the Easter Monday Ball, because she

* The confidante was Sue Bonnie, who lived in a cabin on the outskirts of Leadville and, apparently with Baby's consent or collaboration, composed an account of her life which was later published in a "true confession" magazine.

would be escorted by two young men of respectable families. And Silver Dollar was so beautiful in a blue-silk gown and fur-trimmed coat her mother had made for her.

That was one of the worst nights in Baby's life.

She waited up for hours in the frozen silence of the cold April night. It wasn't until eight o'clock in the morning that Silver Dollar stumbled home looking as though she had fallen down a mine shaft. She was reeling drunk, her silk gown was torn, she had lost her coat—and obviously she had cast off the respectable young men who escorted her to the ball. Baby tried to find out what had happened, but Silver Dollar was too drunk to make much sense. There was nothing to do but help her into bed.

Later that day Baby went down into Leadville to pick up the mail and any clues she might find on what had happened to her daughter. The town was littered with clues. Silver Dollar was the talk of Leadville. She had got "involved" again, this time with a local saloonkeeper, who apparently had spirited her away from the ball.

The term nymphomania was not then in general currency, but Baby was worldly-wise enough to know that her daughter, whom she loved better than anyone living, had developed deep psychic flaws. Raging at her would be no help, it would only make matters worse. The only solution was to channel her drives into something more constructive, more creatively promising. Living in a cabin outside Leadville with no friends of her own age, with no outlet for her creative yearnings, was the worst possible thing for Silver Dollar. She would have to send her daughter away. It took a lot of moral courage to make that decision because Silver Dollar was her only real link to humanity. Nobody and nothing else but the Matchless mattered.

Her daughter was becoming more and more unmanageable. An entry in Baby's diary for March, 1911, told of an appalling tantrum. "Silver and I went to confession," Baby recorded, "and the priest told her not to read bad books. She fell on the floor and screamed in rage, and acted terrible. I scalded my foot through the mercy of God because Silver would not go to communion and

I said I will go on suffering with this foot if you don't, for we must not let the devil conquer after much trouble. She got up and went to communion and conquered the devil. I shall never forget my sorrow and heartaches by the way she acted."

It was during those last years with Silver, in her frequently distraught state, that she began having various visitations she believed were from the spirit world, one frequent vision being that of a "bright purple spark." Her troubled state of mind was reflected in various entries in her diary: "A spirit rang the bell on the No. 5 shaft because no one is on the hill at that time . . . Our Precious Jesus protect my own darling Silver. I went to Dear Father Pious at St. Elizabeth's and gave my darling Silver to Jesus at the Elevation of the Host. God's will be done." Another revealed a religious frenzy of the sort particularly dismaying to the clergy: "Just about 7 P.M. in alley I baptized a man who fell drunk across my path . . . Baptized him with water that lay in middle of alley . . . I wish every saloon was in hell forever."

The question was how to arrange a different sort of life for Silver Dollar and give her the chance to make something of her literary inclinations. Money, as always in recent years, was the problem. The $9,000 she had borrowed from the bank had disappeared into the maw of the Matchless and produced in return only a few ore cars of carbonate rock worth taking to the smelter.

Once again, though indirectly, she would have to turn to her brother Peter (despite the fact that she referred to him in her diary as "Pete the coward," and had sinister dreams about him, including one in which "I dreamed Pete set fire and burned our old house"). Several times when they had been almost destitute she had asked Silver Dollar to write to her uncle for help, and Pete had always complied. With that self-destructive Celtic enthusiasm for pursuing a feud, Baby never could and never would bring herself to contact him in person; she would never forgive him for not answering her appeal for help when Horace was going broke. But once again Pete was her only hope.

She told Silver Dollar to write her uncle and ask for enough money to get her to Denver. There was no opportunity for developing her literary talent in Leadville, she told her daughter, and it was time she struck out on her own. The struggle to make a living might be Silver Dollar's salvation.

Pete was prompt about sending the money, and a week after Silver Dollar's disgrace she and her mother went down to the Leadville station, the scene of so many departures in Baby's life. That day a quarter-century of solitary life began.

For Silver Dollar it seemed like the beginning of what might be a brilliant career. She was as confident of her talent as her mother was of striking it rich with the Matchless.

For weeks, however, she found it difficult to persuade hard-bitten city editors that such a lissome, limpid-eyed girl would make a worthy addition to their staffs. Uncle Peter had met her and advised that the newspaper business might provide the proper training for a writer. She took a room in a small hotel on Eighteenth Street, and every day toured the city rooms of the *Post, Tribune, Times,* and *Rocky Mountain News* to see whether anyone wanted to hire an inexperienced aspirant with a charming little lisp. She caused a stir among the raffish young men sitting at desks in the city rooms, but their editors weren't quite so impressionable.

Finally, perhaps through the intercession of her well-connected uncle, the city editor of the Denver *Times* agreed to put her on the payroll as a reporter at twelve dollars a week. She would spend six months on the staff of the *Times.* There is no need to stress the irony of the fact that most of her assignments were to cover the funerals of various Capitol Hill beldams, who just then were dying off at an alarming rate, and that many of those whom Silver Dollar was required to praise for their charity and benevolence were ones who had consigned her mother to social oblivion.

During those six months, she displayed an un-Baby-like ability in stretching a dollar to its utmost. The readiness of younger members of the *Times* staff to buy her dinner, of course, helped to economize. Out of her twelve dollars a week she not only supported herself and sent her mother $5 weekly but somehow, perhaps through exercising a greater talent for fiddling expense accounts than for journalistic prose, managed also to save a hundred dollars.

Pre-World War I journalism in Denver was a razzle-dazzle of intense competition between the newspapers, circus stunts to attract circulation, outrageous sensationalism (particularly in the *Post*, with its black and red headlines marching two-thirds of the way down the front page), and of some of the brightest reportorial talents in the country. It was the era, still celebrated, when Gene Fowler and Damon Runyon and others were cutting their literary teeth—the era Fowler recalled so vividly and fondly in *Timberline*. The Denver Press Club had its moments when it seemed like a slightly more alcoholic version of the Cheshire Cheese or the Ludgate Hill pub in London. A Denver newspaperman in those days, because of the city's high incidence of journalistic genius, could get a job anywhere.

Silver Dollar Tabor was the prettiest reporter in town but she was too young and inexperienced to thrive in that hectic atmosphere. The sight of her sashaying across the city room floor, her lush figure outlined by a white shirtwaist and a tight black skirt, may have been worth the twelve dollars a week she was being paid, but editorial auditors are mean old men and managing editors worry more about their prostates than about providing entertainment for the help. Silver Dollar and her boss agreed it would be best for her to try something less competitive than daily journalism.

Silver Dollar was ready for that eventuality.

She wrote her mother that what she really wanted to do was to write a novel, which was a shorter route to fame than covering old ladies' funerals. Baby told everyone she knew in Leadville that Silver Dollar was halfway up the slopes of Parnassus and would soon be causing Olive Higgins Prouty and Gertrude Atherton sleepless nights; she had always believed that if you said something fervently enough it was bound to come true.

Certainly Silver Dollar began her novelist's career with method and determination. With the money she had saved, she rented a room in a cheap rooming house on Wentworth Avenue, and every day covered pages of ten-cent notebooks which a girl typist who lived in the same house agreed to type for her.

Star of Blood was the title of her Western melodrama, which drew on all she had seen and heard in Leadville, possibly including the reminiscences of the livery stable proprietor who had ruined her reputation. It centered on the romance between an outlaw killer and his high-spirited girl, Artie Dallas, in whom autobiographical traces could be found.

When the novel was finished, she took it to a Denver printer who agreed to publish *Star of Blood* as a speculative venture. The Tabor name and the publicity Silver Dollar would attract might make it profitable. He was soon disillusioned. The magic of the Tabor name had been dissipated. A few hundred copies were sold in the Denver bookstores, but the reaction of the book reviewers—the few who did not cast it aside as just another floridly written Western melodrama—was generally cool.

Baby always treasured her copy of *Star of Blood*, and she was certain that along with Silver Dollar's four published songs, her poems, and her journalistic experience, it offered promise of a bright and lucrative career. With all the faith she had in her intuitive powers, she did not sense that Silver Dollar had forecast her own fate in the closing passages of her first and only novel. Writing of her heroine, her alter ego, she described the death of Artie Dallas in a backwater of the underworld: "She closed her eyes, her wild, startled black eyes that hopelessly flashed out from her flying dark hair . . . never again would she be found drunk in a Market Street gutter . . . She now lies in an unmarked grave in pauper's field, with only gray rocks to mark her resting place and only weeds to decorate it. No friends visit her lowly grave, but perhaps occasionally a wild bird hovers over the lonely spot, chanting a carol whose plaintive notes ascend into the infinite realms above and invocate, 'Be merciful to her, for she knew not what she did.' "

On the evidence of her mother's diary, Silver Dollar, with her tendency toward alcoholism, was surely headed on the same downward path. Late in 1914, perhaps concerned by reports she had of the kind of life Silver Dollar was leading, Baby came down from Leadville to spend part of the winter in Denver. A $2.50-a-week room at the Milo Hotel served as her winter quarters.

Fragmentary notes scrawled on the margins of a newspaper and on the pages of a calendar survive to indicate the nature of Baby Doe's struggle to lead her daughter away from the primrose path: "Last time I saw Silver was evening of November 4—for only a few minutes she stayed—my heart is broken . . . Up all night hunting for Silver and I slipped in Depot . . . I met her at Phil's flat and begged her to come with me to Milo Hotel but she would not—poor child, she is not in her right mind. God help my poor darling."

On Christmas Day, she was still enveloped in despair over her errant daughter. "God alone gives peace," she wrote on a scrap torn from the Denver *Post*. "Poor lonely me, alone alone alone. Not one soul came to me today . . . and where is my darling child Honeymaid [Silver]? God watch over her—her mind is gone. God will save her for me."

Some weeks later she was writing that her brother—apparently the inimical Pete—told Silver Dollar "not to have anything to do with me, her mother, that she was better off away from me. O my dear God help me bear it. I have only treated her with love and gentle kindness . . . I left her at the door and I have not seen or heard from her since. I have tried and tried and cannot find her."

13. *"Give Me One More Jigger"*

ON the streets of Leadville and Denver, Baby Doe had become a "character," an eccentric remnant of the wild old days. Loneliness would make her more than a little odd-seeming, and she would often slip into the twilight world of mysticism, but there was no reason for people to tap their heads significantly. She had always been indifferent to public opinion, at least in regard to herself, and undoubtedly she would have agreed with Dr. Oliver St. John Gogarty's views on the possible manifestation of the unearthly: "I believe in ghosts: that is, I know that there are times, given the place which is capable of suggesting a phantasy, when those who are sufficiently impressionable may perceive a dream projected as if external to the dreamy mind: a waking dream due both to the dreamer and the spot."

The opinion of respectable people about her habits and beliefs was immaterial. She had once annoyed them by dressing in a too advanced fashion and bedecking herself and her infant daughters with too much jewelry. Now she was considered a public disgrace because she had gone to the other extreme; her costumes seemed to have been plucked from those barrels placed in the vestries of churches in which parishioners could deposit cast-off clothing for the China missions.

Baby occasionally spent a winter in Denver when she was temporarily in funds or had to defend her property on Fryer's Hill against mortgage holders or other creditors. Even then, she did not waste any money on clothing herself because every dollar she could lay hands on had to be spent on protecting and developing the Matchless. People turned to stare at her when she clattered down the street in her men's work boots, even those who didn't know she was the once famous Baby Doe. Invariably she wore a long black skirt turning green with age, a man's khaki shirt and coarse, black cotton stockings. Over this she wore an ancient black cape, with a well-worn woman's motoring cap on her graying blond hair. The cap was equipped with a veil which she drew over her face when she sensed that people were staring at her. In place of the supposed jewels of Queen Isabella and the $90,000 diamond necklace, she now wore an ebony cross strung around her neck on a piece of twine.

Undoubtedly she cut a queer, touching figure as she strode down one of the streets she had once surveyed from the seat of a landau with two coachmen and two footmen in attendance. One thing neither poverty, nor neglect, nor even the advancing years could greatly diminish—the beauty of her face. For this there is the testimony of a photograph of her published in 1927 by the Denver *Post*. She was then seventy-three years old, but her huge blue eyes were clear and unfaded and her face was as smooth as that of a woman half her age.

Perhaps it was her obsessive pursuit of the treasure she believed was locked in the strata below Fryer's Hill that kept her so youthful looking. Nothing could distract her from the Matchless, neither personal tragedy nor the privations of living alone in a clapboard shack on a windswept hillside. When creditors tried to foreclose on the property, she trekked down to Denver and persuaded various lawyers to take her case on a contingency basis. It was a wonder she did not impoverish the whole legal profession in Denver and Leadville, because the Matchless was probably the most encumbered, garnisheed, writ-plastered property in the world. Yet even the most hard-headed barristers would be wheedled into taking up her defense.

And from time to time even the most sensible businessmen would be charmed or bullied into advancing her money to continue tapping away at the Matchless's exhausted veins. Many prominent families with deep roots in Denver can, undoubtedly, produce their own evidence of Baby's influence on a departed ancestor. Such as the one treasured by a local historian dated July 22, 1913, and signed by both Baby and her daughter Silver Dollar: "Received of Mr. William J. Barker the sum of $150 which we promise to return by giving Mr. Barker every other royalty check and settlement sheet from the George W. Casey lease on the Matchless Mine, beginning with No. 65 until said sum with interest is paid."

Baby had no shame about extracting money to keep a few ore-cars trundling up the shaft of the Matchless. One day everyone would be paid off. Besides that, the Matchless was a holy cause, a dedication to the memory of Horace Tabor. It may have been only a series of shafts sunk into a hillside to less perceptive people, but to her it was a kind of temple devoted to worship of a past glory, a sort of mini-civilization in itself which had built the Tabor Grand Opera House in as grand a style as any acropolis or amphitheater of the ancient world. Everything else had been snatched away from Tabor before his death, but the shaft house of the Matchless would serve as his Great Pyramid.

No doubt playing the role of a priestess distracted her from the tragedy of motherhood. When her older daughter Elizabeth married a prospering manufacturer in Wisconsin, they were still estranged and Baby had not been invited to the wedding. Since then Elizabeth had twice made Baby a grandmother, and a temporary reconciliation was arranged. In the later months of 1915 Silver Dollar had temporarily stopped being one of Denver's more hectic party girls, and accompanied her on a trip to Chicago, where they met Elizabeth, her husband John Last, and their children.

It really seemed for a time after that Chicago trip everything might work out all right. One day Silver Dollar came up to Leadville to visit her mother and reveal new plans for the future. She would make one more try at literary success; if it failed she would enter a convent, though it was hard to picture her—sultry black eyes framed by a starched white coif—as a nun.

She planned to start a literary weekly in Denver, and if that didn't pan out, she told her mother, "I think I will enter a convent. You have always been very religious and I am turning in that direction more and more. Perhaps that would be a fine solution for my life."

Baby was delighted by the possibility Silver Dollar raised. Perhaps she sensed that only in worldly success or in its opposite, the cloisters, would her daughter be safe from her self-destructive tendencies.

Silver Dollar then returned to Denver. The last physical memory Baby would have of her younger daughter was as Silver Dollar climbed on the train at Leadville station and gaily waved. Back in Denver, with a few hundred dollars donated by her Uncle Peter or someone else, she started publication of *The Silver Dollar Weekly*, of which she was the editor and sole contributor. The weekly foundered on a shoal of unpaid printing bills after a few issues.

The next Baby heard from her daughter was a letter stating that she was heading for Chicago; she would enter a convent that Uncle Peter had told her about. Uncle Peter would also supply the railroad fare. From then on, Baby would always maintain that her daughter, all evidence sensationally to the contrary, was a Bride of Christ.

Actually, Silver Dollar was journeying to Chicago with ill-defined aspirations to continue her literary career. The only favorable review of *Star of Blood* had appeared in a Chicago newspaper, the literary editor of which had proclaimed that a fine new talent had been born and that her novel showed "a sense of freedom, a disregard of conventions, and an independence of thought."

Odd as it may seem, Chicago in the pre-World War I years had become a literary Mecca, a capital of the artistic renaissance. Young Americans headed for the city on Lake Michigan as a decade later they would seek their creative identities on the Left Bank of Paris. As one of the adornments of that time and place, the late Ben Hecht, wrote in his autobiography: "During its quick and vivid years—there were hardly nine (1913–1922)—Chicago found itself, mysteriously, a bride of the arts. Not gangster guns but literary credos barked. New novelists, poets, painters and critics dotted its pavements and illumined its name."

It was the time when Sherwood Anderson, Carl Sandburg, Theodore Dreiser, Hecht himself, Maxwell Bodenheim, and on the outer fringe, a young advertising copywriter named Ernest Hemingway, were fueling predictions that a new literature would be born under the El. Vast hopes were fermenting, the essence of which H. L. Mencken distilled when he declared Chicago the literary capital of the United States, if not the world. "In Chicago," he wrote for an English magazine, "there is the mysterious something that makes for individuality, personality, and charm. In Chicago a spirit broods upon the face of the waters. Find a writer who is indubitably American in every pulse-beat, snort and adenoid, an American who has something to say and who says it in an unmistakable American way and nine times out of ten you will find he has some sort of connection with the gargantuan and inordinate abattoir by Lake Michigan —that he was bred there, or got his start there or passed through there in the days when he was young and tender. . . ."

What better place to find herself, Silver Dollar Tabor thought, than in a city that seemed to breathe inspiration along with the fumes from the stockyards and the smoke from the immense marshaling yards of the railroads.

Yet there always seems to be danger lying in wait on the

fringes of each new Bohemia, whether it is Greenwich Village, the Left Bank, or the students' quarter of Munich. The glamour of the creative arts attracts not only moths—of which Silver Dollar Tabor was a fairly typical example, with more yearning than talent, more sensuality than sensibility—but creatures of prey. In Chicago the hazy boundaries of Bohemia ran parallel to those of an increasingly violent underworld, and of that sinful quarter called the Levee, where there was a round-the-clock carnival of bordellos, gambling houses, barrelhouse saloons (and later speakeasies), dance halls, penny arcades, pawnshops, voodoo doctors, and tintype galleries.

The sinister aspect of Chicago's underside, underlying its promise as a commercial and artistic capital of the midlands, was sensed by a roving correspondent of the London *Daily Mail*, who wrote, "Chicago presents more splendid attractions and more hideous repulsions close together than any place known to me. It takes elaborate care to present its worst side to the stranger. It makes a more amazingly open display of evil than any other city known to me. Other places hide their blackness out of sight. Chicago treasures it in the heart of the business district and gives it a veneer."

This was the city to which Silver Dollar Tabor, with all her frailty, with an unstable ego all too ready to find its solvent in alcoholic and other escapes, entrusted her future. Perhaps it was a shame that her father had not succeeded in his aim of building a city on Lake Michigan that would turn Chicago into a ghost town.

She made a fairly promising entrance, at that, if only she had been able to exploit it with demonstrable talent and perseverance. Instead of getting herself to a nunnery, she gained entry, possibly through her Denver newspaper connections, to the Chicago Press Club. She met a young reporter there who was naturally influenced by her charm and flamboyantly attractive face and figure. Together they concocted the idea for an interview which would attract attention to her as a fresh and glamorous personality from the Western mountains. It might revive interest in *Star of Blood* and create attention from the publishers for a second book she planned. In the interview, Silver Dollar, whose famous father and mother were mentioned, was pictured as a sort of madcap heiress disdainful of Chicago's new cultural pretensions; for decades English authors had been proving that the American public could be more easily captivated by a poke than a pat. "Money is the god of Chicago," Silver Dollar was quoted as saying, "but manhood and womanhood and character are all that count in the mountains. Chicagoans look sad. They do not know what the buoyancy of right living means. I don't care for the attentions of men, least of all Chicago men. Give me my pony and a wild dash down the mountain trail. Give me freedom to do and dare close to nature, and as nature bids. Chicago disgusts me. Bright lights, music, revelry, have no charm for me. I hear the call of the mining camp, and I want to go home."

Chicago's reaction was to wonder why the "disgusted" young lady didn't just pack up and go back to the snow peaks.

No one expressed any interest in her future literary output, but the "call of the mining camps" was never alluring enough to take her back to Colorado. Chicago, as the ragtime song had it, was her "kind of town." There was no one in the swarming, impersonal metropolis to gossip about one of the Tabors "going bad," or to be concerned about where one spent the night or with whom. Her sister was firmly established as the wife of a stolid Milwaukee burgher, but the eighty-odd miles that separated them might well have been the width of the Indian Ocean.

For a while she supported herself by clerking in the book department of Marshall Field's. That was followed by a variety of jobs during the next year or two. She lived in rooming houses and ate in cafeterias. Almost nightly she attended the studio parties on the fringes of Bohemia, the mean streets around Washington (better known as Bughouse) Square. She became the chattel of one man after another. Her willingness to fling herself into any sort of dissipation made her a popular figure among those failed writers and artists, much like herself, and the pretenders who gathered around them, all united in drowning their frustrations in alcohol or dreaming them away with opium, morphine, or cocaine.

She would spend a decade in Chicago, from her mid-twenties to her mid-thirties, and during that time she kept in touch only occasionally with her mother. Early in 1916 Baby made a diary note that she had finally received a letter from Silver Dollar, adding, "I have not heard from her for weeks and weeks. Thank God she is alive." During the next several years Baby received letters from Silver Dollar reporting that she had been fired from various jobs because her clothes were threadbare. Baby usually answered the hinted appeal by raising $20 to send her daughter.

There may have been some respite from her constant worry in 1922, when Silver Dollar was thirty-three and announced that she had just married. But she didn't suggest a visit from her mother, and it appeared that the "marriage" had neither been blessed by a priest nor legalized by a civil ceremony. "I've planned all along on getting a rich man," Silver Dollar wrote her in what must have seemed like a replay of Baby's own ambitions on leaving Oshkosh for Colorado, "and paying up your mortgage and all our old bills in Colorado and all that. But I couldn't make the grade. God may help us sometime unexpectedly."

All the time Baby was assuring anyone who asked, that Silver Dollar had entered a convent, and in time she managed to convince herself that this was so. People in Leadville wouldn't dare to gossip about a girl, no matter how grievous the mistakes she had made in the past, if she had taken the veil. It was the Tabor name she was bent on protecting. Once she had scoffed at the scandal-makers and dared them to do their worst. It was different now. A scandal involving one of their daughters would reflect on her husband's memory.

The reality of Silver Dollar's Chicago career was indicated by the fact that the only address she gave her mother was "General Delivery, Chicago."

During the first several years after she arrived in Chicago,

Silver Dollar made an effort to capitalize on her sensuous face and figure, her sexual attraction, by trying to gain entrée into show business. She would break in as a dancer, then become an actress. Show business, both live and on film, was booming. Chicago was not only the headquarters of vaudeville and burlesque circuits, but boasted of being the film capital of the world. The motion picture industry was moving West from New York but Hollywood was still in its infancy. It was Chicago where the filmmakers now centered their activity, and one-fifth of the world's film output was produced by such studios as Essanay and Selig Brothers. The North Side film colony included such glamorous figures as Francis X. Bushman, whose appearance in a department store caused a greater riot than a bargain sale, Gloria Swanson, Wallace Beery, Tom Mix, Lewis Stone, Edward Arnold, and Colleen Moore. Western films were shot on the prairies west of Chicago, but others were produced in barnlike studios under artificial light.

If she couldn't make an impression in the literary world, Silver Dollar decided, she might exploit her soubrette's personality and smoldering eyes as a "vamp" to rival Nita Naldi and Olga Nethersole. She took dancing lessons, and began to haunt the casting offices as she had once haunted the city rooms in Denver. One thing her mother had taught her: persistence paid off. In Silver Dollar's case, it resulted in her being hired as a dancer in a few films.

From the fringes of Bohemia and pre-Hollywood her stumbling steps led her to the lower depths of show business. World War I had brought a frenetic gaiety to the cafés and cabarets, where experiments in jazz were being conducted, and the Chicago style, largely imported from the whorehouse district of New Orleans, was being perfected. Silver Dollar was a nightly habitué of those forerunners of the nightclub, usually with a different escort every night. She was in her late twenties and growing desperate; a reckless nymph who danced the nights away and awakened in strange beds with partners who sometimes wore guns tucked under the armpits of their gaudily striped silk shirts. The Chicago of the gangland years and the Prohibition Wars was just in the offing. Silver Dollar would be a witness to, if not a participant in, the booze bonanza which easily outstripped the fortunes made by her father and his fellow silver magnates.

One night she was invited to a private, after-closing party at Colosimo's café on Wabash Avenue. Big Jim Colosimo had risen from pimp to brothel-keeper on the Levee, and was now the kingpin of the underworld over which the Italians and the Irish were contesting for control. Al Capone would take his place after Colosimo was voted a magnificent funeral by his associates.

Colosimo's was respectable enough during the regular business hours and attracted such patrons as Caruso, Tetrazzini, Galli-Curci, and George M. Cohan with its fine food and entertainment. After hours, however, it was the scene of private parties at which the inhibitions of a more innocent America, soon to be more generally dissolved in bootleg alcohol, were cast off.

Silver Dollar attended a party in a private dining room after midnight at Colosimo's. Her fellow guests were the members of a burlesque troupe in from a grueling tour of the provinces. Around three o'clock in the morning the private room looked like a Cossack playpen, with several revelers under the table and some of the girls automatically shedding their clothes. Silver Dollar was urged to perform, and being giddy with champagne complied by stripping off all her clothing except for a scarf she wore around her middle. She then performed a serpentine sort of dance, the choreography of which dates back to Babylon and requires only a few basic undulations. Silver Dollar was a hit. The manager of the burlesque troupe declared she would knock 'em dead on the circuit from Keokuk to Kalamazoo.

The next phase of Silver Dollar Tabor's career saw her billed as "The Girl of the Nile" and for six months displaying as much of her ripely curved body as the various local laws would permit. But even burleycue had its professional standards, and the impresario had to warn Silver Dollar that the discipline of the theater did not permit going onstage drunk on whiskey or floating on a sniff of cocaine. She was fired in Pittsburgh and given her fare back to Chicago.

For the next half-dozen years she found few handholds in her precipitous decline. Pain, degradation, a shifting cast of male characters accompanied her from one cheap room to another on the South Side. Calling herself "Mrs. Ruth Murphy," she drifted from man to man, each lower on the social scale of the speakeasy world. As the kept woman of bartenders and smalltime hoodlums, she was often beaten up and mistreated; she was merely another anonymous drab headed straight for the Cook County morgue.

The end came on September 18, 1925, in a railroad flat on the second floor at 3802 Ellis Avenue, when Silver Dollar was thirty-five years old.

The address was that of a dilapidated frame house in the heart of the South Side's black belt, where she lived under the name of Ruth Norman. A dispassionate headline in the Chicago *Herald-Examiner* told the story: DRINK AND DOPE BLAMED FOR DEATH OF ONCE WEALTHY DAUGHTER OF SENATOR.

Silver Dollar's scalded body was found, nude, on the bed after her screams had attracted the attention of other tenants. A kettle of boiling water was tipped over on the stove in the kitchen. A doctor was summoned. He determined that she had suffered first-degree burns over a large part of her body. Somewhat drunk, according to the doctor's account to police, she told him that she had accidentally scalded herself. Her last words, uttered as she tried to reach for the whiskey bottle on her bedside table, were "Give me one more jigger." A few minutes later she died.

Her death would have been dismissed as one more squalid tragedy of the Tenderloin had it not been discovered that she was the daughter of Senator Horace Tabor, and that on a photograph of a man named Jack Reid, who had operated a saloon until speakeasies came into fashion under the duress of the Prohibition laws, she had scrawled, "In case I am killed, arrest this man." Reid had been one of her paramours, one of the more violent ones. He was promptly arrested. A coroner's jury, however, decided that "From the testimony presented, we, the jury, are unable to determine whether said occurrence is accidental, or otherwise," and recommended the release of the suspect, which was done.

The story made headlines on front pages all over the country, and thus Silver Dollar was spared a burial in potter's field, her uncle Peter McCourt having telegraphed $300 for funeral expenses. No members of the family were present when Silver Dollar was lowered into her unmarked grave, only a few Tenderloin characters and reporters. She had supplied her own epitaph, which survives not on a gravestone but in a surviving copy of her novel in the Library of Congress. It was for her heroine but could serve for its author: "She knew not what she did."

Reporters intent on expanding the story, which naturally caught newspaper readers' fancy, managed to locate her sister Elizabeth, safely and comfortably married in a Wisconsin town. No, Elizabeth told them firmly, she would not attend Silver Dollar's funeral. As she explained to the reporters:

"I haven't seen my sister for years. Not since I was fourteen years old [sic] and she a few years younger. I did not approve then of the life my mother lived. I got my grandmother to let me come and live with her . . . I didn't want to be reminded of my sister, nor of my mother. I wanted a quiet, decent, sheltered life. They didn't. We were just different. . . .

"I never approved of her [Silver Dollar]; she looked at life so differently. I can see no reason now why she should be more to me than just a dead woman down in Chicago. Why should I, who have pride and position, and like only quiet and nice things, have to claim her now in this kind of death?"

Except for that last flurry of sordid headlines, Elizabeth was left secure in her "pride and position."

Nor would Baby claim that "dead woman in Chicago" as her own, though for different, though equally self-protective reasons.

She simply could not acknowledge to herself—or if, secretly, to herself, not the rest of the world—that her beloved younger daughter's life had ended in such tragic squalor.

When the news was retailed in the headlines of the Colorado newspapers, Baby was in Denver staying at a small inexpensive hotel. The clerk showed her the front page of the Denver *Post* with its red headlines: VIOLENT DEATH OF SENATOR TABOR'S DAUGHTER!

Baby didn't even have the price of a newspaper at the moment, but hurried over to the Civic Center to read the newspapers in the Denver Public Library. The facts were all there; "Mrs. Ruth Norman" was positively identified as Rose Mary Echo Silver Dollar Tabor.

Baby, however, had her own concept of truth. To her, "Mrs. Ruth Norman," dead in a slum tenement, was not Silver Dollar unless and until Baby admitted it.

Several reporters were waiting in the lobby of her hotel when she returned from the library, clumping in on her miner's boots. A fierce old lady, with huge blue eyes blazing, confronted them.

What about those stories from Chicago, they asked her.

"All a pack of lies," she shouted at them. "That woman isn't my Silver. She is in a convent near Chicago. I got a letter from her just last week."

Then she wearily climbed the stairs to a shabby room in which the ghosts of memory circled around her. Silver Dollar in her diamond-studded swaddling clothes, being carried by her father to the landau for an airing. Silver Dollar posing for her birthday pictures. Silver Dollar writing poems for her mother's approval. Silver Dollar leaving on the train from Leadville, promising to enter a convent if she did not succeed in her literary career.

All that couldn't end in a flare of red headlines.

From then until her death, Baby would insist that Silver Dollar was still alive, in a convent, and serving Christ in Chicago.

14. *The Recluse of Fryer's Hill*

THERE was a theory abroad that Baby Doe dressed in cast-off clothing adorned only by a wooden cross strung around her neck, and for months at a time lived like a hermit on Fryer's Hill, as a reproach to a neglectful world. Actually it was a penitential gesture, she maintained to Sue Bonnie; she wanted to atone for the vanity with which she had once clad herself in silks, furs, feathers, and diamonds. She had become intensely religious, particularly after Elizabeth and Silver Dollar left her. There were no female hermits in the Catholic pantheon, but living alone on Fryer's Hill brought her closer, she felt, to the eternal mysteries. Irish legend, of which Baby heard so much around the family fireplace in Oshkosh, was full of underground mysteries and fabulous treasure guarded by leprechauns. That gaunt hill outside Leadville was a whole mother lode of superstition to its shabby, aging, but obdurate guardian.

Fryer's Hill was alive with rumors and intimations from the other, unseen world. On the back of advertisements for Nucoa margarine, on Postal Telegraph and Western Union message forms, she recorded dreams and visions in the conviction that they signified something just beyond her grasp. Often, half-somnolent, she had visions of both spiritual and materialistic kinds. There were recurring visions of Jesus Christ and, oddly at variance, those of "two big rich important men" who would soon come to help her develop the Matchless.

A whole montage of encouraging visions occurred to her in April of 1925, for instance, and her "diary notes" indicate how they strengthened her determination to see the Matchless a producing mine again:

"April 6, 1925—I saw in a vision myself down the No. 6 shaft in a drift—244 level—and I saw the most wonderful strike of rich lead ore and another strike close together of rich zinc ore. They [presumably she referred to men working on a lease arrangement on her property] struck zinc ore April 2 and did not tell me. I found it out and saw it."

"April 7, 1925—dreamed I was with a lot of well-to-do society folk. We were going to a big reception. . . ."

"Holy Thursday—April 19, 1925—I dreamed of being with Tabor, Lily, Silver and seeing rich ore in No. 6 shaft."

Often, however, her visions were those of a kind ascribed to the saints. Once she was awakened by a vision of Christ "in front of stovepipe up high . . . He appeared to be nailed to the Cross." She was suffering from cramps in her legs, asked Jesus to take them away and "they instantly left." A few days later, more ominously, she recorded a vision of "two bad wicked men sitting at a table and writing something on a piece of paper to harm us hereabout, planning to steal the Matchless. . . ."

At times it seemed that she could use any number of protective spirits in her efforts to keep possession of the mine. Though it may have been geologically next to worthless, it was under constant assault from Baby's creditors. Keeping it had required a constant rearguard action ever since December of 1899, soon after Tabor's death, when three men seized the Matchless on their claim that the Tabor estate owed them $13,197 and Baby promptly countered with a $3,200,000 suit and somehow hung onto the property. Just after Silver Dollar's death, the mortgage on the Matchless was foreclosed with what seemed to be finality, but she managed to badger a law firm into fighting a delaying action that blocked the foreclosure. Few could understand the intensity of her determination to keep control of a played-out mine.

"Why don't you just let the mine go for the mortgage?" a sympathetic banker asked her. "It's all worked out, it's only using up your energy and destroying your peace of mind."

"I'll never let the Matchless go while there's breath in my body," she replied. "I have no reason for living if I do not have faith in the Matchless. No dear one is left to me. I have only this one legacy of my great love. It is my mission and my life."

Faith, the power of the word, the omnipotence of sheer belief impelled her on a course that would have destroyed any person of lesser fortitude.

Surprising as it may have been to anyone observing her lonely figure clomping down the mountain road into Leadville, she considered herself a happy woman—happier than at any time since Horace had died. Her life, otherwise so full of personal tragedy, had the perfection attained only by a person involved in an all-consuming cause.

Occasionally she would reveal glimpses of that inner serenity. Once she called at the office of an assayer in Denver whom she had known for a long time, bringing a new ore sample from the Matchless. Recently she had driven off the lessees of part of the Fryer's Hill claim because they hadn't lived up to Baby's expectations. But she didn't mention that trifling matter. She wanted to talk about the first motion picture she had ever seen, in a theater near the old Tabor Grand Opera House. The latter was now devoted to boxing exhibitions by Denver's own Kid McCoy, wrestling matches, sabot-fighting and other branches of the performing arts.

"You know that nickelodeon is only a block away from the old Tabor Grand?" the assayer asked. "Many a time I sat in that theater and looked up at your box with the silver nameplate. You were different then, dressed in the heighth of fashion and wearing a fortune in diamonds. Did you think of that?"

"Yes, I did," she said smiling faintly, "but it didn't make me sad. I am happier now than I have ever been in my entire life, except for not having my husband with me. Do you wonder why? It's because I'm a better woman now. I've made my peace with God. I feel no ill will toward anyone, and I hope no one feels so toward me."

She was uncommonly talkative that afternoon, and rambled on: "It's hard sometimes not to feel bitter toward some people who have once been friends. This afternoon I was walking up Sixteenth Street when I met two sisters who were once well known to me. I looked straight at them, and I saw them look straight at me, and then look away. As I passed them, they moved far to one side, drawing their skirts away, so as not to brush me. 'You pose as fine ladies now,' I thought, 'but if I wanted to be real mean I could show you check after check, for hundreds of dollars, all made out by H. A. W. Tabor, all of them canceled, which he gave your father to buy groceries for you and your mother when fortune was not so kind to you.'

"But I am happy now, honestly I am. My daughter is in a Chicago convent serving the Lord, and I still have the Matchless. Why shouldn't I be happy?"

She was approaching her seventy-fifth birthday when the depression preceded by the Wall Street collapse of 1929 began, and not even her talent for bamboozling the money managers could prevail against the economic situation. There would be no more bank loans, no more little syndicates formed to work the Matchless on a royalty basis. The only men she could find to descend into the mine shaft were drifters willing to work on shares of whatever ore assayed high enough to be taken to the smelter. Such temporary helpers were allowed to camp out in another shack on the Matchless property, but Mrs. Tabor treated them like a duchess among the lower orders.

Perhaps the most perceptive glimpse of Baby Tabor in her later years was provided by Caroline Bancroft, the Colorado historian (and author of *Silver Queen*, a biographical sketch written from Baby's viewpoint), who visited the Matchless one day with her father, a mining engineer then conducting a survey for the state. Miss Bancroft was then a schoolgirl, intensely curious about this living legend, initially unpromising though her appearance. It was difficult to believe the tiny woman was the once-glamorous Silver Queen.

Miss Bancroft studied her while Baby and her father discussed the Matchless's prospects, the riches that would be tapped if, as Baby argued, "we could just drift a little further north on the sixth level" or "sink a winze through to that stope on the fourth level." Mrs. Tabor was dressed in a man's corduroy trousers, a soiled and torn blouse, miner's boots, with a bandanna around her head. She had assumed a belligerent stance when she saw them approaching—Fryer's Hill was off-limits to virtually all of humanity, particularly process servers and bill collectors—but welcomed them when she learned who Bancroft was.

Miss Bancroft was startled, as she recalled, by the roughly dressed little woman's flowery speech, once she got off the subject of mining problems, and the intense femininity which displayed itself in flashes like refracted light from an inner Baby Tabor usually concealed from the rest of the world. "The smile, the manner, the voice and flowery speech were anomalous in that strange figure. Her smile was positively, although very briefly, gay and flashing; the teeth, even and white, and the voice clear and bell-like, while the manner I can only describe as queenly despite her diminutive size." It must have been that oddly regal manner, as well as the charm she could exhibit at will, that persuaded so many otherwise sensible men to involve themselves in the tangled affairs of the Matchless.

While her father went back to their car to get a jug of wine, Miss Bancroft took a stroll around the property with Baby and admired the spectacular scenery which surrounded her, with the peaks of Mounts Massive and Elbert off to the west and towering over the whole range. "She did not say anything but she turned her eyes full upon me, the only time I think that she looked directly at me. Again I was startled. They were very far apart and a gorgeous blue, their unusual color preserved through all the violence and drama and bitterness of her then nearly seventy years."

When her father rejoined them, they entered the one-room structure of weathered planks which had been Baby Tabor's home for thirty years. "Her cabin, really no more than a shack, was crowded with very primitive furniture and stacked high in newspapers and mementos. It was quite neat although, to my mind, it could have stood a good dusting and the windowpanes had evidently not been washed since the winter snows. We drank our wine from an assortment of cups, one of them tin. She apologized for their not being very clean and said something about hauling her drinking water from some distance and using boiled mine water for other purposes."

The privations of her life only increased with the years. There was seldom enough money to keep her in the necessities, let alone maintain the Matchless in some kind of working order by pumping out the upper levels, shoring up the tunnels, and greasing the machinery. And the property was under constant assault; if mortgages and other encumbrances had any real weight they would have sunk the shaft house to the bottom level of the mine. Baby was a trifle careless with the paper work. Sometimes she leased two bits of land on the Matchless claim to two different parties. Anyone who objected to her tactics, and was bold enough to present his objections to the lessor in person, was met by her small determined figure marching down the hillside behind a shotgun.

The miraculous way in which the Matchless was rescued time after time only contributed to Baby's feeling that divine intervention was protecting her and her property. Just before the Depression struck in full force, it appeared that her hopes of hanging onto the mine were finally doomed. She would need more than $10,000, she figured, to fend off foreclosure—all judicial delays having been exploited to the utmost—and to keep the tunnels from being swamped by the rising water table.

One more desperate journey to Denver for an interview with a man who just might help her out was undertaken. Her prospective angel was, the saints be praised, at least an Irishman. He was

J. K. Mullen, who had made a million or two as a flour miller
and was a Catholic philanthropist. His wife had recently
died—would that make him more or less likely to share someone
else's burden?

Before approaching his mansion at Ninth and Pennsylvania
streets, Baby stopped in at St. Elizabeth's Church. She knelt and
prayed in a pew in the empty church, fingering, in lieu of a
rosary, the knotted string affixed to her ebony cross.

After asking for God's help in saving the Matchless, she
trudged through the snow to the door of the Mullen mansion.

Mullen himself came to the door, recognized her, and asked
her into the library.

"It's a bad night to be walking the streets," Mullen remarked,
as Baby would recall the conversation for Sue Bonnie.

"It's nothing to the Leadville blizzards," Baby replied, shaking
the snow off her threadbare cape. "I'm used to a hard life."

She gave Mullen a rundown on her financial condition and
her faltering effort to save her last bit of property, explaining that
she held the Matchless "in trust to my husband's memory." That
was not only true, of course, but shrewdly appealing. It touched
the widower's heart.

"Your worries are over, Mrs. Tabor," Mullen told her.

He marched over to his desk and wrote a check for $14,000.
The mortgage was lifted and there was enough money left over to
partly rehabilitate the mine. A photograph of the Matchless
taken around that time shows the shaft house and other buildings
in much better condition than Baby's cabin with its spavined
siding and its rickety lean-to protecting the door against the
winter winds.

The Depression, however, spread its blight not only from the
cities, with their armies of unemployed, to the dustbowl farms
and abandoned ranches of the West, but to the farthest reaches of
the Rockies and into Stray Horse Gulch. The Matchless was
becoming a hopeless proposition in the early thirties. The lessees
of the other mines on Fryer's Hill ran out of money and had to

abandon their workings. Once their pumps stopped operating, the neighboring mines filled with water. Many of the "drifts" which formed the hill were interlocking, and their overflow poured into the tunnels of the Matchless. There was no way of keeping it from becoming waterlogged without first pumping out the other mines.

Leadville itself was becoming as ghostly, as memory-haunted, as the abandoned shaft houses of the mines which had once made it the most famous camp in America. Its population had fallen to less than 4,000, according to the 1930 census, and that was less than a tenth of the number living there during the boom years. Chestnut Street with its once-fine houses was lying in ruins. The stores, saloons, and brothels were mostly boarded up and abandoned. The Tabor Hotel had been renamed the Vendome, the Tabor Opera House had been taken over as clubrooms of the local Elks Lodge. The only local industry that showed any sizable prospects was bootlegging. Leadville moonshine was relished by connoisseurs for hundreds of miles around. The bootleggers operated their copper stills in the abandoned mines around the town. Even that industry would collapse with the election of President Franklin D. Roosevelt and the repeal of the Prohibition Amendment.

And it was beginning to seem that the town's most famous citizen couldn't last another brutal winter above the timberline. Not to any observer, able to spare the thought from his own collection of miseries, who watched her small, bent figure trudging over the snow-covered road from Fryer's Hill wearing an old overshoe on one foot and the other wrapped in burlap.

15. *"Visions of Gold Everywhere"*

VERY late in life, long after she believed the world had forgotten her, Baby Doe regained a measure of the celebrity which had attended her years as the Silver Queen of Colorado. Hollywood had waved its magic wand, leaving a tarnished mark on the Tabor legend but momentarily reawakening public interest in its vanished glory.

Carloads of tourists came up the road to Fryer's Hill and the chatelaine of the Matchless, once assured they were not creditors in disguise (otherwise she would flourish her shotgun), received them graciously, patted their children's heads, and signed their autograph books.

The cause of her emergence from the shadows which had so long enveloped the fallen House of Tabor was a film titled *Silver Dollar*, a somewhat simplistic product of the Hollywood studios.

The film of Tabor's career may or may not have been downright libelous but, to those who valued the Tabor legend, it was a gross misrepresentation down to the last fadeout. Certainly it was careless enough of the truth to show Horace dying on the stage of the Tabor Grand Opera House and falling just below the ominous quotation from Charles Kingsley. It might not have been so bad if it had been a silent film, but the sound track of *Silver Dollar* put words into the mouth of the fictitious Horace that were a libel on his common sense if not his character.

Silver Dollar opened with a splashy premiere in Denver late in 1932. The theater owner and the film's publicists offered Baby her expenses plus a bonus if she would serve as centerpiece at the opening. Possibly her intuition warned that a team of Hollywood hacks would make a hash of it, and though she could have used the money for a winter coat or enough food to see her through till spring, she declined with some asperity. She did agree to let the Hollywood press agents come up to the Matchless and pick up some rocks on Fryer's Hill and haul them off in a gunnysack to decorate the lobby of the theater.

A year later *Silver Dollar* was shown in a theater at Buena Vista, and two friends of hers, Lucille Frazier and Joe Dewar, asked her to drive over to see it, but she refused. Her memories were painful enough without having them paraded, with gross distortion, on the silver screen. Several well-wishers from Denver came up to Fryer's Hill as a delegation. One was a priest she had known for years, and two other men were lawyers. They urged her to sue the producers of *Silver Dollar* on the grounds that the film had maliciously libeled her character, having taken the "shameless hussy" line so popular among her detractors in Denver society during her heyday. Her self-appointed advisers assured her that she was a cinch to be awarded $50,000 for the damage to her self-esteem. They had already drawn up the papers empowering the lawyers to file suit.

Baby, however, handed back the papers and shook her head. "I don't need fifty thousand dollars," she told them. "The Matchless will soon bring me many times that amount."

Later she explained to Sue Bonnie that she couldn't bear the raking up of old scandals which would result from a court battle. The defendant's lawyers would have brought up everything from her clandestine affair with Horace to the sordid death of her younger daughter. Fifty million dollars wouldn't be enough to wipe the mud off the two persons whose memories were the dearest to her.

*   *   *

So Baby Doe Tabor continued to live on stale bread and the cheapest cuts of beef. During the last few years of her life, President Roosevelt's New Deal was proclaimed, but even the wide net of its social programs did not ensnare her. "I have never accepted charity," she would reply to those who suggested that she apply for some form of welfare. For some time, however, she was kept going by the letters from sympathetic persons who had seen *Silver Dollar* or read newspaper accounts of her destitution, and who often enclosed $5 or $10. She used the money, she said, because it did not fall under her definition of charity.

Old-timers in Leadville still remember the indomitable pride with which she confronted the privations of 1933 and 1934.

Henry C. Butler, the editor of the Leadville *Herald-Democrat,* often strolled up to her cabin on Sundays to talk with her and recalled her telling him, "Oh, I cannot accept charity. I believe that I would rather starve. Yes, I would rather die." She was indignant, in fact, if people tried to treat her like a charity case. "Packages left on her doorstep," Butler recalled, "are invariably returned to their donors unopened. With amazing shrewdness the old lady determines who has brought them and back they go. Once when she was unable to trace a box of cast-off clothing, she stopped in and published a notice asking that the donor call for his offering. On the box she wrote: 'Such an insult. I hope never again.' "

She trusted no one, Butler wrote, and "in every unknown visitor she sees a schemer who would get the Matchless away from her."

The glorious past was her present comfort. "She likes to talk of the old days when Tabor was at the height of his fame and the Matchless pouring forth its $2,000 a day. The years seem to fall away from the faded old face. Now she plucks almost daintily at the shabby skirt and I see in the motion the gracefulness of a fine lady gathering her velvet gown about her. I wonder how it can be possible for one who once had so much to now have so little and yet want to live. Then I realize that she lives not in the same world as I, but in a world of her own creation—a world carried over from the past, peopled with the memories of those who have passed on. And in this world is one magnificent figure—Tabor."

Once the most pampered and bejeweled woman on the continent, she was now among the least favored and protected. She made a heartbreakingly forlorn figure as she trudged down the road from Fryer's Hill to Leadville, now wearing burlap sacking on both feet instead of shoes. On a winter's day she would stumble through the drifts in Stray Horse Gulch, with timberline winds blowing at gale force, past the ore dumps and tipples of deserted mines which had once made Leadville one of the wonders of the world and her husband's fortune the envy of his contemporaries.

She would stop at the post office for her mail, then proceed to Zaitz's grocery store with a burlap bag in which to carry back her supplies. Her manner as haughty as when she had patronized the finest shops in Denver and New York, she would order a dozen loaves of stale bread and a slab of brisket, mostly suet, the fat from which precariously fueled her tiny body.

"Charge it," she would tell the clerk.

What she didn't know—or didn't want to know, with her talent for ignoring unpleasant realities—was that her pathetically modest grocery bills were paid out of the town's charity fund.

With the burlap bag slung over her shoulder, she would return to her cabin. On days when it was snowing heavily or was bitterly cold, the storekeeper would assign the delivery boy to take the old lady home. It was only a lonely shack to other people, but in her cabin she was surrounded by the evidence of a glamorous past; the walls were papered with yellowing newspaper photographs, and there were trunks and boxes filled with other souvenirs. Against those memories present privations could be discounted: the cracked cup from which she sipped her tea, the cracks in the walls through which the numbing northers whistled, the small iron stove with its insufficient fuel supply.

The rest of the country might be gripped by the worst depression in its history, but Baby Doe would not abandon hope.

Her powers of persuasion were intact and she was still able to talk men into collaborating with her on reviving the Matchless, waterlogged on its lower levels as it had been for decades. She rounded up seven unemployed miners—James and William Caulfield, Clyde Maney, Tim Riley, Frank Fabian, Henry Freeburg, and A. P. Durning—and convinced them there was a vein of silver which could be tapped by sending down a new shaft into the hillside. They labored for a month, listening to their employer enthuse over the rich new strike they would all share in, and then demanded their wages. Baby suggested that they take promissory notes in lieu of cash. Further enraged by Leadville's amusement over their having been conned into a month's free labor by a little old lady widely believed to be somewhat unhinged, they filed suit against her. She barricaded herself in her cabin and refused service of the papers. The deputies, knowing her defiant attitude toward any law that displeased her, quickly gave up the siege.

The last few years of her life were warmed and made less lonely by the friendship of Sue Bonnie, who had drifted into Leadville early in the thirties, fallen in love with the mountains, and occupied a cabin less than a mile from Fryer's Hill, one of the many refugees from the Depression who settled in such places at a comfortable distance from the breadlines and hunger marches, the agitation and frustration of the cities.

It was the only real friendship with another woman that Baby had tolerated in her long life. In the first place Baby was attracted to Sue, with her curly black hair and lively manner, because she somewhat resembled Silver Dollar. And they had a mutual interest in mysticism; both were convinced they could communicate with the spirit world, with Baby's ouija board often the chosen method of communication.

Baby would attend mass at the Church of the Annunciation in Leadville but only at odd times when there was likely to be few other parishioners around. The parish priest might not approve of such proscribed practices as summoning disembodied presences, but Baby's greatest consolation was trying to reach those she loved, all of them gone except for her brothers Phil and Willard and her daughter Elizabeth. She never heard from Elizabeth, rarely from her brother Willard, but Phil occasionally came up to Leadville in the summer to visit her and scratch around the old mine.

Two or three nights a week she and Sue Bonnie visited each other's cabins, exchanged information on the dreams they had, pondered their significance, and wrote down on scraps of paper the "revelations" they had received from the spirit world. The bulk of Baby's estate would consist of boxes and trunks full of those memorandums, along with a small library of scrapbooks. They also collaborated on a rather sentimental account of Baby's life which they hoped to publish as her autobiography. Eventually it was published serially in one of Bernarr Macfadden's confession magazines.

Thus the last three years of her life were made more tolerable by the friendship of the only woman Baby ever completely trusted.

The last glimpse the world would have of Baby Doe Tabor was on February 20, 1935. A heavy snowstorm was sweeping over the Rockies, but she struggled down the road to town in her torn black cloak on the burlap wrappings which served her as footwear. She bought bread, suety beef, and some turpentine at Zaitz's store. (Her health had always been perfect except for an occasional cold, which she dosed with a mixture of turpentine and lard.) The Zaitz delivery truck gave her a lift beyond the railroad trestle in Stray Horse Gulch, but then was halted by the heavy snowdrifts. She got out with her gunnysack and trudged up the road to her cabin.

It was a bad storm. The scattered cabins in the gulches and on the hillsides around Leadville were isolated for days by the impassable drifts. Sue Bonnie and some of the others who worried about her and were concerned that her slender supply of firewood would run out, recalled the fate of George Schmidt only a year or so earlier. Schmidt was an old prospector whom Baby had allowed to occupy the other shack on her property in return for his services as a watchman. One morning after a similar blizzard she had found his frozen body in the cabin.

For ten days Sue Bonnie, from the windows of her own cabin, could see smoke coming from Baby's chimney. Then another three-day blizzard blew up and blotted out her view of Baby's cabin. On the morning of March 7, the skies finally cleared and Sue Bonnie could see that there was no smoke coming from the cabin on Fryer's Hill. The drifts were so high she had to seek the help of an old prospector named Tom French, who lived nearby, to break a path up the gulch. It took them hours to struggle through six-foot drifts to Baby's cabin.

They peered through a window, saw Baby's body spreadeagled on the floor. Her face was serene. Freezing to death, according to folk wisdom, isn't a bad way to go. There was still some firewood left in the box, so it appeared that Baby had become ill, collapsed on the floor while trying to refuel the stove, and had slowly frozen to death.

Newspapermen who viewed the cabin noted that her last years had been attended by the minimum of necessities for survival. There was a rusty iron-frame bed with a tangle of gray blankets, a table with a leg missing and supported by a wooden box, a sooty oil lamp, net curtains mended with twine. The rear of the one-room cabin was stacked with old trunks, most of them containing bundles of old newspapers in which articles on the Tabors had appeared, and a cardboard box bearing the notation, "In this box was the beautiful, soft, blue and white bathrobe my darling child Honeymaid sent me."

On the inadequately chinked walls of the cabin was found mute but graphic evidence of her struggle to survive the last two mountain winters on Fryer's Hill. Large calendars for 1934 and 1935 hung on the walls and constituted an almost day-by-day record of her physical hardships, of the visions which alternately blessed and tormented her. "Foot frozen" was a frequent notation. March of 1934 had been bitterly cold, and she had barely survived it, as she wrote in one entry on the calendar:

"Went down to Leadville from Matchless mine. Snow so terrible I had to go down on my hands and knees and creep from my cabin door to Seventh Street. Mr. Zaitz drove me back to our getting-off place and he helped pull me to cabin, I falling down through snow every minute. God bless him."

Doubtless the last few years of her ordeal of loneliness and privation were lessened to some extent by the visitations she received from the world beyond. Except for the confidences she exchanged with Sue Bonnie, she kept them to herself, knowing that those less sensitive to psychic phenomena would consider her a mad old hag if she revealed them. Forty years ago, of course, ESP was hardly dreamed of as a scientific possibility, and other forms of communication not conducted by Western Union or Bell Telephone were regarded as the province of superstition-mongers and storefront fortune-tellers. It was obvious, though, that she welcomed such manifestations; they had no more power to frighten her than the disapproval of her contemporaries had to inhibit her years before.

The calendars attested to a tumult of demons mingled with kindlier spirits, gigantic red horses, visions of gold and purple, and what must have been a very small dragon nestled in her coffee cup.

One day in January, 1934, she recorded that "a great vision and I talked to a spirit. She answered me. Two spirits and one bad spirit. She fled."

"Alone, alone," she wrote later that month. "Visions of gold everywhere."

In the blizzard-swept March of that year, she was subjected to demonic presences as well as severe hardships: "Lots of devils all over the cabin. Oh, terrible. No food left. On my hands and knees. Need bread. Cold. Suffered alone. Awful blizzard. I saw purple near the ceiling."

In the gentler April that followed, the phantoms who manifested themselves at Fryer's Hill were less worrisome, but other visions were ominous. "Purple and lots of it. Dark purple on the wall . . . Saint, so big and strong visited here. A vision of the death, death in purple . . . Silver Dollar and big red, gold horse. Oh, so big. As big as four or five horses."

During the winter of 1935 the apparitions were much less troublesome, as if in the waning days of her life the other, unseen world—a curious semi-pagan place inhabited by sprites and demons as well as a pantheon of Catholic saints, animals, and those she loved—was beckoning to her. In the several months before her death, she wrote on the calendar:

"I heard the spirit of Lily Langtry . . . Gold and pink on blue snow . . . I saw a dragon in my coffee cup . . . I had a strange visitor, a lonely cow with a big white heart on its forehead."

"Spirits, spirits, spirits," read her last entry, the final message she would scrawl for posterity.

In one corner of her cabin was evidence that her preoccupation with the spirit world had not entirely eliminated her as a daughter of the Church, a shrine decorated with pine boughs, with a plaster cast of the Virgin Mary, at which she said her prayers. Just below the shrine was a photograph of her brother Philip.

Preparations were made for her burial in Leadville until Phil McCourt, professional gambler, now retired, and the only one of her brothers and sisters she saw in later years, insisted that she be buried beside Horace Tabor in Mount Olivet Cemetery in Denver, to which Tabor's body had been removed when Calvary Cemetery was leveled years before. Father Edward L. Horgan of the Church of the Annunciation conducted services in Leadville before her body was removed to Denver. In Denver the attendance was scantier. The only relative present was her youngest brother Willard. Her surviving daughter, the widowed Mrs. Elizabeth Last, now living in a small apartment in Milwaukee, not only refused to attend the Denver services but denied to reporters that she was Baby Doe's daughter; her father, she said, was John Tabor, Horace's unspectacular brother. Her beloved brother Phil, too ill to attend, was living in a room at the Windsor Hotel two doors down the corridor from the sumptuous suite once occupied by his sister and her husband before and after they were married. "Don't let them say she was foolish or had wild ideas," he pleaded with the reporter who came to interview him.

Her death at the age of seventy-five (Baby Doe's reckoning) or eighty-one (according to her baptismal certificate) was attended by editorials solemnly meditating on the lessons of a picaresque career. It was safe, now, to say that she had been quite a woman. A picturesque survival from the days before New Deal America and its "social conscience" slogans, when it was possible to indulge with an unabashed delight in one's own good fortune without making pious references to the less fortunate. One Denver newspaper rather sensibly commented that Baby Doe "exemplified a pride unparalleled in the romance and hardships of the Old West . . . Her pride was in herself and her memories . . . Men and women are horrified at her 'queer existence' and lonely death. Don't feel sorry for Baby Doe. She who sought no sympathy in life would want none now."

The final and greater glory was that the descendants of the people who wouldn't invite the "shameless hussy" to their homes have made a folk heroine of her, have enshrined the remnants of the career their antecedents deplored, and accepted her as a symbol of all that was recklessly gallant and memorable about the Old West.

Epilogue

BABY Doe had saved a few postmortem surprises for the world which survived her. Some were contained in the immense trove of memorabilia she had collected ever since girlhood. Like the pack rats that succeeded her in possession of the cabin on Fryer's Hill, she apparently saved everything. Seventeen trunks were found in a Denver warehouse, the charges on which she had somehow paid for almost forty years even when she was destitute. In the basement of St. Vincent's Hospital in Leadville, other trunks, boxes, bundles, and burlap bags were found by the administrator of her estate, who fortunately was Edgar C. McMechen of the Colorado Historical Society.

Much of Baby Doe's hoard was junk—gunnysacks stuffed with old newspapers and empty coffee cans—but it also included her silver Tiffany tea set, several bolts of silk dress material she preserved even while dressing herself in cast-off garments, the collars and cuffs of her ermine opera coat (the rest of the coat having been sold for food), and a box of Horace's favorite cigars. There were seventeen scrapbooks, many containing entries written in code. As one of the most diligent communicators with the spectral world, she saved reams of reports on her tea-leaf and coffee-ground "readings," palmists', astrologers', and other sooth-sayers' reports, records of her dreams and visions covering a period of more than thirty-five years. There were 12,500 separate items, a paper blizzard of memos recording everything she observed and sensed in her exploration of the twilight zone between reality and the unseen.

The late Mr. McMechem was determined to preserve Baby Doe's testament for posterity. At the auction held to satisfy claims totaling $3,000 filed against her estate, at which a pair of Tabor's red flannels went under the hammer for sixty cents, he persuaded a group of Denver notables to acquire the bulk of those possessions for $700 on behalf of the Colorado Historical Society.

It was just as well those keepsakes of Baby Doe's didn't fall into the wrong hands. That $700 paid out by the Denver establishment was money well spent, it became evident in 1953, when members of the historical society staff began sorting out her papers.

"The skeletons in some Colorado closets were rattling," the Denver *Post* reported, "as workers at the State Historical Museum sorted through thousands of personal letters. A number of letters—including those of Silver Dollar Tabor—will be 'restricted' material . . . Silver Dollar was known in her girlhood as a 'spirited' young woman and her escapades involved various citizens, some of whom are still living." Elderly gentlemen who had pursued the younger and less conventional Tabor daughter in their youth were assured that their indiscretions would remain privy to their rueful and fading memories.

A year later Father F. M. McKeough of her native parish of St. Peter's in Oshkosh located a baptismal certificate dated October 7, 1854. Since Catholics have their children baptized as soon after birth as possible, it was evident that Baby Doe was born in 1854 rather than 1860, as she had always maintained, and that she had subtracted six years from her age in the passage from Wisconsin. That was one secret she had guarded with particular devotion.

Time has not darkened the Baby Doe legend. Along with the Unsinkable Mrs. Brown, another reject from the old Capitol Hill society, she is an integral part of that legendary Colorado which has been cleaned, gilded, and buffed to a glittering sheen for the tourist industry. Baby Doe, doubtless, would have been pleased by her apotheosis. The tourists who started trekking up to her cabin on Fryer's Hill even before her death had always been welcomed if they minded their manners. Baby Doe's ramshackle quarters outside Leadville have become a sort of shrine to the spirit of the mythical West.

Every summer now the remaining physical evidence of her picaresque career is studied by thousands. In 1954 the pack rats were chased out of her cabin, the depredations committed by treasure and souvenir hunters repaired, and the site of her long vigil over the Matchless mine was "reconstructed" for the benefit of the ten-week tourist season. Other artifacts of the Tabor saga are daily on view, and daily visited throughout the year by droves of schoolchildren as well as tourists, at the Colorado Historical Museum in Denver.

If you walk out along Eighth Street on a spring evening before the tourists descend on Leadville, down the road which Baby Doe often trudged with her gunnysack of supplies, with the snow peaks across the Arkansas Valley coldly glittering under moonlight, you come to the workings of the old Matchless clinging to the hillside. Nearby is her cabin, snugger and tidier now than when it was her shelter against the mountain storms and the indifference or hostility of the outside world.

Easy enough to imagine, in that moonlit scene, that *something* is astir.

If Baby Doe's spirit has joined the thronging shades and clamoring presences which peopled the last decades of her life on that hillside, the visitor may be assured that whether clothed in a white satin gown of her ascendancy or the tattered costume of her later years, it is a small and friendly ghost that beckons him to her last earthly dwelling place.

Notes on Sources

THE complete listing of many sources indicated below under their author's surname may be found in the Selected Bibliography, which follows.

1. The Pocket Venus from Oshkosh

Much of Baby Doe's childhood experiences were related to the friend of the last few years of her life, Sue Bonnie, with whom she apparently had begun collaborating on a biography or autobiography. After Baby Doe's death, Miss Bonnie published the material in *True Story* magazine, January–May, 1938. It seems fairly authentic.

Her exact birthdate is unknown, but the year was 1854, as was established about twenty years ago when the parish priest at St. Peter's, Oshkosh, finally unearthed her baptismal certificate. The priest, Father F. M. McKeough, stated that she was probably born a few days or weeks before she was baptized on October 7 (Denver *Post*, June 17, 1955).

Another early source is her scrapbooks, which she started compiling in girlhood and contained the usual artifacts of a small city's belle. Less usual is the fact that some entries were kept in code. The code was a rather simple affair which was cracked eighteen years ago by Mrs. Frankie Dungan, a Denver cryptographer. For instance, *1 2 3 4 5* stood for *a e i o u*; *6 7 8 9* for *l m n g* and so forth. Among other tidbits revealed when the scrapbook entries were deciphered was her brief romance with W366—that is, Will—which she apparently kept to herself. One entry read: "Will told me a thousand times that I was the most beautiful young woman he ever saw and he would go to hell for me. Oh, how he loved me. Yes, he worshipped me and called me his baby."

The McCourt family background is covered in Karsner, *Silver Dollar,* 138–142; Gandy, *The Tabors,* 255–236; Bancroft, *Silver Queen,* 1–10.

Lumbering history, Oshkosh's disastrous fires are detailed by Austin, *The Wisconsin Story, passim.*

The story of Baby's skating contest victory was related by Bonnie, *True Story,* January, 1938. Hereafter cited as Bonnie.

Her romance with and marriage to Harvey Doe, *ibid.*

2. *The Birth of Baby Doe*

Colorado historian quoted on the influence of "good women" and their discomfiting effect on frontier males, Willison, *They Dug the Gold,* 298.

Account of the Does' honeymoon is from Bonnie, January, 1938.

The marvels of the Teller House in Central City were described on the occasion of its opening by the Central City *Register,* July 7, 1875.

Baby's efforts to get the deed to the mine registered were related by Bonnie, February, 1938.

The hard lot of the miners as described by a contemporary, quoted by Willison, 67.

Baby's determination to help Harvey develop the Fourth of July Lode, Bonnie, February, 1938.

The description of Baby Doe working her half of the mine was published by Central City's *Town Talk,* October 14, 1877.

Harvey Doe's argument for taking a "steady job," Bonnie, February, 1938.

Baby Doe's coded account of her relationship with Jacob Sandelowsky (later known as Jake Sands) is contained in her scrapbooks at the Colorado Historical Museum.

Circumstances of her child's birth and death, her difficulties with her errant husband, *ibid.*

Harvey's letter to his parents, quoted by Hall, *The Two Lives of Baby Doe,* 91–92.

Her divorce from Harvey Doe was granted March 19, 1880, in the County Court in Denver. Obviously her marriage was terminated at flank speed. According to her testimony, she followed Harvey to Lizzie Preston's parlor house, accompanied by police officer Edward Newman, on March 2. Two days later she filed suit on charges of adultery and nonsupport. A few days later she was persuaded to drop the adultery charge.

3. *King of the Mountain*

Eugene Field's description of Horace Tabor, quoted by Barker and Levin, *Denver, An Insider's Look at the High, Wide and Handsome City*, 25–26.

Augusta Tabor's recollection of the hardships of pioneering on a Kansas homestead were published in "Cabin Life in Colorado," *Colorado Magazine*, March, 1927.

Her diary was quoted by Karsner, 12–13, 50–51; Willison, 55–56.

Horace Greeley's observations on the Gregory Gulch diggings are from his *Overland Journey from New York to San Francisco in the Summer of 1859, passim.*

Augusta Tabor on her determination to send their son to school, "Cabin Life," *op. cit.*

The Stevens and Wood operations in California Gulch are described by the Griswolds' *The Carbonate Camp Called Leadville*, 23–24.

The contemporary historian quoted on the effect of the Little Pittsburgh discovery on Tabor's career was Frank Hall, *History of the State of Colorado*, Vol. II, 211.

Journalistic comment on the violence in Leadville, Leadville *Chronicle*, January 10, 1875.

The kidnaping of three Chinese laundrymen was recounted by Willison, 164–166.

Colorado historian quoted on banditry endemic in Leadville's streets, Dill, *History of the Arkansas Valley*, 255.

The Leadville gambler's optimistic letter on Leadville's prospects was quoted by Willison, 202–203.

Luke Short's Leadville career was detailed by Holbrook, *Little Annie Oakley and Other Rugged People*, 157–158.

Doc Holliday in Leadville, Myers, *Doc Holliday, passim.*

The "feed the miners" plea was published by the Leadville *Chronicle*, September 4, 1878.

Mart Duggan's career as city marshal and its aftermath are related by Blair and Churchill, *Everybody Came to Leadville*, 18–19.

The *Chronicle*'s description of the Tabor Light Cavalry's costuming was published February 11, 1879.

Lynching of Frodsham and Stewart, Griswold, 171–175.

The grand opening of the Tabor Opera House was covered by the *Chronicle*, November 23, 1879.

Oscar Wilde's appearance in Leadville is detailed by Lewis and Smith, *Oscar Wilde Discovers America, passim*.

Erba Robeson's unflattering recollections of Horace Tabor on a spree were contained in an interview published by the Leadville *Herald-Democrat*, January 1, 1936.

4. *Silver King Meets Beautiful Baby*

Tabor's purchase of the Brown mansion is described by Barker and Levin, *op. cit.*, 24–25.

Baby Doe described how she met Tabor to Sue Bonnie, *op. cit.*, March, 1938.

Tabor pays out $5,000 for Baby Doe's indebtedness to Jake Sands and for new wardrobe, *ibid.*

Details of the Leadville strike are from Willison, 238–244; David J. Cook's autobiography, *Hands Up, passim*. An objective account of Cook's role in keeping order in the mining camp may be found in Collier and Westrate's *Dave Cook of the Rockies*, 191–200.

An interesting sidelight on the Leadville strike is cast by R. G. Dill, a contemporary historian, in his *Political Campaigns of Colorado* (1895): "In the light of later events it is now scarcely doubted that it was organized rather by certain mine owners than by the miners themselves, and for the purpose of covering up the poverty of some of the mines until the principal stockholders could unload." He did not say whether Tabor was one of them.

The Committee of Safety's decision was reported by the Leadville *Herald-Democrat*, June 4 and 5, 1880.

Denver newspaper which condemned the "bonanza kings" was the *Rocky Mountain News* on June 6, 1880.

Lieutenant Hickman's report to General Cook, Collier and Westrate, 191–200.

Tabor's and Baby Doe's participation in the Leadville welcome to ex-President Grant, Bonnie, *op. cit.*, March, 1938; Leadville *Chronicle*, August, 18–20, 1880.

5. *Career of a Veiled Lady*

A description of the Denver underworld may be found in Parkhill's *The Wildest of the West, passim;* O'Connor, *Bat Masterson*, 138–140.

Eugene Field's satire on the anti-alcohol and anti-tobacco crusaders was quoted by Willison, 249.

Augusta Tabor's denunciation of her husband's strikebreaking activities, as relayed by him to Baby Doe, Bonnie, March, 1938.

That Horace slipped away for an "orgy" in Leadville was also revealed by Baby Doe, *ibid.*

Tabor's participation in completing the Windsor Hotel is related by Barker and Levin, *passim,* and Fowler, *Timberline*, 40–41.

Source of Tabor's inspiration for verse woven into the Tabor Grand Opera House curtain, Perkin, *The First Hundred Years*, 358.

Tabor's habit of shaving after dressing himself was uncovered by Fowler, 45.

A lengthy account of the opening night of the Tabor Grand was published by the Denver *Tribune*, September 6–7, 1881.

Eugene Field's comment on the full-dress requirement, *ibid.*, September 5, 1881.

Tabor's wrangle with Augusta over her suit for a property settlement, Willison, 261.

The means by which Augusta was persuaded to give Tabor the divorce he wanted in Parkhill, *The Wildest of the West*, 162–164.

Newspaper comments on the divorce may be found in Augusta Tabor's scrapbook, which is now on microfilm in the western history department of the Denver Public Library.

6. *The Nuptials of Senator Nightshirt*

For political maneuvers preceding and accompanying Tabor's bid for the Senatorial seat, Dill, *The Political Campaigns of Colorado, passim;* Elmer Ellis, *Henry Moore Teller*, 152–156.

Editorial assaults on the Tabor candidacy were clipped out and pasted into her scrapbook by Augusta Tabor, *op. cit.* The letter from

Teller to Tabor is quoted by Ellis, 154; the *Rocky Mountain News* editorial is quoted by McMechem, *op. cit.,* 24, also by Gandy, *op. cit.,* 231.

Statehouse correspondent's hope that Tabor would "tumble," quoted by Willison, *op. cit.,* 275.

Senator Ingalls' description of Tabor as a "ruffianly boor" is quoted by Parkhill, *op. cit.,* 166.

Tabor's letter to Baby on his "grand dinner party" may be found in one of her scrapbooks in the Colorado Historical Museum.

The comment on that dinner party is from the New York *Herald,* February 25, 1883.

Story of Queen Isabella's jewels is told by Karsner, 214.

The newspaper account of the Tabor wedding was provided by the Washington *Post,* March 2, 1883.

Tabor and Father Chapelle were quoted on the charges of wedding trickery by the *Post,* March 3, 1883.

7. *Not Quite the First Lady of Colorado*

The *Rocky Mountain News* editorial on Tabor's desirability as a Senator is quoted by Perkin, *op. cit.,* 357. Apparently that generally anti-Tabor organ took a kindlier view of him only after his Senatorial hopes had been quashed.

The New York *Tribune* reported Tabor's plans to build a mansion in Washington on March 5, 1883.

Eugene Field's imaginative account of Washington's sorrow over Tabor's departure from the Senate, found in the Denver *Tribune,* March 4, 1883.

Secretary Teller's letter expressing gratitude that Tabor's thirty-day term was over, quoted by Ellis, *op. cit.,* 155.

Tabor's confidence that Baby would be "first lady of the land," Bonnie, *op. cit.,* March, 1938.

The further deflation of Tabor's political ambitions were recounted by Gandy, *op. cit.,* 247.

The interview in which Baby claimed she was "flooded with invitations" from Denver society was quoted by Karsner, *op. cit.,* 231–232.

* * *

8. A Hundred Peacocks on the Lawn

The description of the Tabor mansion and their style of life is from Barker and Levin, *op. cit.*, 26; *The Book of the American West*, edited by Jay Monaghan, 169–170.

The Unsinkable Molly Brown never met Baby Doe, so far as can be determined, but in the early 1920's offered Baby the money to pay off her $14,000 mortgage. Mrs. Brown soon discovered, however, that she had little enough to live on herself. Her husband died intestate in 1922 and most of his estate was gobbled up by other claimants. Mrs. Brown died alone in the room she occupied in a New York women's hotel.

Augusta Tabor's call on Baby was related to Sue Bonnie (April, 1938, installment of the *True Story* series). Some local historians have cast doubt on the story, on the grounds it would have been out of character. Mrs. Augusta Tabor's calling card was, however, found among Baby's possessions when they were sorted out by the staff of the Colorado Historical Museum.

Augusta's denigratory opinion of Baby was delivered in an interview with a Denver *Republican* reporter, an account quoted by the Denver *Post*, October 23, 1953.

Augusta's statement a week later that she was considering legal action to have the divorce set aside, in *Republican*, October 31, 1883.

Tabor's 250 love letters to his second wife are included in the Tabor Collection at the Colorado Historical Museum.

The greatly respected historian Frank Waters is doubtful if contemporaries of Tabor's had an accurate fix on the size of his income. In *Midas of the Rockies: The Story of Stratton and Cripple Creek*, 16, he maintains that Tabor's total income from his Leadville mines was not much more than $5,000,000.

The Eastern financial journal's prediction that Tabor would be the richest man in America was quoted by Willison, 272.

Tabor railroad investments also included such short-lived ventures as the Denver, Utah & Pacific, the Denver, Apex & Western, and the Denver Circle Railroad. He was a founding partner of the Denver Steam Heating Company. The Honduran venture was styled the Honduras-Campbell Reduction Company; what it proposed to reduce was gold, silver, and coal deposits reportedly present on the tract as well as the mahogany forests.

Baby recounted her friendship with theatrical celebrities to Sue Bonnie (April, 1938).

Oscar Wilde's appearance in Denver and his playful victimization by Eugene Field are told in Thompson, *The Life of Eugene Field*, 82–83, and Fowler, *op. cit.*, 94–95.

9. The Crash of a House of Cards

Baby's bitterness over Denver socialites having her Paris gowns copied, Bonnie, April, 1938.

She throws her brother Pete and his friends out of the house, *ibid.*

She has costumes made for her naked statuary to appease a prudish neighbor, *ibid.*

The "silver question" is cogently outlined and analyzed by Hofstadter, *The Age of Reform*, 65–66, 103–106.

Coin Harvey advocated war against Britain in *Coin's Financial School*, 131–132.

Historian quoted on free silver's appeal as "an old policy rather than a drastic innovation," Hofstadter, 104.

Governor Waite's "blood to the bridles" speech and its effects, Fowler, *op. cit.*, 72–73.

Waite at least was original in concocting economic remedies. He suggested the issuance of what he called Fandango Dollars; the state was to buy the output of the silver mines, ship the silver to Mexico, have it milled into dollars and returned to Colorado for circulation. Some people, including those in the U. S. Treasury, might have called it counterfeiting.

The dimensions of Tabor's financial disaster are suggested by the fact there were twenty-one lawsuits against him dealing with twenty-nine unpaid loans. The Tabor Grand Opera and the Tabor Block were mortgaged for $400,000.

Winfield Scott Stratton's $15,000 loan to Tabor, Waters, *op. cit.*, 155–156.

10. "How Can You Do This to Horace Tabor?"

Baby's unsuccessful plea for financial help to her brother Peter, Bonnie, May, 1938.

Tabor's letter to Teller was quoted by Willison, 292–294.

Contemporary quoted on Tabor's openhandedness when he had money, *ibid*, 295.

Baby recalled the family's picnicking in the servantless mansion, Bonnie, May, 1938.

Her furtive gentleman callers after Tabor went to Boulder were recalled for Sue Bonnie, *ibid*.

Stratton's intercession with the Republican bigwigs to get Tabor the Denver postmastership, Karsner, 271–275.

Tabor was converted to the Roman Catholic faith several days before his death.

Account of his death from the Denver *Post* and *Rocky Mountain News*, April 10 and 11, 1899.

11. *Prettiest Widow in Colorado*

The account of Tabor's funeral is from the Denver *Post* and *Rocky Mountain News*, April 13 and 14, 1899. Included in the procession were the First Regiment band, National Guard cavalry troops B and C, the Chaffee Light Artillery, and three infantry companies of the Colorado National Guard.

Baby's search for financial backing to reopen the Matchless mine is related by Barker and Levin, 26.

Her move to Leadville with her daughters, and Elizabeth's objections, Bancroft, *op. cit.*, 62–63.

Elizabeth Tabor had always been fond of her uncle Peter McCourt. Her mother kept in one of her scrapbooks a note Elizabeth wrote at the age of five or six to her uncle: "Peter McCourt you owes Baby [as Elizabeth referred to herself] 200 kisses and unless you pay me I will have you put in jail."

Elizabeth leaves her mother, Bancroft, 64.

12. *The Perils of Motherhood*

Discovery of jewels in forgotten safety-deposit box, Bancroft, 65.

Publication of Silver Dollar Tabor's song saluting President Roosevelt's Colorado tour, Denver *Post*, August 9, 1908.

Silver Dollar's affair with a livery stable proprietor and her Easter Monday ball escapade, Bancroft, 66–67.

The diary entry regarding Silver Dollar's tantrum over the priest's dictum against reading "bad books" may be found in the Colorado Historical Museum (File Folder 897).

Descriptions of her mother's dreams and visions, *ibid.,* File Folder 900.

Silver Dollar's journalistic experience in Denver may be traced in Baby Doe's scrapbooks.

A copy of her novel *Star of Blood* may be found in the western history department of the Denver Public Library.

Death of Silver Dollar's alter ego Artie Dallas, *Star of Blood,* 69.

On her visits to Denver, Baby Doe usually stayed at the rundown Milo Hotel. She always took the cheapest room, at $2.50 a week, without bath.

Her notes on searching for Silver Dollar, diary entries for November 14 and 19 and December 25, 1914, and February 15, 1915, are contained in File Folder 900, Tabor Collection, Colorado Historical Museum.

13. *"Give Me One More Jigger."*

Baby Doe's promissory note to William J. Barker, Barker and Levin, *op. cit.,* 27.

Silver Dollar's decision to enter a convent, Bancroft, 67.

The atmosphere of prewar Chicago is brilliantly recaptured by Dedmon, *Fabulous Chicago,* 251, 279–283; Hecht, *A Child of the Century,* 203.

The visiting English journalist's observation was published by the London *Daily Mail,* December 2, 1911.

The Chicago newspaperman's interview with Silver Dollar was quoted by Karsner, 305.

Letters from Silver Dollar to her mother suggesting her need for money in 1918 and 1919 and telling of her "marriage" in 1922 may be found in the Tabor Collection at the Colorado Historical Museum. In Baby's papers there is much to suggest that her overriding concern was for her daughter's safety and happiness, that she had little hope that Silver Dollar would pull herself together. Her underlying concern was that if Silver Dollar were fated to come to a bad end, then let it be somewhere far from Colorado. She was bitterly aware that she had no power to control her daughter's waywardness.

The account of Silver Dollar's last years and her death was drawn from the Chicago *Herald-Examiner*, September 19–21, 1925; Chicago *Tribune*, September 21 and 22; New York *Times*, September 21.

The interview with Elizabeth Tabor (Last) was published by the Chicago *Tribune*, September 21, 1925.

Elizabeth Tabor lived out her last widowed years in Milwaukee. Oddly enough, so did Baby's first husband, Harvey Doe, who in 1893, after his domineering mother's death, married a Mrs. Kingsley, a widow with three children. Doe worked as a cigar-maker in Oshkosh, then found employment as a hotel detective in Milwaukee, where he died in 1921.

Baby Doe's denial that Silver Dollar was the woman who died in Chicago under scandalous circumstances was published by the Denver *Post*, September 21, 1925.

14. *The Recluse of Fryer's Hill*

The record of Baby Doe's visions and dreams and other manifestations may be found in File Folder 1025, Tabor Collection, Colorado Historical Museum. Those cited were only a small part of the thousands she recorded.

Baby Doe's conversation with the Denver assayer was related by Karsner, 316–318.

Caroline Bancroft recalled her girlhood meeting with Baby Doe in her splendid monograph, *Silver Queen*, 2–3.

Baby's timely loan from J. K. Mullen, *ibid.*, 71–72.

The fame of Leadville's moonshiners, and Leadville as it was in the early thirties, was reported by Willison, 298.

15. *"Visions of Gold Everywhere"*

The film *Silver Dollar* seems to have suffered from a classic case of miscasting. The late Edward G. Robinson, not exactly the rawboned Yankee type, played Horace Tabor. Baby Doe was played by Bebe Daniels, a Latin-type brunette, just the opposite of blond and blue-eyed Baby. With the role of Augusta, the producers hit closer to the mark by assigning it to Aline MacMahon.

A typescript of Baby Doe's conversations with Henry C. Butler may be found in the western history department's Tabor Collection, Denver Public Library.

Aside from recording her dreams and visions, Baby's favorite occupation was clipping newspaper items that interested her. One clipping (Denver *Post*, January 27, 1918) either concerned a woman she had known or indicated a sardonic touch of humor. Its headline read: RACHEL MCLEOD PERISHED OF SUFFOCATION WHEN FIRE DESTROYED HER HOME—STRANGE MAN FOUND DEAD IN HER CLOSET.

She persuades seven miners to work on a new shaft for the Matchless, Associated Press dispatch from Leadville, March 27, 1935, detailing their suit against her estate.

Circumstances of Baby Doe's death, Denver *Post*, March 8–10, 1935.

Notations found on her wall calendars, *Rocky Mountain News*, March 24, 1935.

Elizabeth Tabor's refusal to attend her mother's funeral and her disavowal of the relationship were reported in an Associated Press dispatch from Milwaukee, March 8, 1935.

Denver newspaper's editorial on Baby Doe as exemplifying an unparalleled pride, *Rocky Mountain News*, March 9, 1935.

Selected Bibliography

AUSTIN, H. RUSSELL, *The Wisconsin Story.* Milwaukee, 1957.

BANCROFT, CAROLINE, *Silver Queen.* Denver, 1955.

BARKER, BILL, and JACKIE LEVIN, *Denver, An Insider's Look at the High, Wide and Handsome City.* New York, 1972.

BLAIR, EDWARD, and E. RICHARD CHURCHILL, *Everybody Came to Leadville* (a pamphlet). Leadville, 1971.

COLLIER, WILLIAM R., and EDWIN V. WESTRATE, *Dave Cook of the Rockies.* New York, 1936.

COOK, DAVID J., *Hands Up: or Thirty-five Years of Detective Work in the Mountains and Plains.* Denver, 1897.

DAVIS, CARLYLE C., *Olden Times in Colorado.* Los Angeles, 1916.

DILL, R. G., *History of the Arkansas Valley.* Chicago, 1881.

—— *The Political Campaigns of Colorado.* Denver, 1895.

DRAGO, HARRY SINCLAIR, *Notorious Ladies of the Frontier.* New York, 1967.

ELLIS, ELMER, *Henry Moore Teller, Defender of the West.* Caldwell, Idaho, 1941.

FOWLER, GENE, *Timberline.* New York, 1933.

GANDY, LEWIS CASS, *The Tabors.* New York, 1934.

GREELEY, HORACE, *An Overland Journey from New York to San Francisco in the Summer of 1859.* New York, 1860.

GRISWOLD, DON L., and JEAN HARVEY GRISWOLD, *The Carbonate Camp Called Leadville.* Denver, 1951.

HALL, FRANK, *History of the State of Colorado.* Chicago, 1889. 4 vols.

HALL, GORDON LANGLEY, *The Two Lives of Baby Doe.* New York, 1962.

HOFSTADTER, RICHARD, *The Age of Reform.* New York, 1955.

HOLBROOK, STEWART H., *Little Annie Oakley and Other Rugged People.* New York, 1948.

KARSNER, DAVID, *Silver Dollar.* New York, 1932.

LEWIS, LLOYD, and HENRY JUSTIN SMITH, *Oscar Wilde Discovers America.* New York, 1937.

McLEAN, EVALYN WALSH, with BOYDEN SPARKES, *Father Struck It Rich.* Boston, 1936.

McMECHEM, EDGAR C., *The Tabor Story* (a pamphlet). Denver, 1951.

MONAGHAN, JAY, editor, *The Book of the American West.* New York, 1963.

MYERS, JOHN, *Doc Holliday.* Boston, 1955.

O'CONNOR, RICHARD, *Bat Masterson.* New York, 1957.

PARKHILL, FORBES, *The Wildest of the West.* New York, 1951.

PERKIN, ROBERT L., *First Hundred Years, An Informal History of the Rocky Mountain News.* New York, 1959.

SPRAGUE, MARSHALL, *Money Mountain: The Story of Cripple Creek Gold.* Boston, 1953.

THOMPSON, SLASON, *The Life of Eugene Field.* New York, 1927.

WATERS, FRANK, *Midas of the Rockies.* New York, 1937.

WILLISON, GEORGE F., *They Dug the Gold.* New York, 1931.

Newspapers

Central City *Register*

Central City *Town Talk*

Leadville *Chronicle*

Leadville *Herald-Democrat*

Denver *Tribune*

Denver *Republican*

Denver *Post*

Rocky Mountain News

Washington *Post*

New York *Herald*

New York *Tribune*

New York *Times*

Chicago *Tribune*

Chicago *Herald-Examiner*

Chicago *Journal*

Acknowledgments

THIS book could not have been written without the painstaking efforts of the staffs of the Colorado Historical Museum and of the western history department of the Denver Public Library in collecting and collating the great amount of material which constituted the Baby Doe estate. The work has been completed only in the last few years. The author is indebted to the late Edgar C. McMechem, who was both administrator of her estate and the guardian of her collection at the Colorado Historical Museum; to Caroline Bancroft who has done much research and writing in that field as a regional historian of notable stature; to Mrs. Alice L. Sharp, reference librarian at the museum, and to the group which worked on the Tabor Collection, Lee Scamehorn, its director, Ann Mecherle, Rebecca Pritchard and Ginny Fowler. Also to the staff of the western history department of the Denver Public Library, including Mrs. Aly Freeze, its head, and Mrs. Opal Harber, James Davis, Mrs. Hazel Lundberg, Mrs. Mary Hanley and Miss Eileen White.

Index